D0871964

Additional Praise for **The Power of Passive Investing**

"The retail stockbroker will soon become as extinct as the dinosaur, and good riddance. Thousands of investment professionals, tired of selling the same old lies, and millions of their clients, tired of hearing them, have deserted the brokerage business for a more elegant, effective, and honest way of managing money. Twenty years ago, Rick Ferri helped pioneer that transition. If you're an advisor or a broker, you owe it to yourself to read *The Power of Passive Investing;* if you're an investor, you owe it to your pocketbook."

—Bill Bernstein, author, *The Investor's Manifesto*

"I'm a big fan of Rick's books, and this is his best yet. It's *the* book on how to effectively harness the power of passive investing. Whether you are an individual investor or are responsible for billion-dollar portfolios, this book is critical to your success."

—Allan Roth, author, *How a Second Grader Beats Wall Street*

"Rick Ferri has written yet another terrific book. The numerous studies he reviews provide powerful support for passive investing and guide trustees and other fiduciaries toward this ideal solution."

—W. Scott Simon, principal, Prudent Investor Advisors, LLC

"Passive investments deserve a place in almost all investors' portfolios, but the range of choices has never been so complex or treacherous. There are now every bit as many flawed, gimmicky, or overpriced index funds as there are those from active managers. If you want to navigate this new terrain successfully, you'll find Rick Ferri's *The Power of Passive Investing* an essential text."

—Don Phillips, Managing Director, Morningstar, Inc.

"Powerful! The extensive research behind this book makes a compelling case for a passive investing strategy. Ignore the information in this book at your own peril."

—Mel Lindauer, *Forbes* columnist and co-author of
The Bogleheads' Guide to Investing and *The Bogleheads'
Guide to Retirement Planning*

"Rick Ferri has brilliantly assembled hordes of unbiased, highly technical investment research so that the average investor can understand and benefit from what the smart money has known for decades. If you care about how much you'll retire with, you'll read *The Power of Passive Investing*."
—Mitch Tuchman, CEO, MarketRiders, Inc.

"Rick Ferri has gathered a wealth of research. A passive investment strategy is a great approach because it allows a person to focus on more important things in life."
—Craig Israelsen, author of *7 Twelve: A Diversified Investment Portfolio with a Plan*

"I found this book to be an outstanding resource for the passive investor as well as those who could benefit from this approach. It's another most excellent contribution by Rick Ferri."
—Sheryl Garrett, CFP, AIF, Founder, Garrett Planning Network

"This book is an enormous gem of a history lesson on a profoundly sophisticated (and simple) strategy that has changed the world of investing forever. Rick Ferri's work is a must read for everyone who accepts responsibility for their own financial well-being, giving readers the authority to turn away from Wall Street and make intelligent investment decisions on their own."
—Bill Schultheis, advisor and author, *The New Coffeehouse Investor*

"Enemies of passive investing aren't going to like this book, but who cares what they think? Ferri provides more damning evidence against stock picking and other money-losing strategies that bomb investors' portfolios. In the end, passive investors win."
—Ron DeLegge, host, *The Index Fund Investing Show*

"Having originally been trained in the hedge fund space to think actively, I know there is a large group of investors with an 'active management' state of mind. However, given what I know of many retail investors and a surprising number of institutional investors, I can't help but think that for their own benefit, the passive-oriented approach espoused by Rick in this book is a likely path to minimizing future regret."
—Richard C. Kang, Chief Investment Officer and Director of Research, Emerging Global Advisors, LLC

"'Odds are you'll earn well below market returns in your portfolio over your lifetime if you believe that the mutual funds you're choosing or your advisor selects will beat the markets.' Strong words, but in this eminently readable book, Rick Ferri makes a more than compelling case in favor of passive investing. Wouldn't you like your portfolio to be managed by nothing but managers who shoot par? If you're a professional or a retail investor, following the lessons introduced in this book will unquestionably improve your bottom line."
—Harold Evensky, President, Evensky & Katz

"In this well-crafted book, the author ponders the question of why pay high fees to active managers when index funds—those that follow a real market benchmark, not just a disguised active investment strategy—can do better on a risk-adjusted basis? A strong case is built for passive investing, with arguments backed with market facts and a thorough review of decades of unbiased academic and practitioner studies. At the same time, Rick reminds us of the power of strategic allocation over tactical allocation in meeting a client's long-term financial goals. This book is a valuable resource, and I highly recommend it."
—Seddik Meziani, PhD, Professor of Finance and Economics, Montclair State University

"By focusing on the irrefutable facts, Rick Ferri has put together an unassailable case for *The Power of Passive Investing*. Advisers who implement the principles outlined within this book will strengthen their relationships with clients by delivering solutions in lieu of products."
—Rudy Aguilera, Principal, Helios LLC

The Power of
Passive Investing

Books by Richard A. Ferri

The ETF Book
All About Asset Allocation
All About Index Funds
The Bogleheads' Guide to Retirement Planning (with Mel Lindauer, Laura Dogu, and Taylor Larimore)
Protecting Your Wealth in Good Times and Bad
Serious Money: Straight Talk about Investing for Retirement

The Power of Passive Investing

MORE WEALTH WITH LESS WORK

Richard A. Ferri

Foreword by John C. Bogle

WILEY

John Wiley & Sons, Inc.

Library of Congress Cataloging-in-Publication Data:

Ferri, Richard A.
    The power of passive investing: more wealth with less work / Richard A. Ferri.
      p. cm.
    Includes index.
    ISBN 978-0-470-59220-5 (hardback); ISBN 978-0-470-93708-2 (ebk);
    ISBN 978-0-470-93712-9 (ebk); ISBN 978-1-118-00390-9 (ebk)
      1. Index mutual funds. 2. Investments. I. Title.
  HG4530.F428 2010
  332.63'27—dc22

2010028567

Printed in the United States of America

10 9 8 7 6 5 4 3 2 1

Contents

Foreword

In *The Power of Passive Investing*, Rick Ferri has given us a comprehensive guide to what is proving to be a virtual revolution in investment strategy. Up until the 1980s, "stock picking" was the dominant method of investing by individual investors. Then, through the 1990s, professional investment supervision through actively managed mutual funds was ascendant. But, gradually, index investing—buying and holding a portfolio representing the entire stock (or bond) market, or various sectors of those markets—has attracted the most attention (and dollars) from investors.

Rick's book begins with the historical background of index funds. As one who was present at the creation of the first index mutual fund in December 1975, I can attest to the accuracy of his chronology. (My first decision at the upstart firm Vanguard, which I founded and which began operations in May 1975, was to form the world's first index mutual fund.) We also learn about the other pioneers of the concept of indexing, including Treynor, Samuelson, Malkiel, Ellis, and Sharpe.

The simple fact is that indexing wins because indexing *must* win. After all, we investors as a group are destined to be average. (In a stock market with a 7 percent *gross* annual return, we all divide up that 7 percent.) But after we account for the costs of investing—what I call the "croupier" costs, an estimated 2½ percent—we (again, as a group) earn a net return of 4½ percent. The best index funds win simply because they eliminate management fees and sales loads, and minimize operating costs and portfolio turnover and its costs. In so doing, they provide their services at an annual cost of as little as 1/10th of 1 percent of assets. It is the "relentless rules of humble arithmetic" that drive the theory of passive investing.

But Ferri takes us from theory to reality, providing scores of examples and tabulations that prove that very point. Like many analysts, he finds that it is not past fund performance but low costs that are the best predictor of future (relative) fund returns. In one particularly striking exhibit, he shows that an investor holding a portfolio of five equally-weighted mutual funds has but a 3 percent probability of beating the stock market index over 25 years. (For a holder of 10 funds, the probability is only 1 percent). Again, the historical record confirms the hypothesis.

The Power of Passive Investing also deals soundly with such broad areas as savings and investment, asset allocation, and the use of financial advisers. That is Rick's profession, and he is an outspoken advocate for the indexing approach. By charging minimal fees for his services, he walks the walk that reflects the talk he talks in this fine book. I commend it to you.

John C. Bogle
Valley Forge, PA
September, 2010

Preface

Did you ever buy something because you thought it was a superior product, only to be disappointed with the results? That's the problem with most mutual funds. They don't deliver on their promise.

Investors buy mutual funds in most cases because they believe the fund manager will earn superior returns over a market average. But that's not what typically happens. Most funds that try to beat the market underperform the market, some by a wide amount. Investor hope fades quickly as the reality of mediocre results roll in. Then they search for new funds, finding new hope, and fail again. This vicious cycle has been happening in the mutual fund industry for almost a century.

Odds are you'll earn well below market returns in your portfolio over your lifetime if you believe that the mutual funds you're choosing or your advisor selects will beat the markets. That's not going to happen, at least not in the long term. Perhaps one or two funds will achieve this difficult goal if they survive long enough, but a portfolio of several funds will not beat the markets in aggregate over time. That's almost a certainty.

The advertising from fund companies will always imply that their managers have delivered superior returns and that you can capitalize on this skill and earn superior returns in the future. That's wishful thinking. As a group, mutual fund managers have no special talents and outperformance is more a matter of luck than skill. The academics have been saying this for decades.

There is an alternative. The failure of active fund managers to deliver on their promise of high returns while continuing to charge high fees creates a compelling case for passive investing. Passive investing is all about investing in low-cost passively managed index funds and exchange-traded funds (ETFs) that match the financial market returns less a tiny fee for expenses. This strategy lands your portfolio much closer to the market's return than active fund management, and it ensures that you'll earn your fair share of those returns.

Your goal as an investor is to earn the highest return feasible given the specific amount of risk chosen for a portfolio. A passively managed portfolio holding index funds and ETFs will outperform an overwhelming majority of portfolios using actively managed mutual funds that try to beat the markets with the same amount of risk. Said another way, a passive portfolio will greatly increase the probability you'll reach your financial goals.

This book provides you with the detailed studies and undeniable evidence favoring a passive investing approach. It's filled with academic research and data that goes back many decades. This information clearly shows that trying to beat the market has never been a reliable investment strategy in the past, and there's no reason to believe it will beat a passive approach in the future. Passive investing increases the probability that your portfolio and the portfolios you may oversee for others will succeed. Passive investing IS power investing!

Possible but Not Probable

Wall Street is full of promises. Companies that actively manage mutual funds promote their products based on the perception that they're staffed by very smart and informed people and that they'll earn higher returns than the markets. What investors don't see, and most don't consider, is the academic facts proving that most funds don't achieve this goal. There's only a low probability that any fund will achieve superior returns. While it's possible, it's not probable.

A sign on the highway promoting the Powerball lottery only displays the possible amount you could win; it doesn't tell you the low probability of winning. Most investment opportunities are sold the same way. Wall Street promotes the possibility of earning superior returns—not the probability.

Low odds for selecting a winning mutual fund isn't the only problem for investors. A second problem is payout. The few active funds that are winners don't pay enough excess return over the market's return to make up for the selection risk. There are a large number of losing active funds, and many of those losing funds fall far short of the market's return. The few winning active funds don't perform well enough to make up for the poor results of the large number of losing funds.

A third problem for active mutual fund investors is the short-fall created when multiple funds go into a portfolio. A portfolio of several actively managed funds has lower odds of success than each fund independently. As more actively managed mutual funds are added to a portfolio, the outperformance rate for the total portfolio drops dramatically. This problem compounds over time, and after enough time, the probability for outperforming a passive approach drops to near 0 percent.

Winning actively managed funds are only a small percentage of the total funds outstanding, and identifying these winning active funds in advance is nearly impossible. There are no proven methodologies that accurately predict future winning active funds. Of course, that doesn't stop many market gurus who will claim to have a winning active fund picking formula that they'll sell you for a fee. But that's just marketing spin meant to separate investors from their money.

Attempting to earn above market returns by picking actively managed mutual funds is an inefficient use of time and money. Knowing this fact, and acknowledging it allows you the freedom to go in a different direction—to change religion in a sense.

Passive versus Active Investing

The Power of Passive Investing lays out an irrefutable case for buying low-cost passively managed index funds and ETFs. It amplifies an investment philosophy that's been academically proven over the decades to deliver better returns than beat-the-market fund strategies. With the power of passive, you can build a more profitable portfolio that meets your needs and the needs of the people whose money you oversee.

Passive investing is based on the premise that all financial market participants in the aggregate are better at determining securities prices than an individual who disagrees with those prices and attempts to predict price direction and earn excess profits. It has to be this way. For every buyer of securities there must be a seller. The return of the market is the only return available to investors, and it's shared by all investors. If one person earns a higher return it means someone else missed out. There is no other return.

But there's a problem: Investors don't earn the market return in aggregate. Money management doesn't come free. Take out a few hundred billion dollars per year in expenses to trade securities and manage investments, and you can easily understand why it isn't possible for investors to outperform the markets over the long term. The average investor must underperform the markets given the costs of investing.

You wouldn't know this by reading advertisements from mutual funds; brokerage firms; money management companies; advisors; or what's written in most books, magazines, investment newsletters, and web sites. They make it seem as though everyone is winning. That's simply not true and can't be true.

The Power of Passive Investing makes the case for creating a sound long-term investment policy using low-cost index funds and ETFs that gets you closer to the natural returns of the markets. It's also about clarifying and quantifying the purpose for investing, and then implementing a prudent plan that has the best chance for meeting this goal within a framework of controlled risk.

Mutual Funds Are a Great Idea

Mutual funds are a great investment vehicle. They allow investors to participate in the global financial markets at a relatively low cost by pooling assets together with other investors to gain economy of scale. In addition, fund shareholders have daily liquidity. They can purchase or redeem fund shares any day the market is open.

The modern mutual fund industry had its start in Boston in 1924. Despite its meager beginnings, the industry survived the Crash of 1929 and the Great Depression that followed. Today, there are over 7,000 different distinct mutual funds including about 1,000 exchange-traded funds offered by hundreds of mutual fund companies.

It wasn't until 1976 that the first publicly available index fund was launched by the Vanguard Group. The concept was slow to catch on. However, it didn't take long for investors to realize the value that indexing offered. Today, there are hundreds of index funds tracking practically every asset class, investment category, and style.

Exchange-traded funds had their beginning in late 1993. Most of these products are also designed to track indices. Exchange-traded funds are a type of mutual fund. The main difference between a traditional open-end mutual fund and an ETF is that the ETF shares trade continuously during the day on an exchange rather than at the end of the day with a fund company, as traditional mutual funds do.

Between open-end index funds and exchange-traded products, anyone can create an all-passive portfolio using products that are low cost, tax efficient, and hassle free. Investors who prudently select and maintain a portfolio of low-cost index funds and ETFs will earn higher returns with less risk than those who cling to actively managed funds. It's just a matter of time.

Passive investing with index funds and ETFs works. However, you won't find many passive portfolios in this book. This book makes the case for passive investing. You'll have to read other books for details on asset allocation recommendations and fund selection methods. Several books are highlighted within these chapters.

Index Funds Make Most Active Funds Obsolete

It wasn't necessary for actively managed mutual funds to beat the market prior to the introduction of index funds because they were the only game in town. They were the only option available. Mutual fund companies fulfilled their obligation to investors by offering a broadly diversified portfolio of securities that individuals could not replicate on their own at the same cost. In this regard, actively managed funds were a good deal for investors. But that era has passed.

Today, actively managed funds aren't needed to gain broad diversification in an asset class. Index funds and ETFs perform that function much more efficiently. The costs are lower, diversification is broader, the transparency of fund holdings is superior, and the tax benefit from lower turnover helps investors whose accounts are subject to taxation.

The growth of index funds and ETFs across the spectrum of asset classes has put actively managed fund companies on the defensive. Since the actively managed funds are no longer the most efficient way to gain broad diversification at low cost, the active fund industry has had to fashion another reason for being. This new reason for being is to beat the market.

In a sense, index investing has forced active managers into their difficult beat-the-market mission. After Vanguard introduced index funds in 1976, the active fund industry reacted with some interesting comments. The head of the largest active fund company at the time asked investors why anyone would want just average returns. Another called it Bogle's Folly after Vanguard founder John C. Bogle. Still another fund company went as far as printing a poster that labeled index funds as un-American.[1]

Active funds were no longer the most efficient way to invest in the markets after the introduction of index funds. This put tremendous pressure on the stodgy fund industry. Index funds forced the active managers to prove their worth with outperformance and answer for underperformance. They never had to do that before.

How have active funds performed in the new mission? One word sums it up: terrible. The active fund managers have unilaterally failed in their attempts to beat the market after adjusting for risk. As a group, net of all fees and expenses, their strategies have underperformed the benchmark indexes in every fund category and every style, and across every continent.

In 1975, Charles Ellis labeled active management among professional investors as a "loser's game." Ellis said, "Most institutional investment managers continue to believe, or at least say they believe, that they can and soon will again 'outperform the market.' They won't and they can't."[2] Active investing is a loser's game. The active fund managers don't beat the market, and active investors who try to time mutual fund purchases and sales are equally unsuccessful.

Ironically, the reason active managers don't beat index funds isn't because the managers are dumb. In fact, the opposite is true. The investment industry attracts some of the brightest financial minds in the world. The problem is economics. It is competition and cost. There are too many smart people trying to beat the markets and too few opportunities available. Couple this with high operating expenses and the net result has been and will be below-market returns.

Portfolio management using active mutual funds is obsolete. A well designed and implemented long-term investment policy that uses index funds and ETFs has the higher probability of meeting financial goals. It is the prudent choice for your money and for other portfolios you may oversee. It is your answer to a better performing portfolio.

Overview of Chapters

The Power of Passive Investing is divided into three parts. Part I defines the active versus passive debate, reviews academic literature over the decades, and makes the case for investing in individual index funds and ETFs over individual actively managed funds. Part II focuses on portfolios of active mutual funds verses index funds and the unsuccessful methods people use in their attempts to choose winning active funds. Part III makes the case for passive investing for four different types of investors: individuals, private trusts and charities, pension funds, and investment advisors.

Part I: Active versus Passive

In the beginning, there was only active portfolio management. Index funds didn't exist. People selected individual securities themselves, or hired portfolio managers to select securities, or purchased mutual funds that selected securities.

Over the years, actively managed mutual funds became the product of choice for many investors. It was the economical solution to gain broad diversification at a lower cost than buying individual securities. Fund shareholders pooled their assets together and were entitled to their share of gains and income from the fund. It was a fair system of exchange, even though the results generally underperformed the markets'.

Index funds didn't exist until late in the twentieth century. High fixed commission rates on Wall Street and a lack of computing power made indexing prohibitively expensive. Commission deregulation in 1975 and increased computing power helped foster the first index mutual funds. In 1976 the Vanguard Group launched its first index, tracking the S&P 500.

With the advantage of a bull market at their back and continued lackluster performance by the managers of active funds, index funds began an important growth phase starting in the early 1980s. This was the beginning of a new era for mutual fund investors. Low-cost and broadly diversified index funds became a viable alternative to high-cost and riskier actively managed funds.

Part I tracks the active versus passive debate from its beginnings early in the twentieth century up to the present day. It covers early research through current research. Many exhaustive academic studies are reviewed in this section, some going back to the 1930s. The conclusion of these studies, covering all periods, is that the active managers as a group didn't earn superior returns. There were some funds that did beat the market, but not many, not by much, and not for long, and the winners could not have been identified in advance.

The entire premise for adopting a passive strategy is based on probability and payout. Active funds outperform passive funds only about one-third of the time over a 5 year period. But this is just the beginning of the problem. The winning active funds change from year to year, and the average excess payout for picking a winning active fund isn't high enough to justify taking the risk.

Since the odds are against active funds, it follows that the payouts for the winning active funds make up for the losses derived from selecting losing active funds. But they don't. There are many more losing active funds than winning active funds, and the short-fall from some of the losing active funds is quite large. The returns from winning active funds are far below a fair payout, given the high odds of picking a losing fund and the average performance shortfall from those funds.

It's interesting that two vocal supporters of passive investing come from unlikely groups: famous active investors and the federal government. Investment greats such as Warren Buffett, Peter Lynch, and David Swensen are all outspoken advocates for passive investing. In addition, the U.S. government's Thrift Savings Plan (TSP) for federal employees has only passive investment options available for participants.

Today, there are hundreds of passively managed index funds competing against thousands of actively managed mutual funds. Investors can choose a passive alternative in almost every asset classes and style, including U.S. and foreign equity funds, bond funds, commodities funds, and even currencies.

If low probability weren't bad enough on the fund level, the odds that a portfolio will outperform the market diminish with every extra active fund added to the portfolio. In addition, the longer active funds are held in a portfolio, the worse the performance gets relative to an all-index fund portfolio, until the odds reach a point where there is almost no chance the active fund portfolio will outperform the index fund portfolio.

Part II: Chasing Alpha and Changing Behavior

Naysayers of passive investing will point to some active funds that have outperformed the market. That's absolutely true. There are always active funds that beat the market. Those who know how to pick winning funds in advance will earn excess profits. But that's almost an impossible feat to accomplish with consistency and skill. Seeking winning active funds may satisfy one's competitive spirit but it runs completely counter to achieving a portfolio's investment objective. It's possible that an active strategy will be found that generates consistently high returns, just like it's possible to win the lottery. It's just not probable.

Even when a consistently superior active investment strategy is identified, other investors will copy the methodology and thereby quickly erase its benefit. The very few winning active strategies that are identified always carry the seeds of their own destruction.

Poor market timing decisions by investors also lower their portfolio performance. Many investors attempt to beat the market by tactically shifting their mutual fund weights based on some prediction of short-term market returns. This simply doesn't work. Statistics show that investors lose over 1 percent per year by trying to shift their investment in front of the next market move.

A better strategy is strategic allocation. Fixed weights are assigned to each asset class in a portfolio and they are kept in line through regular rebalancing. Investors who use a strategic asset allocation strategy outperform those who use a tactical strategy by a considerable amount over the long term.

With all the evidence in favor of passive investing, why don't more people use this strategy? They can't bring themselves to do it. As Princeton professor Burton Malkiel explains, "It's hard for people to accept because it's like telling someone there is no Santa Claus, and people don't like to believe that."[3]

Human behavior is the biggest barrier to investment success. Changing behavior takes time and willingness. It is accomplished through education and repetition. That is why a small but growing group of authors write multiple books and articles on index fund investing and continue to publish on all fronts. We may not get top billing at the bookstore, but the truth must be repeated over and over again because lies about investing are constantly being told.

Part III: Passive Investment Policy

Part III begins with a discussion about the purpose of investment policy. A well articulated investment policy leads to a well balanced asset allocation decision and disciplined management. It involves the prudent selection of investments to best represent the asset allocation that's formulated. Finally, a portfolio needs ongoing maintenance and review to ensure that it is following the investment policy and to tweak the plan as circumstances dictate.

The final four chapters discuss passive policies in terms of four different groups of investors. These include individual investors and their families, trustees of charities and private accounts, pension trustees and those who select investment options for employer sponsored pension plans, and professional investment advisors. Each of these four groups has special reasons why implementing a passive investment strategy is better for them.

Individual investors should select a strategy that has the highest probability of reaching their retirement and estate planning goals. There is no reason to believe that an individual investor will find a top money manager who will outperform the markets. That's why it's undoubtedly in the best interest of an individual to create and maintain a portfolio of index funds and ETFs for the long run.

Substantial time is spent explaining why passive investing is a prudent choice for trustees who have a legal responsibility to act in the best interest of the accounts they oversee. This includes charities, private trusts, and pension accounts. Although each of these entities has different goals, the law is very specific about how these accounts should be managed. Trustees have a legal duty to act as a prudent expert in the selection of investments. A passive strategy is clearly the best option for most trusts, and it's a safe option for trustees.

An Irrefutable Case

The case for passive investing is deeply rooted in facts, and those facts are irrefutable. Whether you are acting for yourself or as a fiduciary for someone else, all investment decisions should be based on a sober reading of these facts.

The Power of Passive Investing pulls together decades of academic research coupled with prudent and practical thinking. The results are conclusive: a portfolio of low-cost index funds provides the highest probability for meeting your long-term financial goals. Passive investing IS power investing.

Acknowledgments

I have many people to thank for this book. First, my patient and loving wife, Daria, to whom this book is dedicated. Second, special thanks go to John Bogle for his generous forward, and Mel Lindauer, Scott Simon, and Ed Tower for their meticulous reading of the manuscript and the critical comments that made it better.

I also wish to thank the following people for helping me by providing research, endorsements, or proof reading. They include Rudy Aguilera, Brab Biban, Robert Brokamp, Scott Burns, Jonathan Clements, Shikant Dash, Ron DeLegge, Charles Ellis, Harold Evensky, Rose Marie Ferri, Sheryl Garrett, Craig Israelsen, Richard Kang, Taylor Larimore, Kevin Laughlin, Seddik Meziani, Janet Novack, Travis Pascavis, Don Philips, Allan Roth, Ramiro Sanchez, Bill Schultheis, Martin Sewell, Lawrence Siegel, Mitch Tuchman, and Jim Wiandt, plus the many members of the Bogleheads.org forum, who offered encouragement.

Finally, I wish to thank all the men and women in the armed services for protecting our great nation. They unselfishly put themselves in harm's way and ask for nothing in return except our unyielding support. The royalties from this book are being donated to charitable organizations that assist wounded soldiers, sailors, Marines, and airmen. Lest we forget; freedom is not free.

PART

I

THE ACTIVE VERSUS PASSIVE DEBATE

CHAPTER 1

Framing the Debate

I can't believe that the great mass of investors are going to be satisfied with just receiving average returns. The name of the game is to be the best.

—Edward C. Johnson III

The investment management business is built upon a simple and basic belief: Professional managers can beat the market. That premise appears to be false.

—Charles D. Ellis

The active versus passive debate has all the drama of *West Side Story*, complete with larger-than-life characters and Shakespearean tragedy. Like two rival gangs, the Jets and the Sharks, vying for control of the streets, alternating between dominance and demonization, the opposing active and passive gangs fiercely defend their ideology as they fight for the hearts and minds of all investors. The gangs grapple with each other in the media and needle one another during public speeches and at industry events. No physical brawls have broken out yet - at least that I am aware of.

The tragedy, as passive investors would explain it, comes from the seemingly utter failure of active managers to deliver on their promises of market beating results while enriching themselves with fees extracted from investors who entrust money to them. Active advocates counter that it is possible to beat the market and point to icons such as Warren Buffett as proof. They believe their own superior knowledge and intellect will also lead to above the market returns.

Who's right and who's wrong? To answer this, the opinions of educated and unbiased professionals are needed. This leads us to the halls of academia and to research institutes that study and interpret performance data. Not just any academic or institution will do, because many researchers side with one gang or the other strictly for monetary reasons. They are either paid to write reports that agree with a gang's thinking, or in some way participate in fees and services offered by one side or the other. Unbiased academic opinions are needed from people who aren't compensated by the investment industry. Rather, they exhaustively seek the truth without any preconceived conclusions and make their findings public for the world to judge.

The references to books, articles, and academic studies throughout this book are just a starting point for people interested in this area of study. Sourcing these references leads to a rich treasure chest of data, analysis, and opinion from many of the world's greatest financial minds.[*]

In the Beginning, There Were Active Funds

This book is about mutual fund investing and portfolios of mutual funds, although the arguments can be extended to portfolios of individual securities. Mutual funds are the main focus because they are the optimal investment vehicle for most people. Mutual funds offer diversification, reasonable fees, and liquidity when needed. In addition, there is ample public information available on mutual fund analytics, and that helps in analysis.

The first U.S. open-end mutual fund began operations in Boston, Massachusetts in 1924. The Massachusetts Investors' Trust was a

---

[*]One starting point for reviewing early mutual fund studies is *Mutual Funds: Fifty Years of Research and Findings*, 2005, Seth C. Anderson and Parvez Ahmed, New York, Springer Science and Business Media, Inc. A second source is Martin Sewell's web site at http://finance.martinsewell.com/fund-performance/.

wonderful idea. The new structure offered broad diversification of securities that individual investors couldn't obtain on their own for the same cost. The fund also offered investors full liquidity in mutual fund shares whenever they needed it. Other companies soon followed with similar fund offerings.

In the early years, mutual fund companies weren't in business to beat the market. Rather, their mission was to select superior securities that paid reasonable dividends, to secure profits without undue speculation, and to conserve principal.[1] One reason that beating the market wasn't a goal is because there were no broad based indexes available at the time. There was the 30-stock Dow Jones Industrial Average, but this was a price-only indicator that didn't reflect the entire market of securities or its economic value.

The fund industry reasoned that mutual funds existed to provide all investors the opportunity to own a diversified securities portfolio at a relatively modest cost. The commissions and other trading expenses that an individual investor would expend building the same diversification with individual securities would exceed the cost of the mutual fund shares. According to one source, to buy one share of each of the securities in the 30-stock Dow Jones Industrial Average would have cost $1,800.81 in 1951 with the commission charges on the purchase and resale of shares amounting to 11.16 percent of their purchase price.[2]

From an investor's standpoint, mutual funds were a fair deal. Most people didn't have enough money to buy several dozen stocks, and they didn't have the expertise to keep up with their portfolios. Even the United States Supreme Court agreed. Louis D. Brandeis, Associate Justice of the United States Supreme Court commented:

> . . . the number of securities on the market is very large. For the small investor to make an intelligent selection from these— indeed, to pass an intelligent judgment on a single one—is ordinarily impossible. He lacks the ability, the facilities, the training, and the time essential to a proper investigation.[3]

The mutual fund system worked for the industry and for investors for many years because it was a win-win situation. Investors bought into a diversified portfolio of securities through mutual funds, and the fund companies didn't need to be concerned about losing assets when their managers underperformed the markets because few people monitored the returns that closely.

Passive Investing Makes Its Case

The cozy relationship between Wall Street and Main Street lasted for several decades. Then, in the 1960s, a barrage of brash, young academics began to analyze mutual fund returns more closely and started asking tough questions.

These academics were smart and talented, but they weren't altruistic. Their purpose for deep analysis of fund performance wasn't to discredit active investing—quite the opposite. They were seeking a way to identify investment skill among managers so they could copy those methods and use it for profit. Like everyone else, the academics thought if they dug deep enough, their research would lead to a way to consistently beat the market without taking more risk.

Identifying profitable investment strategies proved harder than it appeared, and what the academics found was much different than what they wanted to find. The details of these early academic studies are the subject of Chapter 2. In brief, the data suggested that few active managers actually beat the markets after adjusting for risk, and that luck couldn't be separated from skill. The academics also started to theorize that most investors would be better off just buying the market itself if they could.

The academics brought their findings to the fund companies. The fund company executives were as unimpressed with the academic research as the academics were with mutual fund performance. When the academics questioned the lagging performance relative to the markets they were quickly reminded by fund company spokesmen that "you can't buy the market."[4] This was a true statement at the time. Index funds didn't exist.

Now You Can Buy the Market

The world changed in 1976 with the introduction of a passively managed S&P 500 index fund by the Vanguard Group. This gave mutual fund investors an option; they could continue to invest in actively managed mutual funds that tended to underperform the market by a considerable amount, or they could buy very close to the market return through the First Index Investment Trust (later renamed the Vanguard 500 Index Fund).

The introduction of index funds to the marketplace was an inflection point in mutual fund history. Not only did index funds give investors a choice, they forced active fund companies to redefine their purpose. When asked if Fidelity would follow Vanguard's lead and offer index funds, Chairman Edward C. Johnson III stated, "I can't believe that the great mass of investors are [sic] going to be satisfied with just receiving average returns. The name of the game is to be the best. "Another large fund company responded to the challenge in a flier asking, "Who wants to be operated on by an average surgeon, be advised by an average lawyer, or be an average registered representative, or do anything no better or worse than average?"[5]

These public statements by active fund companies signaled a titanic shift in industry ideology. For the first time, fund companies took the stand that it wasn't enough to simply offer diversification through a pooled basket of securities that investors couldn't achieve on their own at the same cost. The new mission was to *beat the market*.

Benefits of Passive Index Investing

In 1976, the active versus passive debate spilled over from academia onto Main Street. On the surface, the active fund industry's decision to go head-to-head on performance against index funds was noble. They were determined to beat the market, and they actually thought they could do it. Unfortunately for the active managers, the economics didn't work. The costs were too high, the competition too intense, and there was too little talent among fund managers.

Fortunately for the active managers, the general public didn't know these facts and still doesn't know these facts. Many people continue to believe that the active managers they select will win. Hard facts should have put this debate to rest a long time ago, but it continues to rage on in the battlefield of public perception.

Wise investors know that when one investment strategy can achieve a financial objective with more certainty than another investment strategy given the same risk, they should opt for the strategy with the highest probability for success. Decades of return comparisons and scores of academic studies show passive portfolio management is that strategy.

The benefits of passive management using index funds are numerous. First is the cost. The fee for passive management in a mutual fund is much lower than active management. A fund company typically licenses an index from an independent index provider for a nominal fixed fee or a portion of the assets under management in the fund. In contrast, the active funds must pay economists and analysts to figure out which asset class, which countries, which industries, and which securities to buy and sell. This difference in labor costs keeps the expense ratio for a passive fund very low compared to an active fund. A fund that tracks an index may charge only 0.2 percent in annual fees compared to an active fund with the same investment objective, which may charge 1.2 percent per year.

Bond index funds also operate at a greatly reduced cost structure over actively managed bond funds for the same reasons. The typical bond index fund is about 0.2 percent compared to the 0.9 percent annual cost of an active fund. These figures don't consider sales charges or commissions that an investor may have to pay to purchase or sell funds.

Taxes are another important cost for many investors. Capital gains are distributed to mutual fund shareholders each year based on the net gains from securities sold within each fund. Indexes tend to have low turnover, so index funds have relatively low annual distributions compared to active funds. Distributions from exchange-traded fund (ETFs) are even lower than traditional open-end index funds due to their unique structure. For detailed information on ETFs, including tax benefits, read *The ETF Book* by Richard Ferri (John Wiley & Sons, 2009).

It's interesting to note that active fund turnover was much lower in the years prior to the introduction of index funds. Turnover started rising when active funds started to compete with index funds on performance. In fact, turnover in the active fund industry is about 15 times higher today than what it was in the 1960s.

There's only a finite amount of wealth that's earned in the financial markets each year. Accordingly, the cost to invest has a direct bearing on each investor's return. Since the cost of active management is higher than passive management, after all costs, the average actively managed dollar (or euro, yen, etc.) must underperform the average passively managed dollar (or euro, yen, etc.) in a market. This is according to William Sharpe, Stanford professor and Nobel Prize recipient. It's simple arithmetic, and it's the basis for all arguments that say index funds must outperform active funds in the future.[6]

All about Indexes and Benchmarks

Not all indexes are created equal. There are many different types of indexes to choose from and the selection grows each year. Accordingly, an explanation is needed about index construction before any logical case for index funds and ETFs that follow bench-marks can be made.

An index is a generic term that describes a list of securities that are selected and weighted according to a set of rules provided by an index originator. The index company publishes the price level and the performance of their indexes daily, along with its constituents and any changes to those indexes.

Benchmarks are market tracking indexes that most people envi-sion when they hear the word index. These are broadly based repre-sentations of market activity designed to track the value of financial markets or sectors within markets. A benchmark index is also known in the industry as a plain vanilla index and a beta seeking index.

What qualifies as an index has broadened over the years as more ETFs come to market that follow highly customized non-standard index methods. Today, it seems as though anything can be called an index. An index provider merely creates a mechanical set of rules for security selection, security weighting, and trading, and publishes their back-tested results. For example, an index may be made up of only dividend paying stocks with those stocks being weighted by dividend yield. Or, an index could include companies located west of the Mississippi that have female CEOs under the age of 50. Such an index doesn't exist, but it would if a fund company thought they could sell an index fund or ETF to enough people based on that index.

Buy the Benchmarks

Benchmarks are the only type of index that passive investors should care about because they represent market returns and all subsec-tions of a market. Benchmark indexes are weighted by the value of securities in the index (called capitalization weighted) because this represents the total opportunity set within a market available to all investors.

All index construction methods require constant update and recalculation. This wasn't possible until technology made calcu-lating prices and values easier. There were simple price indicators stretching back to the late 1800s; however, sophisticated market benchmarks that provided broad valuation data weren't available until the late 1950s.

The desire to create a yardstick for measuring general market information has its origins with Charles Henry Dow. His pioneering transportation average began in 1884 with a simple price average of 11 railroad stocks. Dow's average was only a price indicator and not a value measure. However, it did provide a rough barometer of stock market behavior. The indicator was published daily in the *Customer's Afternoon Letter,* forerunner of the *Wall Street Journal.*

In 1896, Dow formed the Dow Jones Industrial Average (DJIA) and renamed his original index as the Dow Jones Transportation Average. The DJIA is still the most widely quoted stock indicator in the media today, even though it still only covers 30 large companies, and those constituents are still weighted by price, not value.

By far, the most important innovation in benchmark construction was made in 1923 by the Standard Securities Corporation (now Standard & Poor's). S&P constructed the first capitalization weighted index that measured market value. There were 90 securities in the original index. This was a huge leap forward from the price-only Dow barometer of market movement.

The S&P index expanded to 500 securities during 1957, and the index level and its holdings became available to the public on a daily basis. The S&P 500 soon became a widely regarded benchmark for valuing the U.S. equities market and the one most often quoted among industry professionals. Not surprisingly, the S&P 500 was chosen as the basis for the first index fund by Vanguard in 1976 and the first exchange-traded fund by State Street Global Investors in 1993.

Starting in the 1970s, more companies entered the indexing business by collecting and tabulating market returns from around the globe and forming benchmarks. These firms included Frank Russell Company, Wilshire Associates, and Morgan Stanley Capital International (MSCI) to name a few. Most indexes created between 1970 and 2000 were intended to be used as benchmarks.

Defining Good Benchmarks

Benchmark indexes are used for many things. They are used as a yardstick to measure active management performance; they're used in economic analysis to measure the level of market activity; they're used by academics to define market behavior; and they're used by investors to set asset allocation policy. Benchmark indexes are also the basis for the low-cost passive index funds and ETFs promoted in this book.

In 1992, Nobel Laureate William Sharpe provided some criteria to be used in benchmark selection when measuring active management performance. He wrote that a proper benchmark should be (1) a viable alternative, (2) not easily beaten, (3) low in cost, and (4) identifiable before the fact.[7]

Benchmarking concepts were further advanced by Laurence Siegel in his 2003 book titled *Benchmarks and Investment Management*. Siegel describes a well constructed benchmark index as one that embodies the opportunity set that active managers have to choose from. The return on the benchmark should represent the return available from the asset class in its entirety and the return that a passive index fund would achieve before costs. The benchmark should also represent, before costs, the aggregation of all active managers who participate in the asset class.[8]

Siegel rightly defends the concept that all relevant benchmarks are capitalization weighted. A capitalization weighted index gives each company a weight in proportion to the total market value of that company's outstanding shares. This weighting method is the central organizing principle of good benchmark construction because it is the only way to represent the investable universe in dollar terms. This is the value set from which all active investors choose.

Other criteria are also included by Siegel as useful in identifying a proper benchmark. They are:

1. **Unambiguous:** The names and weights of securities constituting the benchmark are clearly delineated.
2. **Investable:** The option is available to forgo active management and simply hold the benchmark.
3. **Measurable:** The benchmark's return can be calculated on a reasonably frequent basis.
4. **Appropriate:** The benchmark is consistent with the active manager's style.
5. **Reflective of current investment options:** The active manager has current investment knowledge of the securities that make up the benchmark.
6. **Specified in advance:** the benchmark is constructed prior to the start of an evaluation period.

Passive investors should use index funds and ETFs that track benchmark indexes that reflect market returns. A benchmark may not hold all the securities listed on a market, such as the S&P 500, which holds only 500 stocks. However, as long the index holds enough securities so that it tracks a market closely and is capitalization weighted, then a product tracking that index is a viable choice for a passive portfolio.

Not All Indexes Are Passive

Passive investing as defined in this book means earning a market return in index funds and ETFs that follow benchmarks.

The Morningstar Principia database listed more than 1,100 index funds available to investors as of June 2010. This doesn't mean there are over 1,100 funds following market benchmarks. All benchmarks are indexes, but not all indexes are benchmarks. Many of the new indexes formed over the past decade are active management strategies. Strategy index products have been created and sold to fund providers to compete against index funds and ETFs that follow benchmark indexes. The fees for these newfangled products are double and triple the fees of traditional index funds.[9]

Starting around 2003, the active fund industry decided to expand the definition of an index so that they could compete against traditional index funds on more equal footing. A strategy index may use an active security selection model, or alterative security weighing model, or both. The strategy often consists of highly sophisticated quantitative models that are designed to beat a market benchmark. These strategy products aren't considered true passive investing and should be avoided in a low-cost passive portfolio.

The Portfolio Management Debate

So far we've addressed the active versus passive debate as one between actively managed mutual funds and passively managed index funds. There is another level to this debate. It's at the portfolio management level. It's a question of whether an investor, using any mutual fund type, should use an active allocation strategy or a passive one in the ongoing management of their portfolio.

Investors must make two choices: first, decide which asset allocation strategy is right for them, active or passive, and second, which type of mutual funds they'll use, active or passive. Table 1.1 outlines the four different portfolio management options along with their relative cost.

The first choice investors make is the type of asset allocation strategy they'll use. They can choose either a passive asset allocation strategy that spreads their portfolio across a different asset class using fixed weight allocations or an active strategy that tactically

Table 1.1 Portfolio Management Options

	Passive Funds (index funds and some index-based ETFs)	Active Funds (actively managed mutual funds and ETFs)
Investor maintains a fixed passive asset allocation	Passive funds Passive allocation (lowest cost)	Active funds Passive allocation (high cost)
Investor employs a tactical active asset allocation	Passive funds Active allocation (moderate cost)	Active funds Active allocation (highest cost)

weights allocations to asset classes based on perceived market valuations. For the purpose of this book, tactical asset allocation also includes market timing, which is a strategy that makes complete shifts in and out of asset classes.

The second choice an investor makes is investment selection. Once the asset allocation strategy is set, an investor decides to use index funds and ETFs that follow benchmarks or actively managed funds that attempt to outperform the benchmarks. Some investors may use a combination of both.

The portfolio management strategy recommended in this book is in the shaded box of Table 1.1. Investors should use low-cost index funds and ETFs that track market indexes inside a portfolio that follows a long-term fixed asset allocation strategy. Investments are allocated in fixed amount. When the market moves a portfolio's allocation outside its fixed limits set by the investment policy, the portfolio is rebalanced back to the allocation target. This strategy is commonly referred to as buy, hold, and rebalance.

The strategies in the other three boxes in Table 1.1 employ some type of active management. The hope for investors who choose one of the three active strategies is to generate excess return over the fully passive strategy. An investor who selects actively managed funds hopes those funds will outperform passive index funds, and an investor who chooses a tactical asset allocation hopes that their timing bets will yield higher returns than a fixed allocation to the markets.

All three active management strategies have higher costs compared to the fully passive strategy. The costs are higher due to larger active fund fees, trading costs, and perhaps taxes from higher turnover. There is also a timing cost borne by investors who attempt to time markets, which is a subject of discussion in Chapter 8.

The information in Table 1.1 will be referenced throughout this book. Several chapters will discuss active funds versus passive funds. A few chapters highlight problems that occur when employing a tactical asset allocation over a strategic asset allocation. In the long run, a passive asset allocation implemented with passively managed index funds and ETFs is the best choice.

Summary

The passive versus active debate started in the halls of academia during the 1960s and spilled over onto Main Street in 1976 with the launch of the first publicly available index fund. The active fund companies had to change their focus from providing diversification at a reasonable cost to insisting that their managers could beat the markets. The data consistently suggests that they can't.

The formation of a wide range of benchmarks in the 1970s and 1980s set the stage for an explosion of indexing products over the following decades. Passive investing through index funds and ETFs is now a viable alternative in almost all major asset classes and across styles and sectors. Each year, more market tracking indexes are created, and more of those benchmarks become investable through index funds and ETFs, providing investors with more choices.

The passive versus active debate also includes portfolio management. Investors must choose between passive strategic asset allocation and an active tactical timing method. The ideal choice for investors is a strategic asset allocation implemented with low-cost passively managed index funds and ETFs that follow market benchmarks. This approach provides the highest probability for achieving financial success.

Early Performance Studies

The early pioneers who developed the first portfolio performance measurement techniques were a determined bunch. They didn't have the comprehensive market benchmarks and robust mutual fund databases that we have today. Some of the benchmarks used for performance comparison were crude compared to today's indices, and many academics had to hand collect their mutual fund data by sorting through thousands of documents and recording their results on paper. These shortfalls didn't deter the academics from their mission, and didn't take away from the results because they adequately adjusted for the data shortfalls, sometimes with amazing ingenuity.

This chapter begins with the first in-depth analysis of managed stock accounts and broker stock recommendations from the late 1920s and early 1930s. It then takes us through several decades and mounting evidence against active management. The early research reached a crescendo in the late 1960s, as major breakthroughs in performance modeling were developed when computing power become more available. Some of the models introduced during the Roaring 60s are still the backbone of performance measurement methods used today.

It's worth noting that several young academics mentioned in this chapter went on to distinguished careers in finance. A few won the Sveriges Riksbank Prize in Economic Sciences in Memory of Alfred Nobel, more commonly known as the Nobel Prize in Economic Sciences. Their exhaustive investigative work and groundbreaking analysis became a driving force for future development of passive investment alternatives.

Cowles Commission Report

Alfred Cowles III dedicated his life to elevating economics into a more precise science using mathematical and statistical techniques. He founded the Cowles Commission in 1932 and served as president from its inception. For 10 years prior to founding the commission, Cowles maintained a private organization for statistical research on problems of investment and finance. The Cowles family have held a long association with Yale University. Many of them are Yale University graduates.[1]

The first motto of the Cowles Commission was "Science is Measurement." The first commission report to highlight this motto and attract widespread attention from the investment industry and academics (and still one of its best known of its publications today) was "Can Stock Market Forecasters Forecast?" published in *Econometrica* in July 1933.

For this study, Cowles meticulously collected and analyzed four different independent sources of investment advice from 1928 to 1932. His purpose was to determine if the sources had skill in selecting stocks or timing the stock market:

> These investigations were instituted five years ago as a means of testing the success of the applied economics in the investment field. It seemed a plausible assumption that if we could demonstrate the existence in individuals or organizations of the ability to foretell the elusive fluctuations, either of particular stocks, or of stocks in general, this might lead to the identification of economic theories or statistical practices whose soundness had been established by successful prediction. The forecasters include well-known organizations in the different fields represented, many of which are large and well financed, employing economists and statisticians of unquestioned ability.[2]

In the first of four studies, Cowles charted the weekly individual stock purchase recommendations of 16 established financial services firms from January 1928 to June 1932. There were approximately 7,500 forecasts made during the four and a half year period.

Cowles found the average performance for the 16 services was 1.4 percent below the Dow Jones Industrial Average, with 6 services outperforming the average and 10 underperforming. The ratio of winning services to losing was slightly more than 1 to 2. We see throughout this book that an approximate win-loss ratio of 1 to 2 for active investing recurs time and again throughout history and across all market segments.

Cowles didn't find any predictability in this first study. He concluded that the winning forecasters failed to demonstrate that they had exhibited skill. Their results were no better than that which would have occurred by chance.

In the second of four studies, Cowles measured the common stock investment records of 25 large fire insurance companies for the same period from 1928 to 1932. The investment policies of these companies were based on "the accumulated knowledge of successive boards of directors whose judgment might be presumed, over the years, to have been well above that of the average investor."

Cowles found that the funds failed to exhibit the existence of any skill despite the presumption of investor superiority. To the contrary, the accounts fell behind the Dow Jones Industrial Average (DJIA) by 1.2 percent per year. Of the 20 insurance companies analyzed, 6 portfolios showed outperformance while 14 showed underperformance. That's a win-loss ratio of about 1 to 2, which is the same ratio as in the first study of the financial services firm's stock selection success.

In the third of four studies, Cowles charted the forecasts for stock market performance made by 24 investment newsletters over the same 1928 to 1932 time period. He found that if investors had followed all of them, again with equal amounts of initial capital allotted to each, they would have fallen behind the market average by about 4 percent per year. For 4.5 years ending in June 1932, 8 out of the 24 forecasters exhibited returns higher than the market and 16 exhibited lower returns. This is exactly a 1 to 2 win-loss ratio!

In the fourth and final study, Cowles tested the results of a market timing strategy called Dow Theory, named after its founder, Charles Dow. The data gathered actually followed the predictions of Dow's predecessor, William Peter Hamilton, from 1904 until his death in 1929. Hamilton wrote 255 editorials in the *Wall Street Journal*, where he made market predictions based on Dow Theory.

Hamilton earned a total return of 12 percent per year over the 26-year period while the Dow Jones Industrial Average earned 15.5 percent per year. In all, Hamilton made 90 different market calls to be either long, short, or all in cash. Of those calls, 45 were profitable and 45 were unprofitable. This is the same result that would be expected from flipping a coin 90 times.

The Cowles Commission 1933 report on active management failed to find any individual or organization with the ability to consistently select winning individual securities or foretell the market returns. The results were consistent with chance rather than skill or insight, except for the worst forecasts, which appeared to be lower than expected by chance.

Cowles Updated

The stock market crash of 1929 and the subsequent Great Depression that followed wiped out many stock investors and stock forecasting services by the late 1930s. Nonetheless, Cowles updated his study in 1944 using 11 of the original 24 forecasters that survived through July 1943. He concluded again that these 11 leading financial firms "failed to disclose evidence of ability to predict successfully the future course of the stock market."[3]

Cowles reported that 6 of the 11 surviving forecasters outperformed a random sampling of stocks by 0.2 percent over the period. However, there was likely a strong survivorship bias in the data that resulted in a deceptively high average return for the remaining entities.

Survivorship bias occurs in performance data when the entire return histories of non-surviving entities are deleted from the database as these entities cease to exist. Cowles didn't report the partial period returns from the 13 forecasters who dropped out over the years because of poor performance. Had they been included in the years there was data available, the average return for all the forecasters would likely have been much lower than Cowles reported for only the surviving forecasters.

The Quiet Period

Banks made loans to stock speculators during the 1920s for the purpose of buying the stocks of companies that the banks were underwriting. This activity reached a zenith in late 1929 at about the same time that noted Yale economist Irving Fisher famously predicted, "Stock prices have reached what looks like a permanently high plateau."

Fisher continued to assure investors that a recovery was just around the corner while the stock market and economy collapsed between 1929 and 1932. It took over a decade for the economy and the Dow Jones to recover from the Great Depression.

The 1930s and 1940s were rocky times for whomever was left in the stock market. The Dow Jones did rally substantially in the late 1930s but failed to reach a new high. Stock prices fell back in the 1940s as World War II cast a dark shadow over the country. The Dow eventually climbed back and broke through the old high by 1955. Anyone who bought stocks just before the 1929 market crash didn't see those prices again until a quarter of a century.

As prices waned, academics lost interest in the stock valuation methods. Aside from Cowles's 1944 update, only a few minor studies were published on stock market behavior and the performance of professionally managed accounts during this period.

The Rise of Mutual Funds

Life was slow on Wall Street in the 1930s and 1940s as the country turned its attention to other important matters. However, behind the scenes, significant advances were taking place in the investment industry that would permanently change the way people invest in the markets. The old, highly leveraged bank trusts that caused the demise of so many individual investors during the market crash were going away, and a new way to invest was gaining attention. The new guy in town was open-end mutual funds.

The creation of the Massachusetts Investors Trust in 1924 heralded the arrival of the first modern mutual fund. This fund transformed the market for individual investors and small institutions. The fund eventually became the mutual fund industry giant MFS Investment Management, which is still operating today. State Street Global Investors followed closely behind MFS by starting their own fund in 1924. Scudder, Stevens & Clark would be the first to launch a no-load fund in 1928, which was also the year the Wellington Fund was launched. Wellington was the first mutual fund to include bonds.

By 1929, there were 19 open-ended mutual funds competing for assets. Many of these funds managed to survive through the 1930s despite the market crash and subsequent depression. A couple of reasons why mutual funds survived while bank trusts didn't are because mutual funds weren't leveraged like many bank trusts and the funds weren't used as a dumping ground for toxic assets as many bank trusts were.

Mutual funds gained assets and prominence in the years of economic recovery and through the war years. The Investment Company Act of 1940 helped restore public confidence in the financial system as a whole, and this helped expand the mutual fund industry. In 1940, mutual fund assets reached about $450 million.

After the end of World War II, returning solders exchanged their military uniforms for work boots and business suits, and with new prosperity sweeping the nation, a new generation of investors emerged. By the end of 1950s, mutual funds had reached an impressive $2.5 billion in assets.

Bogle on Mutual Funds

John Clifton Bogle was a college student at Princeton University in 1951 when he submitted his senior thesis as a requirement to obtain an undergraduate degree in economics. His thesis was titled "The Economic Role of the Investment Company." It was a 123-page overview of the mutual fund industry and was full of great information about the growing mutual fund market up to 1950. The thesis is reproduced in its entirety in *John Bogle on Investing: The First 50 Years* (McGraw-Hill, 2000).

One portion of Bogle's research reviewed and commented on the performance of mutual funds during the seven-year period of 1929–1936. He reported that the average per share asset value in 49 open-end funds increased by 6.7 percent.[4] The return for stocks was 7.4 percent over the same period as measured by Standard & Poor's.[*] The paper also examined specific fund returns in later years with mixed results in relation to the market average.

Commenting on this fund performance, Bogle wrote "Funds can make no claim to superiority over the market averages. . . . They state, rather, that their performance must be judged against what the individual could have done at the same cost over the same period, with the same objective as has a given fund."[5] This is important commentary because it captures the primary purpose of mutual fund investing at that time, which was diversification at a reasonable cost, not to beat the market.

Bogle also observed that "management can scarcely be expected to buy so that the fund can stay ahead of the market when the very

---

[*]Bogle did not include the S&P 500 return in his study. The index was added by this author for comparison purposes. Annualized data for the S&P 500 was provided by Standard & Poor's, a division of McGraw-Hill and Company, Inc.

securities that it buys are a part of that market."[6] Bogle saw this picture clearly. The supply of market returns is known. All participants in the market share in these returns, although not equally. There are winners and losers, and these inequalities zero out. For every investor who beats the market before expenses, one must underperform before expenses. Thus, after expenses, in aggregate most investors must underperform the market. It's simple arithmetic. This same logic would be used years later by several leading academics to support a passive indexing approach, including William Sharpe, winner of the Nobel Prize in Economics Sciences in 1991.

The Roaring 60s

Interest in the stock market was renewed in the late 1950s as the Dow broke though its old 1929 high. A new generation of post–WWII investors started buying into the market through customer's men working from local investment offices that were popping up on nearly every Main Street in America. Merrill Lynch, Shearson, Kidder Peabody, and Lehman Brothers became household names. Easy access to the markets through these local reps brought vigorous growth to the mutual fund industry. Over 100 new funds and billions of dollars in new assets flowed in during the 1960s. This growth provided a rich data source for academics to study, particularly young PhDs and PhD candidates looking to make a mark in the world.

These bright young people wanted to know what worked on Wall Street and what didn't. They sought to understand securities pricing and identify those investment strategies that consistently outperformed. It was assumed that some winning fund managers had skill and some were just lucky. The academics wanted to identify those who had skill and isolate the factors that made them better, and then capitalize on this information. This analysis would require new quantitative tools for comparing portfolio returns across hundreds of funds at the same time to effectively sort the skilled managers from the unskilled and the lucky ones.

The natural tendency for comparing results would be to evaluate returns in relation to market indices. However, while comparing mutual fund performance to a broad benchmark is an adequate way to gauge the returns of a mutual fund in general, it misses one important element: risk. A portfolio manager who takes higher risk should be expected to outperform a manager who takes lower risk. Should this extra return from taking extra risk be attributed to manager skill? That depends on the amount of extra risk taken and the amount of extra return.

The academics decided that actively managed portfolios needed to be risk-adjusted before determining if a manager had investment skill. The tools for doing this didn't exist. New methods were needed for digging under the surface of fund performance and comparing returns on a risk-adjusted basis.

What would occur in the 1960s was a revolution in how portfolio performance was measured. Risk was now going to be an important factor in evaluation along with return. This new area of performance research would be aided by increased computing power at colleges and universities.

Armed with 30 years of accumulated data on mutual fund performance, plus data from bank-managed trust accounts, insurance company funds, and pension funds, researchers had a rich source of data to conduct their analysis. Much of the early work on portfolio analysis centered on finding common risk elements that occurred across all these portfolios. If common risk elements were found across all portfolios, they could be incorporated into mathematical models and used to compare the results of many portfolios at the same time. It was an efficient way to approach the problem.

The following sections are synopses of the efforts by select researchers to better measure portfolio performance and make risk adjusted comparisons. There were so many advances in portfolio analysis that occurred in the 1960s that this short section doesn't do them justice. For the bigger picture, read Peter Bernstein's fabulous book about the origins of modern Wall Street titled *Capital Ideas* (Free Press, 1992). Bernstein's follow-up book, *Capital Ideas Evolving* (John Wiley & Sons, 2007) expands on this rich history and explores new frontiers of risk management to the current time.

Harry Markowitz

The huge leap that occurred in the understanding of stock prices, portfolio theory, and risk and return measurement techniques had its roots in a 1952 thesis Ph.D. written by an unassuming student from the University of Chicago. Twenty-five-year-old Harry Markowitz wrote a revolutionary research paper entitled "Portfolio Selection."[7] This short, initially unnoticed 14-page paper would eventually change the way institutions managed portfolios, the way colleges and universities would teach portfolio management, and the way analysts would measure portfolio performance.

Markowitz's paper was revolutionary because it explored the idea that portfolio risk is as important a part of portfolio management as portfolio return. He noted in his paper that there is a direct correlation between risk and return, although a portfolio should try to eliminate as much risk as possible, observing that ". . . the investor does (or should) consider expected return a desirable thing *and* variance of return [i.e., risk] an undesirable thing." Markowitz's basic theory was that a portfolio is efficient if no other portfolio provides either (1) a higher expected return and the same risk or (2) a lower risk and the same expected return.

As obvious as this concept seems today, until Markowitz pointed out that risk is equally as important as return in portfolio management, academics and portfolio managers had only considered the risk of each individual security. No study had explored overall portfolio risk as it relates to portfolio return.

Markowitz makes the case for a broadly diversified portfolio that is spread across multiple industry sectors to decrease its overall portfolio risk. As he states in his paper, this portfolio ". . . gives both maximum expected return and minimum variance, and it commends this portfolio to the investor." In today's world, Markowitz would be making the case for a total market index fund that holds all tradable securities because this is the maximum expected return and minimum variance [i.e., risk] portfolio.

Harry Markowitz expanded his thoughts in his 1959 book entitled *Portfolio Selection: Efficient Diversification of Investments* (John Wiley & Sons, 1959). It extended his theory of minimum variance as a factor in portfolio construction. This work spawned many new ideas among academics and market researchers.

Eugene Fama

Eugene Fama was another early pioneer in portfolio theory. He received his undergraduate degree from Tufts University in 1960, and his Masters and Ph.D. from the University of Chicago in 1965.

Fama's meticulously researched Ph.D. thesis was published in 1965 and titled "The Behavior of Stock Market Prices." The purpose of the paper was to test the theory that stock market prices are random and follow what's commonly referred to today as a *random walk*.[8]

Fama's work led to the formation of the efficient market hypothesis (EMH), which is a theory of efficient security pricing in free and open markets. The theory states that all known and available information is already reflected in current securities prices. Thus, the price agreed to by a willing buyer and seller in the open market is the best estimate, good or bad, of the investment value of a security. Any new information is nearly instantaneously incorporated into market prices. This makes it almost impossible to capture excess returns without taking greater risk or having inside information about securities.

One of Fama's tests was to review mutual fund performance for randomness in return. The idea was that if mutual funds exhibited random returns, then that's further evidence that stock prices within mutual funds are also random because no portfolio manager could consistently capitalize on inefficiencies or trends.

Fama reviewed domestic equity mutual funds that had at least 10 years of performance from 1951 to 1960. He classified a fund as domestic equity if it held no more than five percent in bonds. There were 39 funds that met his criteria. He then compared the performance of the 39 funds to an equal-weighted New York Stock Exchange (NYSE) index. An equal-weighted index assumes the same amount is invested in each NYSE stock regardless of the market value of each company. Figure 2.1 illustrates the returns of the 39 funds to the NYSE equal-weight index and the capitalization-weighted S&P 500.[*]

On average, the 39 funds performed slightly better than the equal-weighted NYSE index. However, there were 17 funds outperforming and 22 underperforming, providing a 44 percent success rate. The average outperformance for the 17 funds was 1.9 percent, and the average underperformance for the 22 funds was 1.6 percent. Fama concluded:

> Thus, funds in general seem to do no better than the market; in addition, individual funds do not seem to outperform consistently their competition. Our conclusion, then, must be that so far the sophisticated analyst has escaped detection.[9]

---

[*]Fama did not include the S&P 500 return in his 1965 study. The index was added by this author for comparison purposes. Annualized data for the S&P 500 was provided by Standard & Poor's, a division of McGraw-Hill and Company, Inc.

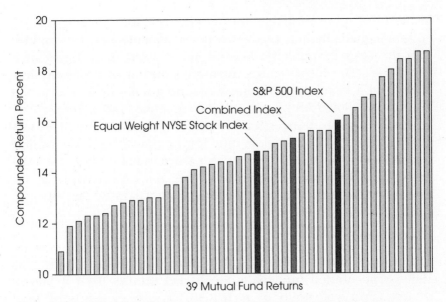

Figure 2.1   Annualized Returns for 39 Domestic Equity Funds from 1951–1960

In my opinion, Fama gives the funds more credit than they deserve. The 39 funds likely held a greater weight in the large company stocks that dominate the market by value than to an equal-weight NYSE index favoring mid and small cap stocks by value. Since 1951 to 1960 was a period when large company stocks outperformed mid and small company stocks, it's a fair conjecture that the funds likely held a greater weighting of large cap stocks than mid and small cap stocks. If this assumption is correct, then the funds would have performed worse than a capitalization weighted index.

In fact, the 39 funds didn't perform well against the capitalization-weighted S&P 500 included for comparison in Figure 2.1 (the S&P 500 return was not included in Fama's study). Only 9 funds outperformed the S&P, and 30 funds underperformed, providing a 23 percent success rate. The average outperformance for the 9 funds was 1.6 percent and the average underperformance for the 30 funds was 2.4 percent.

A composite index shown in Figure 2.1 represents the half-way point between the capitalization weight S&P 500 and the equal weight NYSE. I created this benchmark because I believe it's a closer representation to how the 39 funds would have actually invested their assets by capitalization. In other words, the stocks in the funds were probably not market capitalization weighted or equal weighed. Rather, they were likely someplace in the middle with the largest companies holding more assets than the smaller companies. The fund returns themselves hint at this presumption although I have no direct evidence of fund holdings.

An S&P 500/NYSE equal weight composite index resulted in 13 funds outperforming, 25 underperforming, and 1 tie. This was approximately a 1 to 2 win-lose ratio for these surviving funds, which is consistent with other active versus passive index studies. The outperforming 13 funds achieved a 1.7 percent excess return while average underperformance of the remaining 25 was 2.0 percent.

William Sharpe

The performance valuation models created by researchers in the 1960s concentrated on separating market returns from manager returns. Every portfolio of securities has two elements of risk: systematic risk, which is the risk of the market in general, and unsystematic risk, which is risk created from the individual securities in a portfolio. To make things simple, I'll refer to systematic risk as market risk and unsystematic risk as non-market risk.

Market risk is visible in individual security returns and small groups of securities. It's the risk that each individual security carries in addition to market risk. For example, a randomly selected portfolio of 50 stocks may have 80 percent market risk and 20 percent non-market risk.

Non-market risk can be mitigated away in a portfolio by adding more securities. For example, adding more stocks beyond our random 50 stock portfolio would increase its market risk while decreasing its non-market risk.

Market risk is risk of the entire asset class. It cannot be diversified away by adding more securities of the same asset class into a portfolio.

Figure 2.2 illustrates how broad diversification reduces non-market risk. As the number of securities in a portfolio increases, non-market risk decreases to a point where only market risk remains.

William Sharpe chose the Greek letter beta (β) to represent market risk.[10] Sharpe said the market's beta is always equal to 1.0 regardless of periodic high or low volatility in securities prices. The market cannot become more or less risky than itself.

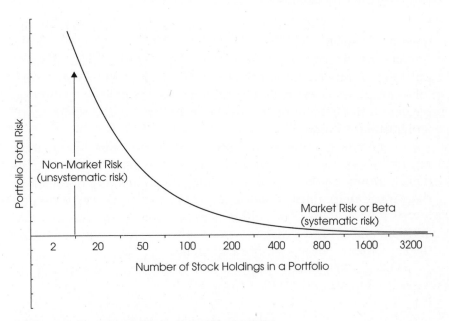

Figure 2.2 Market Risk and Non-Market Risk

Since the market always has a beta of 1.0, the risk of individual securities and of portfolios can be expressed in relation to market beta. For example, if a mutual fund is broadly diversified across hundreds of large company's stocks in different industries, it will likely have a beta close to 1.0 because the portfolio structure is very close to the market structure. When the market goes up 10 percent, the portfolio will likely go up by close to the same amount because it has a beta of 1.0. On the other hand, if a portfolio holds only a few small company stocks in select industries, it may have a beta of 1.3, which means the portfolio price moves more than the market even though it's market risk that's moving the portfolio. If the market goes up 10 percent, the small stock portfolio will likely go up by roughly 12 percent because it has more market risk (it's not a one-to-one formula).

Every portfolio has its beta regardless of the number of securities in it, and even a single security portfolio has a beta. The relevance of beta depends on how broadly a portfolio is diversified. A portfolio with only a few stocks may have a beta of 1.0, but the returns of the portfolio may vary widely from the market return because of the high non-market risk in the portfolio. In contrast, a portfolio of hundreds of stocks may also have a beta of 1.0, but there's much less non-market risk and beta will have a large influence on the portfolio's return.

Sharpe's beta measure can be uses to compare all securities and portfolios to one common risk factor. This makes risk-adjusted portfolio comparisons easier and faster. Beta is elegant, logical, and simple, and it has been applied extensively over the decades in finance and business valuation.

In summary, there's only one market risk and one market return. No excess return or excess risk exists in the market. This makes all non-market risk a zero sum game. For every non-market risk winner there must be a non-market risk loser. However, no one invests for free. After fees and expenses, most non-market risk takers (i.e., active fund investors) must underperform the market by the costs they incur. It's simple arithmetic.

During 1964, Sharpe applied beta in his revolutionary Capital Asset Pricing Model (CAPM) for which he was awarded the Nobel Prize in Economic Science. This model defines a company's estimated cost-of-capital in relation to that company's specific beta. The Capital Asset Pricing Model remains the backbone of modern price theory for financial markets. It's applied extensively in valuation models of both public and private enterprises and has become an important tool for business decision making.

Jack Treynor

Jack Treynor was a mathematics major at Haverford College before graduating from Harvard Business School with distinction in 1955. He later studied at MIT under another great researcher, Franco Modigliani, an economist at the MIT Sloan School of Management and MIT Department of Economics, and winner of a Nobel Prize in Economic Sciences in 1985.

Treynor created a formula for fund evaluation using beta in 1965, which became known as the Treynor Ratio. His findings were published in the *Harvard Business Review*.[11] The article was entitled "How to Rate Management of Investment Funds."

Here is how the Treynor Ratio works: Take any portfolio's return and subtract a risk-free rate of return (usually the Treasury bill yield); then divide the result by the portfolio's beta. The result is the ratio of a portfolio's excess return to market risk as measured by the portfolio's beta.

The Treynor Ratio can be used to compare many portfolios to one another and sort the results by the best risk-adjusted returns.

The funds with the highest ratios have the highest returns per unit of market risk; this is an indication of the managers who may have skill. The ratio is used to weed out bad managers from potential good ones, thus making an investment consultant's job much easier.

William Sharpe developed a similar formula for evaluating risk-adjusted returns of portfolios. Ironically, rather than using his own beta formula as the denominator in the equation, Sharpe used a portfolio's standard deviation of return. Perhaps this was because Treynor beat him to the punch. Sharpe's formula became known as the Sharpe Ratio.

An interesting 1966 paper published by Sharpe in the *Journal of Business* evaluated the performance of 34 mutual funds over a period from 1954–1963 using the Sharpe ratio; the Treynor Ratio; and a third factor, fund expenses.[12] Sharpe's intent was to compare the three methods and perhaps determine which was better at determining skill among mutual fund managers.

Sharpe found sufficient evidence that all three ratios had some predictability for selecting funds relative to each other, although no one method isolated funds that consistently outperformed the market as measured by the DJIA (Sharpe doesn't disclose why he chose this limited market indicator when the more comprehensive S&P 500 existed). Sharpe acknowledged that the DJIA had no transaction cost or administrative expenses; however, he also noted that the fund returns were calculated without deducting their sales commission, which for most was 8.5 percent. Here are the results:

- The market as measured by the DJIA was less than 11 active funds and better than the remaining 23 funds. Basically, there was one winning fund for every two losing funds, a win-loss ratio of 1 to 2.
- The Sharpe Ratio for the Dow was 0.67 while the average ratio for the 34 funds was only 0.63. This means the Dow had a better return per unit of risk than the average mutual fund in the study.
- The Treynor Ratio returned results similar to the Sharpe Ratio.

Sharpe also tested fees as a predictor of return. He makes this important observation about fees near the conclusion of the paper:

> While it may be dangerous to generalize the results found during one ten-year period, it appears that the average mutual fund selects a portfolio at least as good as the Dow-Jones

Industrials, but that the results actually obtained by the holder of mutual fund shares (after the costs associated with the operation of the fund have deducted) fall somewhat short of those from the Dow-Jones portfolio. This is consistent with our previous conclusion that, all things being equal, the smaller a fund's expense ratio, the better the results obtained by its stockholders.

Sharpe's observation about mutual fund expenses in the last sentence is noteworthy because it set the stage for much discussion on the topic in the future. If professionals select stocks at least as good as the market, but in doing so incur fund expenses that erode performance, then expenses become an important determinant in predicting active fund performance. John Bogle made a similar observation in his 1951 Princeton thesis.

Michael Jensen

If a portfolio has a higher return than predicted by its beta, this excess return could be an indication of manager skill. This excess return has been given a name. It's called *Jensen's Alpha* after Michael C. Jensen, a University of Chicago-educated PhD. The name was shortened to *alpha* by practitioners over the years.

Jensen published his research paper introducing alpha in *The Journal of Finance* in 1967. He agreed with Treynor and Sharpe that a portfolio's return should be risk-adjusted to properly measure a manager's skill. Riskier portfolios are expected to have higher returns over time than less risky portfolio, and outperforming managers shouldn't be credited with having skill just because they took more risk.

Jensen thoroughly analyzed 115 surviving fund returns from 1945 to 1964 to test his formula. He found the average fund earned about 1.1 percent less per year than the S&P 500.[*] This was a lower than expected return given the average fund's level of risk as measured by its beta. In other words, the average fund manager didn't generate alpha.

---

[*]Prior to March 1, 1957, the S&P index was based on only 90 securities in Jensen's study (50 industrials, 20 rails, and 20 utilities) and hence for the earlier period, the index is a less reliable estimate of the returns of the market portfolio.

Net of fees and risk-adjusted, 39 surviving funds beat the market while 76 funds underperformed. That's a 1-to-2 win-loss ratio in the funds before the risk adjustment and a 1-to-2 win-loss ratio after risk adjustment. The median winning fund outperformed the market on a risk-adjusted basis by 0.6 percent while the median losing fund underperformed the market by 1.6 percent. It is interesting to note in Jensen's study that fund managers fared no better or worse in their risk-adjusted returns than their unadjusted performance.

Jensen summed up his findings in his study's abstract:

> The evidence on mutual fund performance indicates not only that these 115 mutual funds were on average not able to predict security prices well enough to outperform a buy-the-market-and-hold policy, but also that there is very little evidence that any individual fund was able to do significantly better than that which we expected from mere random chance.[13]

Alpha is an indication of a manager's potential skill. However, it's not a guarantee of manager skill. Alpha doesn't differentiate skill from luck. A certain number of managers will outperform the market due to randomness, and there's no telling when their luck will run out. Even if Alpha did indicate skill, that's history. There's no way to know which managers will show skill in the future. Chapter 7 explains why past performance is not an indicator of future returns.

Alpha is always a zero sum game across the investment industry before fees and expenses. The cost of acquiring relevant investment information, analyzing the information, and making trading decisions is expensive. Even if active managers are correct on their analysis, the cost of active management often overwhelms whatever alpha they find.

It should be emphasized that neither Jensen nor any other academic was out to debunk active management. To the contrary, their research was conducted with the intent to identify skilled managers and alpha generating strategies. Instead, the academic evidence pointed to a different conclusion. It showed that active management strategies added more risk than investors were compensated for. In a nutshell, the act of active management created uncompensated risk.

There were several other studies conducted during the 1960s and 1970s that lead to the same conclusions about actively managed funds. Using only funds that survived and discarding the funds that closed or merged, the probability of selecting a winning actively managed fund is about one winner for every two losers, and the payout for success isn't nearly as high as it should be given the poor odds for success and survivability. The academics all agreed that investors would have been better of just buying the index if it was possible. The problem was that index funds didn't exist—but that was about to change.

Summary

The early performance analyses presented in this chapter point to a few basic conclusions that appear to always be true: (1) in the aggregate and before expenses, active management appears to add little value over market benchmarks, (2) after expenses the probability for adding value drops precipitously, and (3) the excess returns earned from the few winning funds are not high enough to compensate investors for the high shortfall from the losing funds.

Active management was exposed as a loser's bet many decades ago by the academic community. The more bets that an investor makes on actively managed funds the lower their probability for outperforming the markets. It's a mathematical certainty.

The references in this chapter are just the tip of the iceberg for readers who wish to investigate further. Sourcing these references leads to a treasure chest of data, analysis, and opinion from many leading academics, researchers, and practitioners.

CHAPTER 3

The Birth of Index Funds

Index investing emerged in the early 1970s in a series of fits and starts. Trading costs within mutual funds were high because brokerage commission rates were regulated by the federal government. An index fund holding several hundred stocks would have incurred high internal expenses. A couple of institutional index portfolios were started by banks, but they had limited access and limited success. The deregulation of fixed commission rates in 1975 lowered mutual fund trading costs, and by 1976 the first publicly available index fund was launched. This chapter is a brief overview covering the birth of index investing, the first publicly available index mutual fund by the Vanguard Group, and the huge success that this fund has enjoyed.

The First Indexed Portfolios

In 1971, John A. McQuown and William L. Fouse from Wells Fargo Bank pioneered the first private index portfolio with a $6 million account for the Samsonite Corporation pension fund. The account was designed to track an equal weighted index of New York Stock Exchange equities, similar to the method described in early research papers from the 1960s. Unfortunately, the execution of this strategy was a nightmare due to high commission costs from government directed fixed rates. The method was abandoned in 1976 and replaced with a market-weighted S&P 500 Index.

Batterymarch Financial Management of Boston also independently pursued index investing in 1971. The developers were the firm's co-founders, Jeremy Grantham and Dean LeBaron. There were no takers for the strategy, which led *Pensions & Investments* newspaper to award the firm the Dubious Achievement Award in 1972. Two years later, in December 1974, Batterymarch attracted its first client to the strategy.

American National Bank in Chicago also created a common trust fund in 1974 that tracked the S&P 500 Index. The fund was the work of Rex Sinquefield, an MBA graduate of the University of Chicago. The minimum investment was $100,000, which was too high for most individual investors, but at least the fund was open to the public.

In 1981, Rex Sinquefield became chairman of Dimensional Fund Advisors (DFA) and McQuown of Wells Fargo joined DFA's board of directors. DFA develops low-cost index-based investment strategies for advisor clients through mutual funds and for institutional clients through privately managed portfolios.

The First Index Fund

In his bestselling book, *A Random Walk Down Wall Street* (W.W. Norton, 1973), Princeton professor Burton G. Malkiel published his own in-depth mutual fund analysis. His conclusions were similar to all the other academics who studied the data. Where was the skill? Most active fund managers don't beat the market and can't beat the market.

Malkiel's book targeted the court of public opinion, and he was an exceptionally successful communicator. Individual investors began to understand how the mutual fund deck was stacked against them. Malkiel laid out several advantages for the formation of an index fund that matched the market's return, and even made a plea to mutual fund companies to sponsor an index fund, noting that "fund spokesmen are quick to point out you can't buy the market averages. It's time the public can."[1]

Malkiel was not the lone voice pleading for index funds in the early 1970s. Several other prominent voices called out for passive options.

One voice was MIT's Paul Samuelson. He wrote a short and punchy 1974 article in the *Journal of Portfolio Management* entitled "Challenge to Judgment." Samuelson struck at the heart of professional money managers by stating, ". . . the best of money managers cannot be demonstrated to be able to deliver the goods of superior portfolio-selection performance. . . . Superior investment performance is unproved." He goes on to suggest that, "at the least, some large foundation should set up an in-house portfolio that tracks the S&P 500 Index—if only for the purpose of setting up a naïve model against which their in-house gunslingers can measure their prowess."[2]

Charles Ellis, then president of Greenwich Associates and a respected investment advisor to charitable trusts, added to this chorus with his famous 1975 article, "The Loser's Game." It was an admission of sorts from a leading industry insider that the current method wasn't working for investors. What Ellis wrote shook the very foundation of the investment management business:

> The belief that active managers can beat the market is based on two assumptions: (1) liquidity offered in the stock market is an advantage, and (2) institutional investing is a Winner's Game. The unhappy thesis of this article can be briefly stated: Owing to important changes in the past ten years, these basic assumptions are no longer true. On the contrary, market liquidity is a liability rather than an asset, and institutional investors will, over the long term, underperform the market because money management has become a Loser's Game.[3]

Associate Editor A.F. Ehrbar of *Fortune* magazine chimed in with his thoughts in a July 1975 article entitled "Some Kinds of Mutual Funds Make Sense." Ehrbar pointed out that, "while funds cannot consistently outperform the market, they can consistently underperform it by generating excessive research costs and trading costs."[4] He wasn't optimistic that the fund industry would change anytime soon.

Along Came John

As Ehrbar predicted, the pleas for an index fund available to all investors were largely ignored by the established mutual fund firms. Active management was the only game in town, and it was profitable to those firms, so why ruin a good thing? The stubbornness of the old-line firms created an opportunity for one enterprising person who was paying attention. That person was John Clifton Bogle.

John Bogle began the quest for an index fund by first doing his own number-crunching to confirm the performance numbers that others had pointed out. He calculated by hand the annual returns generated by the actively managed mutual funds over the previous

30 years and compared those returns with the Standard & Poor's 500 Index. The funds underperformed the index on an annual pre-tax margin by 1.5 percent. This shortfall was virtually identical to the costs incurred by fund investors during that period.[5]

The Vanguard Group would launch Bogle's index fund in 1976 even though the firm wasn't set up for this purpose. Formed in May 1975, Vanguard's purpose was to direct the day-to-day administrative, financial, and legal operations of what had been previously known as the Wellington Group of Funds. Vanguard itself wasn't allowed to manage mutual funds or market them as part of its agreement with Wellington. However, Bogle saw an opportunity to run an unmanaged index fund under this agreement because the stock selection in the S&P 500 was done by another firm.

Bogle and his tiny staff met with Wellington's board of directors in the fall of 1975. They explained that no advice would be involved in an index fund offering, and that the fund's underwriting and marketing would be handled by an outside syndicate of brokerage firms so that Vanguard would not be breaking its agreement with Wellington. Bogle argued that the offering would be within the mandate that Vanguard agreed upon with Wellington.

The board accepted this view, and a Declaration of Trust for the Vanguard First Index Investment Trust was filed with the U.S. Securities and Exchange Commission on December 31, 1975.

Ironically, the world's first low-cost index mutual fund would have to be sold through the high cost brokerage industry because Vanguard couldn't market mutual funds per their Wellington agreement. The selling brokers would earn a sales commission of 6.0 percent on the amount they sold, which at the time was distinctly below the typical commission rate of 8.5 percent commission paid to brokers for selling actively managed mutual funds.

Selling through brokers and offering them a below average commission was a big risk. The University of Pennsylvania Wharton School released a major study in the early 1970s suggesting that broker recommendations to clients were heavily influenced by the size of the sales commission. The study also noted that high commission funds produced lower returns than low commission funds when the commission was included in fund performance. Tying these two facts together suggested that yield-to-broker was more important than yield-to-client.[6]

The brokerage industry acted exactly as the Wharton School study predicted. Brokers were turned off by the commission haircut and largely ignored the Vanguard First Index Investment Trust. The initial offering attracted only $11 million in assets, far below the $150 million target. Nonetheless, a bold decision was made by Vanguard to launch the fund. On August 31, 1976, the world's first index fund became available to the public.

Vanguard changed direction in February 1977. The contract with Wellington restricting direct sales was terminated and the brokerage distribution channel was dropped, along with the sales commission. From then on, all investors would have direct contact with Vanguard and they would not have to pay a sales load. In addition, the Vanguard Group would be owned by the funds it administered. The firm would operate on an at-cost basis, putting the shareholder in the driver's seat. The shackles were off as John Bogle and his small crew at Vanguard set a new course to sail into unchartered waters.

Vanguard 500 Index Fund's Proven Record

In 1976, the passive versus active debate moved from academia to Main Street as the battle for the hearts and minds of investors' began. Who's been winning the battle? Let's start by looking at the performance of Vanguard's first index fund over the past 25 years.

There were about 260 actively managed domestic equity funds available to investors at the time the Vanguard 500 Index Fund launched in late 1976, according to Lipper, a financial markets research and wholly owned subsidiary of Reuters Group PLC. About half of those funds have closed or merged over the years, leaving 136 surviving funds as of December 2009. Figure 3.1 illustrates how these remaining funds have performed relative to the Vanguard 500 Index Fund over a 25-year period ending in 2009 according to Lipper data.

Figure 3.1 doesn't include the closed or merged funds. It only includes data on funds that have survived since 1976. The first strike against active funds is their relative performance. The Vanguard 500 Index Fund placed in the 34th percentile of surviving funds over the 25-year period. The actively managed funds to the right of the Vanguard 500 achieved higher returns and the funds to the left earned lower returns. These are nominal pre-tax returns, not risk-adjusted after-tax returns.

Exactly one-third of the surviving funds outperformed the index fund and two-thirds underperformed. This win-loss ratio of

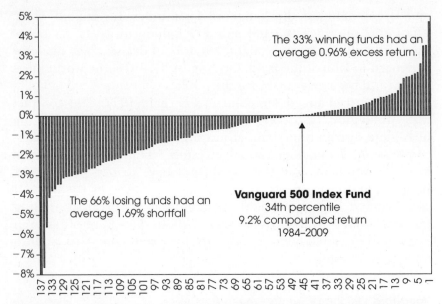

Figure 3.1   Active Funds Performance Relative to Vanguard 500 Index Fund (1985-2009)

1 to 2 is right in line with what all the academic studies from the 1960s and 1970s predicted, showing that passively managed index funds do perform as expected.

Closed and merged funds were not included; however, studies on closed and merged fund performance show that a large majority of these funds considerably underperformed their benchmarks in the years leading up to their demise. Chapter 6 provides performance data on terminated mutual funds prior to closing or merging.

Including terminated fund performance in the data up to each fund's termination date would eliminate the survivorship bias and change the outcome in Figure 3.1. Without survivorship bias, the Vanguard 500 Index Fund beat over 85 percent of actively managed funds during the 25 year period.

The second strike against active funds in this sample is the small excess returns of the winning active funds relative to larger short-falls from the losing funds. The excess return for picking a winning active fund is far below a fair payout given the high probability of selecting a losing fund and the average shortfall from losing funds. The winning funds won by an average of 0.96 percent, while the losing active funds fell short by 1.69 percent on average.

Given a win-loss ratio of 1 to 2 for surviving actively managed funds, a fair payout for winning would be double the potential shortfall from losing. In this real-world example, the winning active funds should have provided an average fair payout of 3.38 percent return given the 1.69 percent average loss. In fact, the average winning fund delivered only 0.96 percent in excess return—less than one-third the fair payout! That's like betting $1 on a coin flip and only getting $1.30 when you win when you should be getting $2. The payout isn't aligned with the odds.

The third strike against active management is sales loads. The Vanguard 500 Index Fund had no sales load in 1985. Many of the surviving 136 in Figure 3.1 did have a sales load. Had sales load been included in the performance data, the Vanguard 500 Index Fund would have beat 88 percent of the active funds over the 25-year period.

The fourth strike against actively managed funds is risk. Had the active fund data been adjusted for risk using the various risk-adjusted models described in other chapters, fewer active funds would have outperformed the Vanguard 500 on a risk-adjusted basis. This is due to the fact that most of the 136 active funds held stocks with smaller market capitalizations than the S&P 500. Small cap stocks have greater risk, and therefore there needs to be a risk adjustment in the data, as we will learn in Chapter 4.

The fifth and final strike against the active funds is taxes. Mutual funds distribute dividends and capital gains to shareholders each year as they are realized. Index funds are inherently tax efficient compared to actively managed funds because index funds do not turn over securities on a regular basis. The annual turnover of the S&P 500 is about six percent compared to an annual turnover of about 50 percent for active funds. Greater turnover in a mutual fund generates greater costs, which must be paid for by investors in the fund.

The Morningstar Tax Cost Ratio measures how much a fund's annualized return is reduced by the taxes investors pay on distributions. The data goes back 15 years in the Morningstar Principia program. The 15-year tax cost ratio for the Vanguard 500 Index Fund was 0.5 percent per year versus a 1.5 percent per year average tax cost for the 136 active funds. Including the after-tax returns for the sample, and assuming the closed and merged funds also had lower after-tax returns, I estimate that the Vanguard 500 Index Fund beat over 90 percent of the active funds over the 25-year period.

The 25-year Vanguard 500 Index Fund study is a classic active versus passive illustration. The win-loss ratio for active funds compared to the index fund is 1 to 2 even before making adjustments for terminated funds, risk factors, sales loads, and taxes. To add insult to injury, the average underperformance from the losing funds was greater than double the outperformance of winning funds, meaning the winning fund payout was only about 30 percent of what would be expected in a fair game.

The picture that starts to emerge from this data and from the previous chapter is that actively managed mutual funds are the wrong choice for long-term investors. The odds of choosing a winning active fund are low, the average potential reward for picking a winning fund is below a fair payout, and the longer actively managed funds are held the worse their relative performance becomes. It doesn't pay to play with actively managed mutual funds.

Summary

Index investing had a difficult start in the early 1970s. High fixed commission rates on Wall Street made management expensive, and the entire concept was slow to catch on with investors. Increasing calls for a low-cost index fund open to all investors were dismissed by the old-line mutual fund industry.

John Bogle heard these calls. In 1976, he and his crew at the Vanguard Group pushed for and successfully launched the first index fund available to all investors. The fund was called the First Investors Index Trust and later re-named the Vanguard 500 Index Fund.

The Vanguard 500 Index Fund has performed exactly how the academics anticipated. Low fees in the fund and low turnover propelled the fund into the top echelon of fund performance over the years, and a new era of mutual fund investing emerged.

Advances in Fund Analysis

The early research from the Roaring 60s has led to further development in risk-based portfolio analysis with the help of faster computers and more complete databases. Academics have made huge progress in isolating new risk factors that together with beta help explain portfolio returns more completely. Two prominent risk factors that have been quantified in recent decades are the firm size factor and the value factor. More recently, momentum has garnered a lot of attention, although capturing this factor in real time may prove to be difficult due to trading costs.

The Early Years in Review

The early academics worked hard to create a simple risk-based model for evaluating active manager performance so they could more easily identify skill. These efforts lead to several models that are the backbone of analysis today, including the Capital Asset Pricing Model (CAPM), Sharpe Ratio, Treynor Ratio, and Jensen's Alpha.

These efforts began with Harry Markowitz's pioneering work on portfolio construction in the 1950s. He asserted that both risk and return were equally important in portfolio decisions. The tactic taken by most researchers subsequently has been to adjust a portfolio by its market risk factor called beta; this will highlight any excess return that could signal manager skill. Market risk was symbolized by the Greek letter beta (β) and the excess return that managers created over market risk was symbolized by the Greek letter alpha (α).

Beta is the dominant factor driving the returns of all broadly diversified portfolios. A portfolio with a beta greater than the market beta, which is deemed to be 1.0, should outperform the stock market over time simply because there is more market risk in the portfolio. The risk-based formulas from Sharpe, Treynor, and Jensen don't give credit to managers for beating the market if they were simply taking more market risk, nor did they penalize a manager for underperformance when the portfolio had less than market risk.

Ironically, none of the models succeeded in their original intent to find a proven risk-adjusted method for consistently beating the market. The academics were unable to isolate consistent outper-formance among active managers after adjusting for market risk. What alpha they did find was not more than would be expected by chance. It was even difficult to say that the best performing manag-ers weren't simply lucky.

Building on Success

Beta models do explain a significant portion of a diversified mutual fund's return. However, there's a lot of wiggle room in the data. Even William Sharpe concedes that a single factor model alone doesn't capture all the risks in a diversified portfolio.[1] Other common risk factors are also at work, and those risks could be factored into a valuation model as well. Finding these other common factors and quantifying them became the main focus for academics in the 1980s and beyond.

The Firm Size Factor

Small company stocks have had higher returns than large com-pany stocks. Much of this excess return is explained by higher betas in small stocks, and some isn't. Research shows that stocks in small companies have generated higher returns than can be completely explained by beta.

The excess return was first documented by Rolf Banz in 1981. Banz conducted a study of U.S. equity returns over the 40-year period of 1936 to 1975. He found that small firms had considerably higher returns than large firms, and that this excess return could not be fully explained by their higher betas. There was another risk fac-tor driving the returns of small company stocks higher than what the risk models estimated. He coined the phenomenon the *size effect*.[2]

The database Banz used included all New York Stock Exchange (NYSE) stocks. The smallest 20 percent of the firms on the NYSE earned a beta-adjusted return that was about 5 percent per year higher than the remaining firms. He also noticed that this difference varied considerably. At times the size effect was positive and at times negative; other times it disappeared altogether within the 40-year period.

Also in 1981, another researcher, Marc Reinganum, analyzed a broader sample of 566 NYSE and American Stock Exchange (Amex) firms over a much shorter period from 1975 to 1977.[3] He found during this three-year period that the smallest 10 percent of firms outperformed the largest 10 percent by 1.6 percent per month. Reinganum calculated that 0.6 percent of this excess return was due to higher beta in the smallest companies, while the remaining 1.0 percent per month was due to a size effect.

No one could definitively explain why the size effect occurred. The academics surmised that small company stock had higher returns than large company stock, and that part of the excess return could be explained by higher beta, but they couldn't agree on what the other part was. Banz theorized that higher uncertainty from insufficient information about small companies may have caused the extra premium. Others theorized that it was a liquidity premium in the market, meaning that small stocks have lower trading volume than large company stocks and are subject to higher trading spreads and bigger price swings as a result. Still others believe there is a greater business and credit risk in small companies, and thus higher return on capital is required.

Whatever the reason or reasons for the small stock premium, all the researchers agreed that it was due to a risk factor that wasn't accounted for by the market risk factor alone. This discovery led to the introduction of new models that used two factors to explain portfolio performance: beta and firm size.

A portfolio heavily weighted in small cap stocks would appear to have generated alpha if only beta was used in the risk-adjustment model. However, if a two-factor model is used that includes firm size and beta, and the portfolio alpha diminished or disappeared altogether, then the two-factor model would be a more precise measurement than the one-factor beta model.

The size factor has been added as a new tool for researchers in their quest to accurately detect manager skill. The academics concluded that it took no special skill to overweigh a portfolio with small cap stocks. Thus, managers who outperform simply because they hold an overweighting with small cap shouldn't be recognized as having investment talent. The same portfolio performance could easily have been achieved by investing in a small cap index fund.

The Value Factor

Value investing has been a popular investment strategy for more than a century. This strategy involves the study of financial data to determine appropriate company valuation and investing in those companies that appear to be good value. John Burr Williams was one of the early pioneers of value investing, and one of the first economists to estimate stock prices by their *intrinsic value*. Williams was also the first to document a theory of cash flow valuation using dividend payments. He is best known for his 1938 book *The Theory of Investment Value* (Harvard University Press), which was the basis of his Harvard Ph.D. thesis.[4]

Benjamin Graham was also a true believer in fundamental analysis and is considered one of the pioneers of value investing. Graham began teaching his theories at Columbia University Business School in 1928 and subsequently refined this application with David Dodd through their famous book *Security Analysis*.[5] Graham's most successful and well-known student is Warren Buffett, the billionaire chairman of Berkshire Hathaway Inc. Buffett credits Graham for much of his investment success.

In the late 1970s, academics began to analyze value investing from a broad market perspective to isolate the premium paid in the marketplace for stocks that exhibited certain fundamental characteristics. Computing power greatly enhanced this task due to the amount of data mining required for this analysis.

In 1977, Sanjoy Basu tested the notion that value factors explained differences in portfolio returns that were unrelated to beta or the size effect. He identified a positive and consistent relationship between price-earnings ratios (P/E) and portfolio return that couldn't be explained by these other risk factors.[6]

Marc Reinganum's paper, mentioned earlier, confirmed and extended Basu's findings in 1981, as did several other academics conducting research on value premiums during this period. In summary, these findings identified a significant positive relationship between portfolio returns and fundamental variables such as price-earnings, price-to-cash-flow, and price-to-book (P/B). Stocks with high fundamental value relative to price (value stocks) outperformed stocks with low fundamental value relative to price (growth stocks) by a considerable amount over the long term.

Eugene Fama and Ken French released ground-breaking research in 1992 that, among other things, measured book-to-market

(BtM) returns for the highest BtM (or value) stocks compared to the lowest BtM (or growth) stocks from 1963 to 1990. They found excess returns of value stocks over growth stocks to be more than 5.0 percent per year in the United States equity markets.[7] Fama and French also confirmed Basu's finding that higher P/E value stocks did outperform lower P/E growth stocks; however, P/E was not as strong as BtM as a factor. Their research led to the next step in valuation models, the Fama-French Three Factor Model, to be discussed later.

The value effect in its many forms has been reproduced by numerous researchers over many different sample periods and across most major global securities exchanges. Researchers still don't know exactly what causes the value premium, but they do know it's not the same factors that cause beta and size risks.

Academics have theorized many reasons why a value premium exists. Some say it occurs because value companies are fundamentally weak. They tend to be slow growing firms in old-line businesses that have high debt and are prone to financial setbacks. Others argue from the other side, saying that growth stock expectations are overestimated so the outperformance of value is due to the underperformance of growth stock. There's also the view that value companies don't gather much attention from Wall Street analysts because those firms are not doing much investment banking business. Consequently, value companies don't get the table-pounding buy recommendations from these analysts that growth companies receive.

Whatever reason the value premium has occurred isn't vitally important. What is important is that the premium has been well documented in the United States and abroad. Most academics do agree that the premium paid to value stocks reflects an inherent risk and is not a fleeting market anomaly. Value stocks have outperformed growth stocks by a wide margin, and this outperformance is a result of a new risk factor that's independent of beta and firm size.

The Three Factor Model

Eugene Fama and Kenneth French compiled the three factors of beta, firm size, and value (BtM) and created a new blockbuster valuation model called the *Fama-French Three Factor Model*. One use for the model is to compare a mutual fund performance to three distinct risks factors and isolate how much of a fund's return was due to these three factors and how much was due to the fund manager.

Fama and French found that, on average, beta alone explained about 70 percent of a diversified portfolio's performance. When they measured how much exposure that randomly created portfolios were influenced by the three risk factors of beta, size, and BtM, they could explain within about 95 percent accuracy how a diversified portfolio should have performed in relation to the stock market without knowing the actual return of the portfolio. All they needed to know was the amount in each risk factor.

The results were a blow to active portfolio managers, who until this time touted their stock-picking prowess as the primary reason for generating alpha. The new three-factor model left surprisingly little excess return to be explained by a manager's individual skill at security selection. It was all about the three factors.

Factor Benchmarks

Special Fama-French Benchmark Factor indices are now available to the public that track these three risk factors of beta, firm size, and value. The complete data library is available online at no cost from Ken French's web site at the Tuck School of Business at Dartmouth College. It is a treasure trove of information and insight for students of portfolio management.[*]

The Fama-French indices can be used as inputs for the three-factor model. The market factor is determined by taking the total stock market return and subtracting the T-bill return; the size factor is measured by subtracting small cap stock returns from large cap stock returns; and the value factor is measured by subtracting high book-to-market (value) stocks from low book-to-market (growth) stocks. Figure 4.1 shows how these three risk factors varied over a five-year period from 2005 to 2009.

The Fama-French Three Factor Model provides a new and powerful tool to measure the performance of investment portfolios.

---

[*]Kenneth R. French is the Carl E. and Catherine M. Heidt Professor of Finance at the Tuck School of Business at Dartmouth College. He and co-author Eugene F. Fama from the Booth School of Business at the University of Chicago are well known for their research into the value effect and the three-factor model. Data is available free of charge from French's faculty homepage at http://mba.tuck .dartmouth.edu.

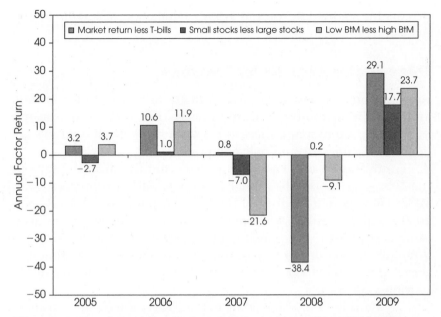

Figure 4.1   Fama-French Risk Benchmark Factors from 2005–2009

The data in Figure 4.1 can be used to measure a mutual fund's return and separate the portion attributed to the market factor, size factor, value factor, and any residual amount that may be attributed to manager decision making.

If a mutual fund had excess return after accounting for the three factors, then the fund had alpha and the fund manager potentially had skill. If there was no excess return, then the fund didn't produce alpha, because the same returns could be engineered in a portfolio through a combination of a total market index fund (beta exposure), small cap index fund (size factor exposure), and value index fund (value factor exposure).

If approximately 95 percent of diversified fund performance can be explained using the three-factor model, and active management contributes very little, if any, to return then why pay high fees for active management when you can engineer the same risk exposures using low-cost index funds?

How to create a three-factor portfolio using index funds is beyond the scope of this book. There are several books available on this investment strategy including one that I wrote, *All About Asset Allocation*, 2nd Edition, 2010, from McGraw-Hill. The book is available in bookstores and from on-line booksellers including Amazon.com.

Three-Factor Analysis for Everyone

Research on size and value factors made its way out of academia and into the investment industry during the 1980s. This research first showed up in new indices as research firms sliced their market benchmarks into size and style components.

Frank Russell and Company became the first firm to segment the U.S. stock market by capitalization size and investment style in 1982. They created the Russell 1000 large cap index and the Russell 2000 small cap index. A couple of years later, Russell introduced value and growth style benchmarks for those indices. Russell uses a multifactor model to differentiate value from growth, although they'll also allocate a portion of a stock to value and the remaining portion to growth.

Standard & Poor's wasn't far behind Russell with the introduction of size and style indices. The company created the S&P MidCap 400 index and the S&P SmallCap 600 index in 1990 to complement the primarily large cap S&P 500 index. Together, these three size indices compose the S&P 1500 index. Soon after, the firm then teamed up with Barra Inc. to create growth and value style indices for these four benchmarks. The S&P/Barra style indices used price-to-book ratios as their differentiation factor, which was similar to the measure used by Fama and French. In late 2005, S&P phased out the single factor methodology and began using a multi-factor method for their renamed S&P/Citigroup style indices. S&P/Citi also introduced a Pure Style index series which are mutually exclusive, meaning that all stocks are either wholly growth or wholly value.

Today, more than a dozen index providers offer size and style benchmarks covering the global equity markets. Each provider has their own methodology for deciding what's a small cap and large cap stock and what's value and growth. All style indices are designed to do essentially the same thing regardless of the methodological differences.

Size and style indices give investors a better benchmark to measure performance against. For better or worse, active managers are now pigeonholed into a particular investment style so that their performance can be compared to a style benchmark as well as other active managers who have been classified the same way.

Mutual Fund Scorecards

Research firms began publishing ongoing active versus passive return reports based on their style indices during the 2000s. The following highlights two companies that provide this information to the public at no charge. They are Standard & Poor's and Morningstar, Inc.

Standard & Poor's Indices versus Active   S&P started publishing the Standard & Poor's Indices Versus Active (SPIVA) report in the early 2000s. The report compares active managers to their appropriate S&P style and size indices and tallies the number of winners and losers. It was an innovative idea that's now widely read by investors and advisors, and results in interesting media commentary from believers in active investing and passive investing.

The SPIVA scorecard compares the quarterly performance data of more than 3,500 actively managed mutual funds covering U.S. equities, international equities, and fixed income funds to their appropriate market benchmarks. The analysis includes size, style, and sector indices. This methodology is designed to provide an accurate and objective apples to apples comparison.

The U.S. equity funds are segregated into 13 different categories including large cap, mid cap, and small cap indices. The groups are then benchmarked to the S&P 1500, S&P 500, S&P 400, and S&P 600 style indices and one real estate investment trust (REIT) benchmark. Comparisons between the funds and the style indices are conducted over one-, three-, and five-year time periods. Funds that had a style change during one or more of these periods are omitted from this performance comparison.

The SPIVA scorecards show both equal weighted and asset weighted averages for the funds. Equal weighted fund data represents the average return from all fund choices available to investors during the period. It represents the universe of investment choices that an investor has. Asset weight represents the actual dollar amount invested in each fund during the period. Funds with more invested received a higher weighing than those funds with less invested.

Overall, the S&P benchmarks outperformed the active managers in most style and size groups over most periods. There were some periods when active managers outperformed, but it wasn't by much and not for long.

S&P uses the CRSP Survivor-Bias-Free U.S. Mutual Fund Database, which accounts for funds that may have merged or liquidated over the years. This information was used by S&P to report fund survivability data figures for each category. It also shows the number of funds that changed style. Some of the S&P survivability information is provided in Chapter 7.

Srikant Dash is an S&P analyst and the current author of the SPIVA study. He summed up the results of this study by explaining that over a complete market cycle, actively managed mutual funds outperform the indices only about one-third of the time.[8] This independently derived win-loss ratio of 1 to 2 is consistent with all other performance studies to date.

The Morningstar Box Score Report   A second ongoing active versus passive report is provided biannually by Morningstar, Inc. It's called the *Box Score Report* (BSR) and compares actively managed funds to Morningstar Style Box indices, a style classification methodology that's been popular in the mutual fund industry since 1992. Visit www.Morningstar.com for details on Morningstar Style Box methodology.

BSR compares active fund performance against Morningstar Style Box indices similarly to the way S&P compares performance to their indices in the SPIVA report. BSR also builds on this analysis by adjusting the active funds using two risk models: Jensen's Alpha and the Fama-French Three Factor Model modified to Morningstar indices.

Jensen's Alpha adjusts each mutual fund for its sensitivity to market beta while the Fama-French Three Factor Model adjusts each mutual fund for its sensitivity to beta, size, and style exposures as measured by Morningstar. The three-factor adjustment helps indentify true alpha within the active fund universe.

Figure 4.2 provides an eye-opening comparison using BSR data ending in 2009. The figure compares the number of winning active funds using the three analysis methods. The left grid shows the percentage of active funds that outperformed the style box index nominally over a three-year period ending in 2009; the center grid shows the percentage of active funds that outperformed the same indices after applying Jensen's Alpha to adjust for beta exposure; and the grid on the right shows the percentage of active funds that outperformed the indices after adjusting for the three-factor model.

Figure 4.2 is interesting in several ways. You can see how different risk models affected the percentage of active funds that

	Value	Core	Growth
Large	81%	22%	38%
Mid	54%	42%	38%
Small	28%	37%	46%

Straight Comparison

	Value	Core	Growth
Large	85%	25%	39%
Mid	45%	42%	39%
Small	29%	39%	32%

Jensen's Alpha Adjusted

	Value	Core	Growth
Large	36%	39%	41%
Mid	49%	34%	39%
Small	38%	29%	17%

Three-Factor Adjusted

Figure 4.2   Three-Year Box Score Results through 2009

outperformed their benchmarks by reading across from left to right in each grid.

Let's take the large-value box of the leftmost grid in Figure 4.2 for example. Unadjusted, 81 percent of active funds beat the Morningstar large-value index. By adjusting only for differences in fund beta using Jensen's Alpha, the percentage went up to almost 85 percent, a great showing for active funds. However, the number of outperforming active funds dropped radically to about 36 percent once the size and style biases in the mutual funds were eliminated using a three-factor model.

Dunn's Law   History shows that active managers perform the best when the style they are compared to performs the worst. Over the three-year period ending in 2009, large-value stocks were the worst performing category among the nine Morningstar style boxes. The underperformance of large-value stocks in general helps explain why a high percentage of actively managed funds outperformed this category before making risk-factor adjustments.

This phenomenon has a name. It is called *Dunn's Law* after Steve Dunn, a friend and cohort of William Bernstein. Dunn's Law is as follows: "When an asset class does relatively well, an index fund in that class does even better. In contrast, when an asset class does poorly, the active managers do better." Bernstein immortalized Dunn's Law in an insightful *Efficient Frontier* article in 1999.[9]

William Thatcher of Hammond Associates built on Dunn's Law and gave it a new name in a *Journal of Investing* article published in 2009. Thatcher labeled the phenomena as "The Purity

Hypothesis."[10] He explained that the reason more active managers beat their benchmark in underperforming styles was because the benchmarks were pure plays on that style, while the actively managed funds often were not. The impurity of actively managed funds creates a style bias in the fund when a straight comparison is used. The active funds show better performance than is expected when the style performs poorly and worse results than expected when the style performs well.

Morningstar's three-factor analysis does a good job of removing style impurities from active funds and helps level the results across all categories. We can see this in Figure 4.2. Comparing active results within each grid shows that the percentage of winning funds in each style are closer to each other using the three-factor model than the straight comparison data and the adjustments by Jensen's Alpha. In no style box did a majority of managers beat the benchmark after three-factor adjustments.

Deeper analysis of the BSR results finds that after adjusting for three-factor risk, on average, the active funds on average underperformed by just about the fees they charged. This should be no surprise. John Bogle hinted at this in his 1951 Princeton thesis and Nobel Laureate William F. Sharpe drove the point home in a three-page paper he wrote 1991, observing "properly measured, the average actively managed dollar must underperform the average passively managed dollar, net of costs. Empirical analyses that appear to refute this principle are guilty of improper measurement."[11]

BSR author Travis Pascavis made a comment in the second half 2009 report. His observation appeared at the top of the first page: "After accounting for the sensitivity to risk, size and style as well as costs, *only about a third of active funds in the study had positive alpha over the past three years*" [italics added].[12] The 1 to 2 win-loss ratio shows up yet again.

Morningstar X-Ray   Morningstar.com provides a useful portfolio management tool called *X-Ray*. Type in a list of mutual funds and the amount in each fund and X-Ray provides the portfolio's exposure to size and value stocks. These factors will determine about 95 percent of the portfolio's risk and return over the long-term according to Fama-French findings. Any investor can create an index fund or ETF portfolio that has their desired size and value characteristics by using tools such as X-Ray, and can do it for a fraction of the cost of active management.

Three-Factor Analysis from the Source

Fama and French recently conducted a detailed study on mutual fund performance using their three-factor model as well as other tools. The report is titled "Luck Versus Skill in the Cross Section of Mutual Fund Returns." It's expected to be published in 2010 in the *Journal of Finance*.[13] The study analyzes the past performance of 3,156 mutual funds spanning 23 years from 1984 to 2006.

Mutual fund performance is measured in multiple ways using several risk-based models in this meticulously researched paper. The funds were first categorized by the amount of money invested in each according to small, medium, and large amounts. They were then ranked into 10 deciles based on the amount of alpha using different risk models. Funds in highly rank deciles earned excess returns after adjusting for risk, and funds in the lower rank deciles had no excess return after adjusting for risk.

Figure 4.3 illustrates this ranking using the three-factor model, net of fund fees. The highest alpha generating funds were in the 99th percentile, and the worst funds were in the 1st percentile. This fund group held assets between $250 million and $1 billion.

The funds in the deciles from left to right up to the 70th percentile exhibited no alpha. This means approximately 70 percent of

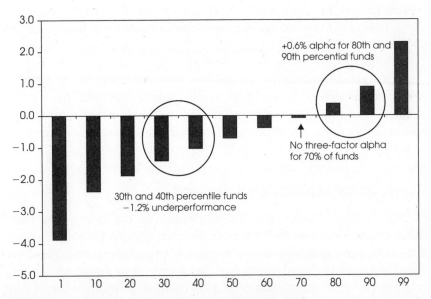

Figure 4.3 Fama-French Mutual Fund Study Results

the funds underperformed the three-factor risk model. The funds in the 80th and 90th percentiles did show alpha, meaning there were unexplained excess returns above the three-factor model return. The top funds with the highest excess returns are at the far right.

Overall, I'll give the benefit of the doubt to active funds and say that about one-third of the funds outperformed the three-factor model. This is a win-loss ratio of approximately 1 to 2. The median excess return for the outperforming funds was approximately 0.6 percent, as shown between deciles 80 and 90. The median percent underperformance was approximately 1.2 percent as shown between deciles 30 and 40. Thus, the benefit of selecting a winning fund was about one-half the opportunity cost of selecting a losing fund on a risk-adjusted basis.

Given a win-loss ratio of 1 to 2, and given that the median risk-adjusted underperformance by the losing funds was 1.2 percent, it would be fair to say that the median winning fund should deliver 2.4 percent to make betting on active management a fair bet. In reality, this level of alpha was reached only by the best performing funds in the 99 percentile. The median excess return was only 0.6 percent. That's much too low to compensate investors for the potential underperformance.

The clear message conveyed over and over again by the academics is that investing in actively managed funds creates uncompensated risk in a portfolio. Trying to select an actively managed fund that provides enough alpha to compensate for that risk carries overwhelmingly low odds.

Fama and French reiterate in their study that fees are an important driver of investment return in the long-term. From 1984 to 2006, active mutual funds in aggregate held a portfolio that, before expenses, mimicked a market portfolio. The return to investors though, was far lower. Fees and expenses took away any chance for a fair bet.

Four-Factor Models and Beyond

A fourth factor uncovered by academics in the 1990s was price momentum. Momentum is the tendency for individual stock prices to follow a trend at times, either up or down. These tendencies have been documented and quantified using various momentum models.

Simply put, momentum is the finance industry's answer to Newton's first law of motion: A body in motion tends to stay in motion unless it is compelled to do otherwise. Investors who believe they can capture momentum in stock returns attempt to do so by jumping on a trend and staying there until the trend changes. Of course, when a trend changes, many investors are slow to react and often feel the painful experience of Newton's third law: For every action there is an equal and opposite reaction.

Mechanical trend following has been tested and retested by academics and quantitative analysts for years. There are those who believe they have captured this element of performance as a market factor and can profit from it. However, momentum strategies typically require high turnover, and that means trading costs. So, while the momentum factor appears to exist on paper, it remains to be seen if it can be captured in reality.

The first paper published to target momentum in stock prices was published by Narasimhan Jegadeesh and Sheridan Titman in 1993 using stock data from 1965 to 1989.[14] They showed that simple relative strength strategies that rank stocks based on their past 3 to 12 month cumulative raw returns predict relative performance over the next 3 to 12 months.

The Jegadeesh-Titman study suggests that relative winners tended to continue as relative winners up to 12 months, and recent relative losers tended to continue to be relative losers. These excess returns could not be explained by CAPM or other known risk factors at the time. This phenomenon would later be called the *momentum effect*.

Fama and French studied momentum in 1996. They found that a momentum effect wasn't captured by their three-factor model.[15] The research led to the creation of the Momentum Factor (Mom) index that is now included as part of the Fama-French factor database available on Ken French's web site.

The basis behind calling momentum a risk factor in mutual fund analysis requires some cynicism about the way some active fund managers try to beef up returns. Theoretically, it doesn't take any skill to buy stocks that have recently outperformed the market. This information is widely known in the public domain, and anyone can follow it. In addition, many services offer momentum stock data for a nominal fee. If a manager is simply jumping on the bandwagon and buying hot stocks, and those stocks cause a portfolio to outperform, why should we herald the manager as having investment skill?

Mark Carhart was the first researcher to use momentum as a factor in explaining mutual fund returns in his 1997 Ph.D. thesis for the University of Chicago. Carhart incorporated momentum into the Fama-French Three Factor Model to create a four-factor model, and then drilled into the performance of 1,892 funds that existed between 1961 and 1993.

After adjusting for beta, firm size, style, and momentum factors, Carhart concluded that an equal weighted portfolio of the mutual funds underperformed by 1.8 percent per year for the period covered. This was close to the fees and expenses of the funds. The following is in his conclusion in the *Journal of Finance*:

> Overall, the evidence is consistent with market efficiency, interpretations of the size, book-to-market, and momentum factors notwithstanding. Although the top-decile mutual funds earned back their investment costs, most funds underperform by about the magnitude of their investment expenses. The bottom-decile funds, however, underperform by about twice their reported investment costs.[16]

One added benefit from Carhart's exhaustive study on mutual fund performance was the creation of the first survivorship-bias-free mutual fund database. The database was initially funded by Eugene Fama and compiled by Carhart. Unlike other databases at the time, the CRSP Survivor-Bias-Free US Mutual Fund Database included the returns of closed and merged funds. This represented the true opportunity set that investors had to choose from over the years.*

Fama and French also included a four-factor model in their recent study on mutual funds mentioned earlier. Like Carhart, they added a momentum factor to their three-factor model and then tested 3,156 mutual funds spanning 23 years from 1984 to 2006. The data from this research was used to form Figure 4.4, which illustrates the differences in observed mutual fund alpha based on three risk-adjustment models: beta only, three-factor model, and a four-factor model that includes momentum. The funds in the figure held assets between $250 million and $1 billion.

---

*Including closed and merged mutual funds in a database lowers the performance of the average fund over time by as much as one percent. A significant amount of effort has been expanded over the past decade to correct mutual fund database biases universally. The three major mutual fund database providers, CRSP, Morningstar, and Lipper, are now survivorship bias free.

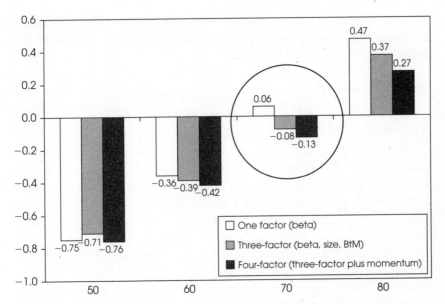

Figure 4.4   **Three Models Explaining Mutual Fund Performance from 1984–2006**

Figure 4.4 has several interesting points to discuss. First are the three measures of alpha: (1) beta only as a risk factor; (2) a three-factor model of beta, firm size, and style (BtM); and (3) a four-factor model of beta, firm size, style, and momentum.

The alphas for all three models were similar; however, differences arise in the explanatory power of the models. At the 70th percentile level based on alpha rankings, the positive alpha number using only beta implies that fund managers at this point have some skill (0.06 percent alpha). However, alpha is nonexistent at the 70th percentile level using a three-factor model (–0.08 percent alpha) and measurably negative using a four-factor model (–0.13 percent alpha).

The difference between the one-factor model based on beta and the four-factor model based on beta, firm size, value, and momentum was 0.19 percent. That's not a lot, but noteworthy nonetheless. It implies that the four-factor model had more explanatory power for fund returns than the other two models and that the odds of selecting a winning active fund worsened as the models provided more explanatory power.

Momentum is an investment style that has been studied extensively by academics for many years but remained largely undiscovered as a mainstream building block for index portfolios. This appears to be changing, as momentum is now being recognized as a risk factor in addition to value and firm size.

Momentum on Trial

Cliff Asness received an MBA with high honors and a Ph.D. in Finance from the University of Chicago where he was Eugene Fama's student and a teaching assistant for two years. Asness is a true believer in momentum investing. He has published several leading papers on the subject including his Ph.D. dissertation in 1994. Asness co-founded AQR Capital Management in 1998 along with several of his former co-workers from the Goldman Sachs quantitative group. AQR is an institutional money manager.

AQR launched three momentum index funds in July 2009 that specifically attempt to track three AQR momentum indices covering small cap stocks, large cap stocks, and international stocks. Whether these index funds will actually capture momentum returns remains to be seen, particularly after fees and expenses. In addition, an investment in a pure momentum fund does require taking capital away from other market factors that have proven track records.

Does Anyone have Skill?

There have been other recent academic papers that attempt to separate outperforming manager skill from luck. Some papers conclude the task is impossible given the lack of mutual fund data in existence, while other studies attempt to quantify the number of managers that have luck verses those that don't.

A recent paper published by the Swiss Finance Institute entitled "False Discoveries in Mutual Fund Performance: Measuring Luck in Estimated Alphas" attempted to quantify the number of skilled managers from the number of lucky managers. The research set was a database of 2,076 U.S. equity mutual fund returns over the 1975 to 2006 period. The authors' conclusion was that only 12 fund managers exhibited skill over this time period. Table 4.1 is a breakdown of the results.[†]

[†] Source: Barras, Laurent, Scaillet, O., and Wermers, Russ R., False Discoveries in Mutual Fund Performance: Measuring Luck in Estimated Alphas (April 20, 2009). *Journal of Finance*, Forthcoming; Swiss Finance Institute Research Paper No. 08–18.

Table 4.1   Number of Skilled to Unskilled Managers

	No Alpha	Alpha	Alpha from luck	Alpha from skill
Proportion of Funds	75.4%	24.5%	24.0%	0.6%
Number of Funds	1,565	511	499	12

An interesting aspect in the Swiss Finance Institute was the decreasing number of managers who the researchers claim exhibited skill over the decades. Specifically, the authors' observed that the proportion of skilled funds decreased from 14.4 percent in 1990 to 0.6 percent in 2006, while the proportion of unskilled funds increased from 9.2 percent to 24.0 percent. So, at least according to this study, some active managers had skill in the past, but they don't have it anymore.

Summary

Researchers are constantly improving performance methods that slice away the alphas that winning active managers are claiming. New studies on active versus passive investing improve upon the earlier research and expose more risk factors that are used by active management to compete with index funds. The probability of finding consistent alpha in active management diminishes as research advances and more multi-factor risk models are formed.

The past several decades have also seen the proliferation of low-cost index funds and ETFs that adequately capture these risk factors. Investors can now easily create a passive portfolio that provides the same risks and return expectations as active management for a fraction of the cost.

5

Passive Choices Expand

There was no question in my mind that bond index funds would come to meet a major need in the marketplace, because most bond mutual funds were grossly overpriced, often carrying both high expenses and excessive sales charges.

—John C. Bogle

No longer can active managers use the excuse that "you can't buy the index," because today you can buy almost any market exposure at a reasonable cost. Passive investing has exploded since John Bogle launched the First Index Investment Trust in 1976. Today, there are well over 1,000 index funds and ETFs available from dozens of mutual fund companies. These products cover multiple asset classes, styles, and sectors. This rich source of indexing products allows investors to build low-cost passive portfolios based on any risk and return parameters desired. This chapter explores how growth in the index fund marketplace occurred and where it might be going in the future.

The Growth of Indexing

It isn't easy to create a market for a product that doesn't exist. Most companies that venture into the unknown struggle through the first few years. Vanguard was no exception. The active fund industry did everything they could to discredit Vanguard and the indexing idea. John Bogle was used as a punching bag by competitors. They called his index fund Bogle's Folly and even un-American. The tactic almost worked.

It was touch and go for the fledging First Index Investment Trust. The fund had attracted barely $17 million in total assets one year after its launch. That wasn't even enough money to buy all 500 stocks in the S&P 500 index. Only after the Wellington Board of Directors approved a $58 million merger with another Vanguard administered fund in late 1977 did the fund have enough capital to complete its index replication strategy.[1]

The fund had grown to $110 million in assets by the end of 1982 despite the difficult market in 1981, and it looked as though Bogle's Folly might survive. Reaching the $100 million mark was a big number in the fund industry at the time. It was a milestone that helped to position the fund in the marketplace.

A bull market in stocks began in 1982 and continued for 18 years almost without interruption. This was a huge boon for the Vanguard S&P 500 index fund. Not only did interest in index investing start to catch on, the index fund itself outperformed three-quarters of all active funds from 1983 to 1986. This run brought increased publicity to Vanguard.

The unexpected asset growth at Vanguard made competitors rethink their opposition to index funds. Wells Fargo was the first to launch a competing fund in 1984. The fund had expenses of almost 1 percent per year and attracted few assets. Two other index funds were formed in 1985, although they were only offered to institutional investors. Eight new index funds were launched by competitors in 1986, which marked the beginning of true competition. A few traditional active mutual fund companies that had lampooned John Bogle in the past reversed course and launched their own index funds lineup. These firms included rivals Fidelity, Dreyfus, and T. Rowe Price.

Vanguard expanded its U.S. index fund lineup into an extended market index in 1990. This index tracked the Wilshire 4500 Index, which is composed of all investable U.S. stocks not held in the S&P 500. Within a couple of years Vanguard had also launched the first index fund to track a foreign stock index as well as the first total U.S. stock market fund that tracked the Wilshire 5000 index, a measure of the total U.S. stock market.

ETFs Line Up to Compete

ETFs are mutual funds that trade continuously during the day on a stock exchange rather than once at the end of the day with a fund company. ETFs broke into the index fund marketplace in December 1993 when State Street launched the SPDR 500 (Ticker: SPY). SPY became the first widely accepted ETF on the market. It should be no surprise that the fund tracked the popular S&P 500 index.

ETFs differ from traditional open-end funds and closed-end mutual funds. Open-end funds trade once a day at the end of the day, and all trades go through the fund company. Closed-end funds and ETFs trade on exchanges during the day while the markets are open. The difference is that the Security and Exchange Commission (SEC) has granted ETFs special regulatory relief that allows trading of ETF shares during the day and the creation and redemption of fund shares during the day. Closed-end funds don't have an ongoing share creation and redemption feature. The ability for an ETF to create new shares and redeem old shares intra-day keeps the ETF's market price very close to its net asset value (NAV) and eliminates the deep discounts and premiums to NAV that are the hallmark of closed-end mutual funds.

There are hundreds of exchange-traded funds available today that track various induces. Many of those induces are beta seeking representations of the stock and bond markets, and several others are alpha seeking induces that follow active management strategies. More information on this is presented later in this chapter and detailed information is available in *The ETF Book* (John Wiley & Sons, 2009). For more information, visit www .theETFbook.com.

The First Fixed Income Index Fund

Index funds had their world premiere event in 1976 with the release of the Vanguard First Index Investment Trust starring the S&P 500 index. The sequel wouldn't take place for another 10 years when Vanguard launched the world's first bond market index fund, the Vanguard Total Bond Market Index Fund (originally launched as the Vanguard Bond Market Fund). The fund was benchmarked to the Lehman Aggregate Bond Index, now the Barclays Capital Aggregate Bond Index. The Lehman Ag, as it was known, represents a broadly diversified index of investment grade bonds trading in the U.S.

Ironically, the SEC wouldn't allow Vanguard to include the word *index* in the name of the fund when it was first launched. The Lehman Aggregate Bond Index held thousands of bonds, and most were not traded regularly. Vanguard's strategy was to use a securities sampling technique composed of tradable bonds in an attempt to track the index performance. This created an issue for the SEC staffers. They couldn't get their heads around the idea that a large index holding thousands of bonds could be closely tracked by a fund that held only a small relative sampling of those bonds. Rather than fight the SEC, Vanguard dropped *index* from the title, and were given the go-ahead to launch the Vanguard Bond Market Fund.[2]

The Vanguard Bond Market Fund tracked the Lehman index closely, which has allowed it to outperform most actively managed bond funds and provided justification for changing the name to the Vanguard Total Bond Market Index Fund. Within ten years, this index fund became one of the largest bond mutual funds on the market. The success of the first bond index fund led to the creation of more bond index funds from Vanguard and its competitors. Today there are sector bond funds tracking various security types, credit quality, and maturities, as well as municipal bond index funds.

The academic evidence supporting bond indexing does not have a long history like stock indexing, but it has robust conclusions. The first major study on active bond fund performance was published in the *Journal of Business* in 1993. "The Performance of Bond Mutual Funds" by Christopher Blake, Edwin Elton, and Martin Gruber analyzed the performance of 41 surviving bond funds during a 10-year period ending in 1988.[3]

The 41 funds were compared to the index that was most appropriate for each fund according to Morningstar analysis. Overall, 8 funds outperformed their benchmark and 33 underperformed. That is a win-loss ratio of about 1 to 4, which is twice as poor as the 1 to 2 win-loss ratio for stocks. Figure 5.1 illustrates the under- and outperformance relative to the benchmark performance.

The alpha for the average outperforming bond fund was 0.5, and the average underperforming fund was 1.2 below the benchmark. The average annual underperformance for all funds was 0.9 below appropriate bond indexes. This is not a wide range considering the large percentage of funds that underperformed. However, remember that we're talking about bond funds, not stock funds.

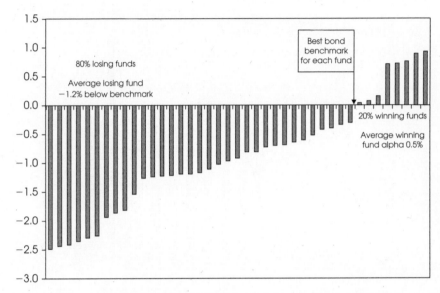

Figure 5.1   Active Bond Returns Relative to Appropriate Indexes

The payouts for winning active bond funds are horrendously low given the low odds for success and the average 1.2 percent underperformance by the losing funds. A fair payout for selecting a winning bond fund should be 4.8 percent. In practice, this payout is only 0.5 percent, and no fund achieved an alpha greater than 1 percent.

Figure 5.2 is provided only to emphasize the difference in the range of returns between active stock funds and active bond funds. This figure illustrates the 10-year returns for U.S. large cap growth stock funds and intermediate-term general corporate bond funds ending in 2009, according to Morningstar Principia data.

Figure 5.2 shows that bond fund returns fall in a much narrower range of return than growth stock funds. This is due to the low dispersion in individual bond returns relative to the high dispersion in individual stock returns.

Blake, Elton, and Gruber concluded their study with two observations. First, the overall 0.9 percent underperformance of bond funds compared to their benchmarks was, on average, approximately equal to the average management fee of the funds. Second, they found no evidence that past performance in bond funds predicted future returns.

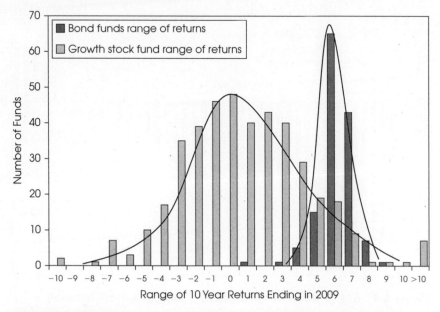

Figure 5.2   Dispersion of Growth Stock Fund Returns to Bond Fund Returns 2000-2009

Marlena Lee, a research associate at Dimensional Fund Advisors with a Ph.D. from the University of Chicago wrote an unpublished study on bond fund returns in 2009. Lee analyzed 2,353 bond funds over the period from January 1991 to December 2008. The data included investment-grade, high-yield, and government bond funds from the CRSP Survivor-Bias-Free U.S. Mutual Fund Database. It excluded municipal bond funds, money market funds, index funds, and asset-backed funds.[4]

Lee used a five-factor risk model for her analysis. The five-factor model was based on the Fama-French Three-Factor Model plus two bond specific risk factors: term risk and default risk. This model was modified from an earlier five-factor model introduced by Fama and French in 1993.[5] Lee concluded that the average underperformance of actively managed bond funds was 0.9 percent after adjusting for risk. Government bond funds performed worse with average underperformance of 1.1 percent risk-adjusted.

The average cost for the bond funds was 0.8 percent annually, which explained most of the underperformance. Lee concluded in her report that adjusted for risk, "overall, there is strong evidence that the bond mutual fund industry as a whole does not sufficiently enhance returns to compensate for fees and expenses."

There have been several bond fund studies since the Blake, Elton, and Gruber analysis, including Lee's work. All of the studies come to the same conclusions: (1) the average bond fund under-performs by an amount roughly equal their cost, (2) outperform-ing funds do not outperform by a meaningful amount, and (3) past outperformance typically does not persist.

International Equity Index Funds

Index funds expanded into international markets in 1990 when Vanguard introduced a European index fund and a Pacific Rim index fund. The company also launched the first emerging market indexes fund four years later.

An early study of mutual fund performance by international funds was conducted by Robert Cumby and Jack Glen in 1990. Their study was appropriately titled "Evaluating the Performance of International Mutual Funds."[6] What makes this study unique is that it appears to be one of the first papers where an international benchmark was used rather than a U.S. benchmark to compare international fund performance. The index was the Morgan Stanley Capital International World Index. The study made the case for using an international benchmark to compare foreign funds rather than a U.S. equity benchmark. This may seem obvious to investors today but it wasn't in 1990.

Cumby and Glen examined the performance of a sample of 15 U.S.–based internationally diversified mutual funds from 1982 to 1988 using two performance measures, Jensen's Alpha and an alternative measure called *positive period weighting* that attempts to identify managers skilled at market timing. The positive period weighting measure was remarkably similar to Jensen's Alpha, both in magnitude and statistical significance.

Figure 5.3 illustrates the range of monthly Jensen's Alpha for the 15 funds. No evidence was found that the funds provided investors with consistently superior performance that surpassed the interna-tional equity index over this sample period. There were funds that outperformed the market, although the consistency of those returns wasn't great enough to confirm that the managers had skill. Cumby and Glen also concluded that none of the 15 managers had market timing ability.

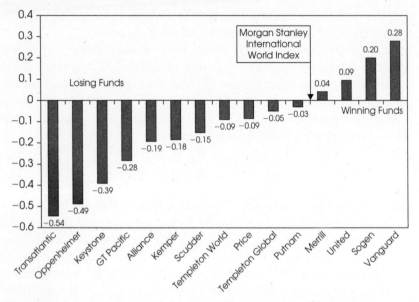

Figure 5.3 Monthly Jensen's Alpha from 15 International Funds 1982–1988

The pattern of returns in Figure 5.3 is strikingly familiar. As with all performance reviews thus far in this book, the underperforming funds to the left of the index had greater underperformance than the outperformance of the few winning funds to the right of the index. In other words, the alpha created by the winning funds was much lower than a fair game would pay given the low probability of selecting a winning fund.

The Vanguard Group also performed a detailed analysis of international indexing in 2009. The analysis included the United Kingdom and Japan, as well as the European and Asian regions excluding those countries. Figure 5.4 illustrates the percentage of actively managed funds that outperformed appropriate benchmarks over a 10-year period ending in 2008. The data was not risk adjusted.[7]

The percentage of surviving active funds that underperformed in a particular region varied somewhat, although all regions combined averaged about 35 percent. In the long term, the number of international active managers that outperformed their benchmarks is consistent with a win-loss ratio of 1 to 2.

A study of Canadian mutual funds from 1985 to 1996 showed similar underperformance.[8] The 2002 study looked at 325 funds

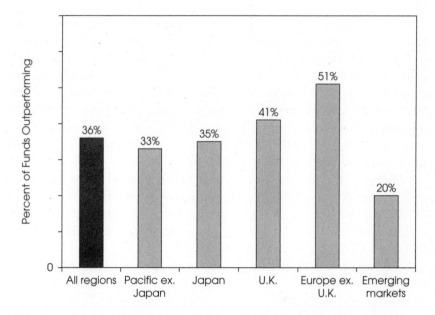

Figure 5.4   Percentage of Actively Managed Foreign Stock Funds Outperforming Their Country Indexes over 10 Years Ending in 2008

over three different time periods and across four different asset classes or styles. There were 163 funds classified as equity, of which 61 outperformed over the period. This is consistent with a win-loss ratio of about 1 to 2.

The authors came to the same conclusion about Canadian mutual funds that researchers had already reached about U.S. stock funds: "Canadian mutual funds, in general, have not exhibited any stock picking or market timing ability during the study period."

Three-Factor International Portfolios

There has been extensive work conducted on the size and value effects in international markets. Some of these studies concentrated more on the value premium and others on the size premium.

Fama and French studied the value premium for the United States and 12 major Europe, Australasia, and Far East (EAFE) countries using MSCI accounting ratios (book-to-market, price-earnings, etc.) for at least 10 firms in each country from 1974 to 1994. They found strong evidence of a consistent value premium in international returns. The average return on the global value portfolios (including the United States) was 3.1 percent to 5.1 percent per year higher than the average return on the global market portfolio.[9]

Elroy Dimson, Paul Marsh, and Mike Staunton produced an excellent chronology of international risk premiums in several foreign markets in their informative and well illustrated book, *Triumph of the Optimists: 101 Years of Global Investment Returns.*[10] The book encompasses annual real and nominal returns on equities, bonds, and bills, as well as GDP, inflation, and exchange rate data over 100 years (1900 to 2000) for 16 countries.

Dimson, Marsh, and Staunton reported that value stocks (those with higher dividend yields and/or higher ratios of book-to-market value) earned higher returns in the long run than did growth stocks, and that small cap stocks outperformed large cap stocks in all but 1 of the 16 countries studied.[*]

Mathijs A. van Dijk listed 23 separate studies in his 2007 paper on the size effect in international markets.[11] Those studies covered estimates of the monthly size premiums for 18 individual countries and two groups of countries (emerging markets and Europe). According to van Dijk, the international evidence on the size premium is remarkably consistent. Small firms outperform large firms (on a risk-unadjusted basis) in 17 of the 18 countries investigated as well as in a sample of emerging markets and in Europe.

Size and value factors can play a role for investors who are comparing the results of international mutual funds. In addition, it is now possible for investors to create an international three-factor portfolio using a variety of available international value and small cap index funds and ETFs. The annual cost of these investment products is a fraction of the cost to gain the same risk exposures using actively managed investment products.

Real Estate Investment Trusts

When President Eisenhower signed the 1960 Real Estate Investment Trust Act into law, it established qualifying Real Estate Investment Trusts (REITs) as pass-through entities for tax purposes. This provision eliminated corporate taxes for real estate management

---

[*]Dimson, Marsh, and Staunton use data from Hawawini and Keim in their "The Cross Section of Common Stock Returns: A Review of the Evidence and Some New Findings" published in a book by Keim and Ziemba entitled *Security Market Imperfections in Worldwide Equity Markets* (Cambridge University Press, 2000).

companies as long as they paid out 90 percent of their free cash flow to shareholders. The law has remained relatively intact with minor improvements since then.

REITs initially remained a small and rather obscure market due to regulations requiring the separation of management and rental property owners and the fact that pension funds were not allowed to invest in REITs. Deregulation by the Tax Reform Act of 1986 allowed REITs to manage their properties directly, and in 1993, investment barriers to pension funds investing in REITs were eliminated. These developments opened the door for new capital investment in REITs and to a flurry of new REIT offerings.

Vanguard launched the first real estate specific index fund in 1996 to track all U.S. property REITs that trade on U.S. exchanges. No mortgage REITs or hybrids (debt and property) were included in the fund. Figure 5.5 illustrates the performance of 30 actively managed REIT mutual funds relative to the Vanguard REIT index for 10 years ending in 2009.

REITs are a relatively new asset class, and there isn't much comparison data yet. Nonetheless, the returns for the Vanguard REIT Index Fund are shaping up as one would expect in that it's outperforming a majority of actively managed REIT funds. Figure 5.5 shows that there is a win-loss ratio of about 1 to 2 for the actively managed REIT funds.

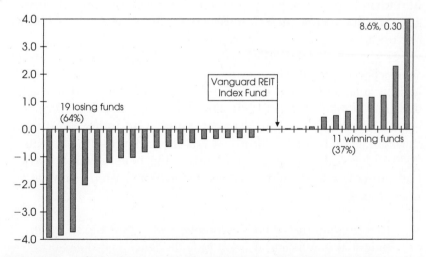

Figure 5.5   10-Year Return of Active REIT Funds Relative to the Vanguard REIT Index Fund

The Vanguard REIT Index Fund was the number 12 best-performing fund out of 31 total funds. Figure 5.5 also shows three poor performing funds and one fund that exploded to the upside. The single outperforming fund beat all others by a wide margin, although with much more volatility in its annual returns than the average REIT fund.

Figure 5.5 also shows a poor payout for most winning actively managed REIT funds in relation to the shortfalls from underperforming active funds. The average winning active fund beat the index fund by 0.7 percent, not including the big top performing fund. In contrast, the average losing fund fell short by 1.1 percent not including the bottom performing fund. Aside from the single big active winning fund, the poor payouts for winning are in line with other asset class returns.

U.S. Small Cap

The range of returns for small cap funds is much wider than large cap funds because the variability of return in individual small cap companies is greater than large cap companies. This is particularly true during volatile markets.[12]

Some would argue that small cap stocks are inefficient and that this wide dispersion of returns makes it possible for active managers to outperform more frequently. I disagree. While greater dispersion in returns among small cap stocks may increase the probability that greater value can be added in the small cap universe, simply having this opportunity does not guarantee alpha.

Not every index fund works exactly as hoped, and the first U.S. small cap index fund is a good example. Vanguard converted an actively managed small cap fund into an index fund that tracked the Russell 2000 index in 1989. This conversion didn't go very well.

The problem with the Vanguard Small Cap Index Fund wasn't the management of the fund—it was the index itself. The Russell 2000 index didn't make a good investable benchmark because it had annual reconstruction issues. William Bernstein summarized these issues:

> It turns out that there's a problem with the Russell 2000 Index—it is rebalanced every June 30. Since it is defined as the 1001st through 3000th stocks ranked by market cap, and since it is the most widely used small-cap index, savvy traders

can easily predict which stocks will be added and dropped from the index, bidding these stocks up or down before June 30, adversely impacting the indexers who must buy or sell these stocks after June 30, lest they incur increased tracking error.[13]

There has been significant analysis conducted on the reconstitution of the Russell 2000 index and the tough issues that index managers face.* Tracking the Russell 2000 is "the equivalent of an Army obstacle course, complete with water hazards, balance beams and hand-to-hand combat" according to one *New York Times* journalist.[14]

Vanguard fund managers were able to deftly outperform the Russell 2000 index because of the way they traded around the reconstitution period as mutual fund industry insider Gary Gastineau explains:

> For the ten years ending in 2001, the Vanguard Small Cap Index Fund beat its Russell 2000 benchmark index by an average of 76 basis points or 0.76% per year. . . . The outperformance that Vanguard achieved came largely from recapturing part of these embedded transaction costs. It did this by making annual reconstitution transactions at a time other than the market close on the last trading day of June when Russell index rebalancing is formally implemented.[15]

Kudos to Vanguard for smart trading practices that reduced some costs, but this didn't solve the big issue of the Russell index. The active managers still beat the Russell 2000 rather handily.

Vanguard made a bold decision to dump the Russell 2000 index in 2004 and switch to the MSCI Small Cap index. The move to MSCI paid off. Performance improved relative to active funds. Figure 5.6 highlights the relative performance of the new Vanguard Small Cap Index Fund relative to active funds for five years ending in 2009.

The dispersion in small cap fund returns is broader than large cap fund returns because the range of stock returns that make up

---

*For a good review of Russell 2000 reconstitution issues and their effects on index fund performance, see Ananth Madhavan, "The Russell Reconstitution Effect," *Financial Analysts Journal* 59, no. 4 (July–August 2003): 51–64.

those funds is greater. The average winning small cap active fund outperformed the Vanguard index fund by 2.1 percentage points per year. That's more than double the outperformance for the average large cap active fund. On the losing side, the average small cap active fund underperformed by about 2.8 percent, which is also more than double the average large cap fund underperformance. So, while the opportunity for greater outperformance in the small cap fund universe exists, the risk for greater underperformance also exists.

The new Vanguard Small Cap Index fund landed in at the 42nd percentile for all funds over this five-year period. This is better than the average actively managed small cap fund, and the data doesn't include the 20 percent or so active small cap funds that closed over the period in question.

The same shape forms in Figure 5.6 for small cap performance as all other asset classes despite a relatively short performance period study. More than half the small cap active funds underperformed the Vanguard Small Cap Index fund for five years ending in 2009, and the outperforming funds did not return enough to make up for the shortfall from the losing funds.

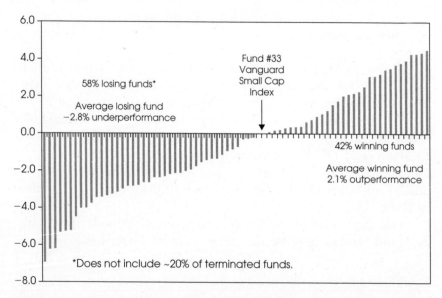

Figure 5.6   Five-Year Relative Performance of Small Cap Funds Ending in 2009

Revisiting SPIVA Performance Studies

Chapter 4 introduced the Standard & Poor's Indices Versus Active (SPIVA) report. This study tracks one-, three-, and five-year active mutual fund performance across several different asset classes and is derived from a survivorship-bias-free database. The semiannual SPIVA report includes U.S. equity, U.S. real estate, U.S. fixed income, international equity, emerging markets equity, and international fixed income.

The SPIVA report constantly reminds us that indexing has had remarkable success in all asset classes and style sectors over the years, albeit with varying results over different time periods. Over the long-term, index funds outperform the average active fund in every asset class, sector, and style. There are periods when active funds shine as a group, but they don't shine by much and not for long.

The conclusions drawn from academic studies and ongoing reports such as SPIVA make it clear that a low-cost passive approach works across every asset class. Combining index funds from a number of asset classes into a portfolio and maintaining that portfolio provides the highest probability for meeting an investor's financial objectives.

Active Management Invades Indexing

There is one smear on the impressive growth in index funds and ETFs. It's the invasion of active management into index fund space. Up until 2003, all index funds and ETFs tracked traditional benchmark indexes that were designed to reflect the value of financial markets and market sectors. Then, in 2003, one ETF company boldly changed the definition of an index fund by launching ETFs that track active management strategies and called them strategy indexes.

Products that follow these strategy indexes are not passive investments.[16] They were never designed to measure market returns or to be used as a proxy for market beta. Nor do they have a role in academic research or as benchmarks to measure the performance of active managers against. Strategy indexes are active management in drag that were created for one purpose: to capitalize on the popularity of passive index fund investing.

The fund companies that use strategy indexes often claim these methods are better performing than traditional benchmark indexes.

The salespeople for the active fund companies that run strategy index products say traditional benchmarks are *inefficient* and *flawed* and that their new strategies are better. This is nonsense, of course. It's the same sales spin that active managers have used since Vanguard launched the first index fund in 1976.

The SEC did investors no favor by allowing the marketers of these strategy index products to re-label their active methodologies as indexes and launch strategy index funds straight into the heart of the passive indexing industry. It is as though the SEC invited the foxes into the henhouse.

As expected, these newfangled index funds created tremendous confusion for would-be traditional index fund investors. Many didn't understand the strategies or what the added costs were. All they heard was that these new index products were supposedly better than the old index products, and this was the exact message the product issuers wanted the public to hear. It's wrong for securities regulators to allow this public deception to continue.

Since 2003, there have been hundreds of ETFs and mutual funds launched that follow actively managed strategy indexes. The labeling of these strategies include clever names such as Intellidex, AlphaDEX, fundamental indexing, dividend indexing, quantitative indexing, and a host of others.

Repacking active management in the form of an index does not change the underlying problems with active management. The active methods are not proven to generate alpha, and the cost of strategy index products is much higher than the cost of passive funds that follow benchmark indexes. It's a repackaged loser's bet. Passive investors would be wise to avoid these pseudo-index funds and stay true to the lowest-cost index funds and ETFs that follow market benchmarks.

Summary

In every asset class, the odds of beating index funds are low, and the payout for being right is well below what a fair payout should be. The only conclusion one can draw from this data is that active management cannot compete against passive management in any asset class, style, or sector in the long run.

Only U.S. equity index funds were available to investors up until the 1980s. Investors had no choice except to purchase high-cost actively managed mutual funds for most asset classes. This is no longer true. Today, there are hundreds of low-cost index funds and ETFs that cover a wide variety of asset class, styles, and sectors. Choose funds that follow understandable market benchmarks, have low fees, are fully liquid, and tax efficient.

CHAPTER 6

Portfolios of Mutual Funds

The most important questions of life are indeed, for the most part, really only problems of probability.

—Marquis de Laplace

More than 50 years ago, Harry Markowitz revolutionized portfolio management by observing the way securities act together in a portfolio to reduce risk. He proposed that portfolio management should have more to do with overall portfolio risk than the risk inherent in each individual security in a portfolio. The same concept can be applied to a portfolio of mutual funds.

Investors typically don't own one mutual fund; they own a portfolio of mutual funds. How does the performance of a portfolio of actively managed funds compare to a portfolio of index funds? Do more active funds in a portfolio change portfolio risk relative to index funds? This chapter extends the passive versus active debate from one mutual fund to portfolios holding a number of funds.

Data on portfolio performance from multiple passive funds compared to multiple active funds yields important information for all investors. A portfolio of actively managed funds has a lower probability of outperforming a portfolio of index funds than a single active fund has of outperforming a single index fund. As the number of actively managed funds increases, the odds that a portfolio will outperform decreases. In addition, the longer active funds are held, the worse the odds become for the active fund portfolio, until eventually there's practically no chance of outperformance.

Efficient Portfolios

Eugene Fama coined the term *efficient market* hypothesis in his landmark 1965 thesis on the behavior of stock prices. Fama said that an efficient market exists when (1) information about the securities trading on a market is widely and cheaply available to all, (2) all known and available information is already reflected in security prices, (3) the current price of a security is agreed upon by a buyer and seller in a market, and it is the best estimate of the investment value of that security at the time, and (4) security prices will almost instantaneously change as new information about them appears in the market.[1]

Fama's paper sparked a long debate over whether markets are efficient, and index fund advocates were naturally dragged into this debate. Indexers, as they are called, generally side with the efficient market hypothesis while active investors point out that there are many market inefficiencies. Ironically, Fama himself has helped document some of those inefficiencies over the years. Warren Buffett's success in active management is often cited as proof that markets aren't efficient. Yet, Buffett himself is a strong proponent of index fund investing for most individual investors. Accordingly, after almost 50 years the only conclusion that can be drawn from the efficient market debate is that the debate will likely continue for another 50 years.

In my opinion, the important question for investors is not if markets are efficient. Rather, it's a question of efficient investing, meaning creating and maintaining an efficient portfolio that has the highest probability for success. That's the purpose for investing.

Portfolio Choices

As I previously stated, most people don't own just one fund; they invest in a number of mutual funds. And they don't just buy one style of fund; they diversify across different asset classes.

There are two basic choices that we all make as fund investors. One is an asset allocation decision and the other is a securities selection decision. We decide which asset classes to own and then decide how to own them. Some people spend many hours on portfolio construction. They isolate desirable assets classes first, and then search for the right finds for each asset class. Other investors don't give it much thought. They muddle through the process without any asset allocation or fund selection strategy. Nevertheless, in the end, everyone ends up with a portfolio of sorts.

Let's assume all investors are logical in their asset allocation decisions and diligent in their fund selections. Table 6.1 is a 2 × 2 matrix that illustrates how these two decisions fit together. The columns represent fund selection strategy and the rows represent asset allocation strategy. These four methods of portfolio management represent the investment strategies used by all mutual fund investors even if they don't realize it.

Starting with asset allocation first; there are two schools of thought. The first follows a fixed passive allocation also known as *strategic* asset allocation. In this approach, investments are allocated to a fixed allocation of asset classes that's based on long-term needs and are held at that allocation through regular rebalancing. In contrast, a *tactical* asset allocation is all about actively shifting mutual fund weights based on near-term predictions of asset class returns. A tactical asset allocation decision may last from a few days to a few years.

On the fund side, investors can choose between passive index funds and ETFs that follow benchmarks and actively managed mutual funds and ETFs that try to beat the benchmarks. Much of this book explains the difference, so I won't elaborate here.

Both fund asset allocation strategy and fund selection methodology have a major influence on portfolio return. Specifically, the more active bets made in a portfolio either through fund selection or tactical allocation, the lower the expected portfolio return. This chapter looks at portfolio returns using active and passive funds while Chapter 8 takes a closer look at asset allocation decisions.

Table 6.1 Four Portfolio Choices for Investors

	Passive Funds (index funds and benchmark based ETFs)	Active Funds (mutual funds and actively managed ETFs)
Maintain a Fixed Passive Asset Allocation	Passive funds Passive allocation	Active funds Passive allocation
Employ a Tactical Active Asset Allocation	Passive funds Active allocation	Active funds Active allocation

Portfolios of Active Funds

Finding an actively managed mutual fund that delivers alpha is a challenge for any investor. Trying to select a portfolio of active funds that outperforms a portfolio of index funds is another matter entirely. The odds of a portfolio using actively managed funds outperforming an all index fund portfolio is much lower than a single fund, and the odds drop with each additional active fund added to a portfolio, and the longer the funds are held. A portfolio holding several active funds for several years has only a negligible chance of beating an all index fund portfolio.

The first attempt to quantify portfolio return probabilities in an active portfolio was conducted in the early 1990s by Larry L. Martin and published in the spring 1993 issue of *The Journal of Investing*.[2] In "The Evolution of Passive versus Active Equity Management," Martin used fund fees and simulation to estimate how well a portfolio of active funds would perform against a portfolio of indexes. Table 6.2 highlights the results.

Table 6.2   The Probability an Actively Managed Portfolio Will Beat Indexes as Measured by Martin in His 1993 Study

	1 Year	5 Years	10 Years	20 Years
One Actively Managed Fund	41%	29%	22%	14%
Three Active Funds Portfolio	33%	17%	9%	3%
Five Active Funds Portfolio	29%	11%	4%	1%

Author and financial advisor Allan Roth also quantified these portfolio questions and found strikingly similar results as Martin. His data is published in his enjoyable book, *How a Second Grader Beats Wall Street*.[3] Roth designed a Monte Carlo simulation model that calculated the probabilities a randomly selected portfolio of actively managed funds would beat an all index fund portfolio. The model takes into account the range of active fund returns as well as the possibility that some funds will close or merge. Table 6.3 highlights the results of Roth's study.

Table 6.3   The Probability an Actively Managed Portfolio Will Beat Index Funds Based on Roth's Study

	1 Year	5 Years	10 Years	25 Years
One Actively Managed Fund	42%	30%	23%	12%
Five Active Funds Portfolio	32%	18%	11%	3%
Ten Active Funds Portfolio	25%	9%	6%	1%

Source: Allan Roth, Wealth Logic, LLC.

According to Roth's model, the chance that a single actively managed fund will beat a comparable index fund over any single year is 42 percent. The success rate drops to 30 percent over 5 years, 23 percent over 10 years, and just 12 percent over 25 years.

As mentioned previously, most investors don't own just one mutual fund in their portfolio. They own five or ten funds. This is where Martin and Roth's data becomes interesting. Averaging the two studies resulted in a portfolio composed of five actively managed funds having about a 30 percent probability of beating an all index fund portfolio over 1 year, about 15 percent probability over 5 years, 8 percent probability over 10 years, and just 2 percent over 25 years.

The odds get progressively worse as more active funds are added. Assume you own 10 actively managed funds. According to Roth's data, the odds of beating an all index fund portfolio are 27 percent over one year, 9 percent over five years, 6 percent over 10 years, and an incredibly low 1 percent over 25 years.

Martin and Roth's estimates appear to be accurate when put to the test in the real world. A 25-year study on the Vanguard 500 Index Fund performance discussed in Chapter 3 found that only about 12 percent of general U.S. equity funds outperformed that index fund over a 25-year period ending in 2009 after adjusting for terminated funds. This is in accordance with what Roth's simulation model had predicted.

Modeling the Active Bet

I took a different approach to modeling portfolio performance and found results very similar to Martin and Roth. First, I created a model to simulate the five-year compounded returns of 100 active mutual funds in a generic asset class using actual results from many fund categories over multiple time periods. Second, I randomly created thousands of portfolios using 3, 5, and 10 funds and compared the results to an all index fund portfolio with the same number of funds. Third, I assumed my model was wrong and made adjustments that were heavily in favor of active funds. Fourth, I tested the model in real time using actual 15-year active fund returns.

Figure 6.1 is a mutual fund return model that I developed to illustrate the range of returns for all actively managed funds within a generic asset class. The model is based on a five-year period. The point of intersection of the bars and the horizontal axis is the return of a comparable index fund. The data points to the left are the losing funds and the data points to the right are the winning funds. Once more, this demonstrates the 1 to 2 win-loss ratio in active funds.

Thousands of actively managed fund returns were used over many asset classes and time periods to create this generic 100 fund model. The index fund return noted in the graph isn't intended to represent any particular market or investment style. Rather, it's where the index fund return tended to fall relative to actively managed fund returns across many fund categories.

The model also includes terminated funds because they were a choice investors had at the time. The annual rate of return used

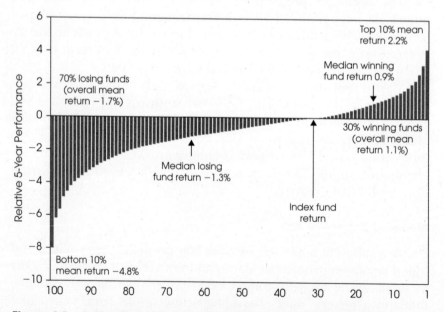

Figure 6.1   Active Fund Five-Year Relative Performance Model

in a terminated fund until its termination date was four percent per year below the index, which is the average performance as calculated by academics in a detailed study on fund persistence.[4] Fund terminations were spread over the full five-year period. It was assumed that the proceeds from each terminated funds were reinvested in the index fund for the remainder of the period.

Mutual fund relative returns are shown from left to right starting with the top performing fund at the 1st percentile on the far right and the worst performing fund at the 100th percentile on the far left. The remaining actively managed funds plus the index fund fall in between. The index fund itself was ranked at the 30th percentile in performance.

The shape of the relative return model illustrates how actively managed mutual funds perform relative to an index fund. There are more losing funds than winning funds, and the worst underperforming funds fall short by about twice as much as the best outperforming funds exceed the index fund.

The mutual fund returns are risk-adjusted. This discounts fund performance that resulted solely from a fund manager taking more market risk (beta). Sales commissions and taxes aren't considered.

Overall, Figure 6.1 shows that the winning active funds earned a mean excess return of about 1.1 percent per year over the index fund while the mean losing fund underperformed by 1.7 percent. The median of the winning funds earned an excess return of 0.9 while the median losing fund underperformed by 1.3 percent.

The two ends in Figure 6.1 are interesting. This is where the best and worst active funds reside. The winning funds progressed steadily higher until about the 10th percentile and then they accelerated. Their return for the best fund was about 4 percent over the index fund. The bottom funds had a steady downward march until about the 85th percentile and then the drop accelerated until it hit −8 percent for the worst fund. The model mirrors the real world quite well. There are roughly twice as many losing funds as there are winning funds, and the average losing fund gives up about 50 percent more than the average winning fund gains.

The model also assumes random expense ratios for the actively managed mutual funds. The average was 1.1 percent, with the worst performing funds having higher fees than the average. The fee for the index fund was assumed to be 0.2 percent, which is a reasonable average estimate for an all-index fund portfolio. It is no coincidence that the return difference between the average active fund and the index fund is –0.9 percent, because that's the average fee difference. This is consistent with the broadly documented and widely accepted notion that, on average, actively managed funds underperform their benchmark by the fees they charge.[5]

Figure 6.2 is a simplified version of Figure 6.1. It divides the 100 funds into 5 equal quintiles, each representing 20 actively managed funds. The median return for the top 20 funds beat the index fund by 1.3 percent. The next 20 funds had no meaningful difference in return. The remaining 60 funds all had returns measurably below the index fund return. The bottom 20 funds had very poor relative performance, falling 3.3 percent behind the index fund over five years.

Modifications to the Model

Modifications could be made to the model studying each asset class separately if a researcher preferred. The volatility of an asset class is a good proxy for making model adjustments. The lower the volatility of an asset class, the fewer active funds outperformed and the tighter the active fund range of returns compared to the index

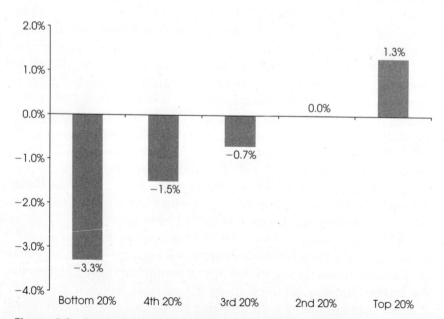

Figure 6.2   Ferri's Simplified Relative Performance Model

fund, and vice versa. It's the same model with adjustments for asset class volatility.

Bond funds have lower volatility than stock funds. Based on the bond fund data presented in Chapter 5, an index fund would be expected to outperform about 80 percent of the actively managed bond funds. In addition, outperforming bond funds would have had approximately a 0.5 percent median excess return while under-performing funds would have fallen short of a bond index fund by about 1.2 percent.

A single model illustrated in Figure 6.1 still works for portfolio analysis because it assumes that a portfolio holds a large cap stock fund, small cap stock fund, bond fund, and other asset classes. The models for individual assets differ slightly based on asset class vola-tility. Overall, the high and low volatility of different asset classes cancel each other out to form this single generic model.

Random Portfolio Results

I conducted multiple tests using the model in Figure 6.1. My intent was to determine the probability that a portfolio of randomly selected active funds would outperform a portfolio of comparable index funds. Each test generated 10,000 randomly selected portfo-lios from the 100 data points in the model. All of these simulations have a margin of error of ±2 percent.

The first test looked at two portfolios held for five years. One tested the probability that a portfolio of five randomly selected active funds would outperform a portfolio of comparable index funds, and the second tested a portfolio of 10 randomly selected active funds. Table 6.4 shows the results.

For the 5 fund portfolio, only 16 percent of portfolios holding all active funds outperformed an all-index fund portfolio. A mere 5 percent of those portfolios won by 0.5 percent or more, while 63 percent underperformed by at least 0.5 percent.

Table 6.4 Probability That an Active Fund Will Beat Index Funds over 5 Years

	Winning Portfolios	Won by 0.5% or More	Lost by 0.5% or More
5 Actively Managed Funds	16%	5%	63%
10 Actively Managed Funds	8%	1%	70%

For the 10 fund portfolio, only 8 percent of portfolios holding all active funds outperformed an all-index fund portfolio. A stark 1 percent of those portfolios won by 0.5 percent or more, while 70 percent underperformed by at least 0.5 percent.

My overall winning percentages were between Martin and Roth's estimate for a 5 fund portfolio and very close to Roth's estimate for a 10 fund portfolio (Martin didn't calculate results for 10 funds). This analysis provides further evidence that as you add more active funds to a portfolio, the probability the portfolio will outperform an all-index fund portfolio drops. It's hard to believe that anyone could make a compelling case for using actively managed mutual funds given these low odds and low payouts.

Changing the Model

Naysayers to my simulation model may contend that there's a greater than 30 percent probability that an active fund will beat an index fund. Some of these people insist that their smarter-than-mortal-man fund selection methodology works. Others may say the odds can be improved significantly by eliminating the high fee funds from the selection list.

To answer these critics, I modified the model in two ways and ran the numbers again. One modification is based on 40 percent probability that active funds will outperform index funds, thereby giving credit to the smarter-than-mortal-man selection theory. The second modification assumes that the highest-cost funds are eliminated from the selection, thus, by default, removing some of the poorly performing funds from the data.

The smarter-than-mortal-man 40 percent model leaves all 100 fund returns intact while decreasing the return of the index fund so that it intersected at the 40th percentile. This provides a win-loss ratio of 2 to 3, which is slightly better than a win-loss ratio of 1 to 2 found throughout the academic studies. Table 6.5 highlights the results.

Table 6.5   Tests Using a 40 Percent Winning Active Fund Expectation

	Winning Portfolios	Won by 0.5% or More	Lost by 0.5% or More
5 Actively Managed Funds	26%	10%	51%
10 Actively Managed Funds	18%	3%	52%

Assuming that 40 percent of active funds beat index funds didn't help the case for active mutual funds very much. Overall, the odds for selecting a winning combination of active funds only went up by 10 percent in both 5 and 10 fund portfolios over a five-year period. There was still greater than a 50 percent probability that the active fund portfolio would underperform an all index fund portfolio by 0.5 percent or more.

The second model assumes that the 10 highest-cost active funds were deleted from the database, leaving only 90 active funds with lower expenses. To fairly eliminate funds based on fees, I deleted funds across the range of returns with a generous number deleted from worst performing funds. The academic research on fees suggests that about 40 percent of the highest-cost funds are in the bottom 25 percent of funds, with 20 percent in the bottom 10 percent. Thus, most of the funds were deleted from those deciles. Table 6.6 highlights the results.

Table 6.6 Tests Deleting the 10 Highest-Cost Funds

	Winning Portfolios	Won by 0.5% or More	Lost by 0.5% or More
5 Actively Managed Funds	20%	6%	59%
10 Actively Managed Funds	10%	1%	62%

Deleting highest-cost funds to find winning active funds isn't as promising as the active fund advocates may suggest. Overall, the odds for selecting a winning combination of active funds only went up by 4 percent in the 5 fund portfolio and 2 percent in the 10 fund portfolio. The number of active fund portfolios that beat the index fund portfolio by 0.5 percent or more hardly budged, while the number that underperformed by 0.5 percent or more remained very high.

The Real Deal

Finally, I conducted an independent real-world test of a randomly selected actively managed fund portfolio versus an all index fund portfolio. I used the actual fund returns from three fund categories going back 15 years. I constructed an index fund portfolio using the funds and weights in Table 6.7. My test compared this index fund portfolio to thousands of randomly selected active funds from the Morningstar list, in the correct weightings.

Table 6.7   Model Index Fund Portfolio Used in the Live Study

Index Fund Name	Percent Allocation
Vanguard Total Stock Market Index Fund	45%
Vanguard Total International Stock Index Fund*	15%
Vanguard Total Bond Market Index Fund	40%

* The Vanguard Total International Fund had its first full year under management in 1998. The FTSE All-World ex-US Index Fund (less 0.4 percent fee) is substituted for the years 1995 through 1997. The allocation of the FTSE ex-US could have been replicated using three other Vanguard international index funds that were in existence over the entire time period. The difference between the simulated fund and the actual funds was negligible.

Using the Morningstar Principia database ending in December 2009, I screened each asset class for actively managed funds that were in the same fund category and had the same investment objective as each index fund. The active funds also had the same Morningstar style box to ensure an apples to apples comparison. Table 6.8 has the number of actively managed funds in each category and the percentage of these funds that beat their respective index fund.

As noted in the footnote for Table 6.8, only surviving actively managed funds are included and sales loads were excluded. The active portfolios didn't include closed and merged active funds, which are typically poor performers according to data compiled in

Table 6.8   Active Funds Used in the Live Study

Actively Managed Funds	Number of Funds*	Percent That Beat the Index Fund**
Large Cap U.S. Stock	50	30%
Diversified International Stock	35	51%
U.S. Investment Grade Bond	38	34%

*This data has a survivorship bias because closed and merged fund performance was not included. Using S&P survivorship data, it's estimated that U.S. large cap and diversified international mutual funds closed at about a 4 percent annualized rate over the 15 year period. This means roughly half the funds in existence in 1995 didn't make it through 2009. Closed and merged fund performance was not included in this study.

**These numbers are higher than what an investor should expect going forward today because they only included surviving funds and sales loads were not deducted. Had the closed and merged funds been added and sales loads been deducted, then the percent of equity funds that beat the market in those two categories would be less than half what is shown in Table 6.8. Bond funds survivorship rates are higher and loads are lower. Nonetheless, including these factors would have reduced the number of winning bond funds to roughly 20 percent.

Chapter 7. In addition, sales loads were excluded from the performance analysis. Knowing in advance which funds will survive and not paying a sales load affords the best-case scenario for an active fund investor in this test, even though it's an unrealistic scenario since it isn't possible to know today which funds will survive 15 years into the future.

This test gives us a real-world look at the probabilities that an actively managed fund portfolio would have outperformed an all-index fund portfolio over the past 15 years. The study randomly created 25,000 portfolios using three actively managed funds. Each portfolio held a U.S. large cap fund, an international stock fund, and a general bond fund. The portfolio allocation assigned to each active fund in each asset class were the same as those assigned to the index funds for each asset class. Table 6.9 shows the result of this study.

Table 6.9   Results of the Real-World Three-Fund Study

Portfolio Results	Percent
Active fund portfolios that beat the index fund portfolio–overall	27%
Active fund portfolios that won by 0.5% or more	11%
Active fund portfolio that lost by 0.5% or more	46%

Despite the huge advantage provided to active fund buyers in this study by eliminating closed fund returns and using preload performance figures, only about one-quarter of active fund portfolios beat the Vanguard index fund portfolio, and only 11 percent outperformed by 0.5 percent or more. In contrast, almost three-quarters of the active fund portfolios underperformed the all-index fund portfolio, and almost half underperformed by 0.5 percent or more. I also ran more tests using different asset allocations than those shown in Table 6.7. The results weren't materially different.

It's interesting to note that the surviving actively managed funds fared better in each individual category than they did as part of a portfolio. About 30 percent of active large cap U.S. stock funds beat the Vanguard Total Stock Market Index Fund, 51 percent of active international funds beat the Vanguard Total International Stock Fund, and 34 percent beat the bond index fund. So, on average 38 percent of active funds outperformed their equivalent index fund. Yet only 27 percent of 3 fund active portfolios beat the all index fund portfolio. This shows that as more active funds are added to a portfolio, the lower the probability that the active fund portfolio will outperform an equivalent index fund portfolio.

The win-loss ratio of active fund portfolios would have been reduced considerably more if the closed and merged fund performances were included in the data, and load-adjusted returns were used for active funds rather than assuming there were no sales loads. I calculated that the win-loss ratio for the active fund portfolios over five years would have plunged to about 15 percent. This is right in line with Martin's estimate and my Active Fund Relative Performance Model estimate (Roth's data didn't include three fund probabilities).

The Bottom Line Is Your Bottom Line

I believe your bottom line is much more important than the bottom line of Wall Street. Investing isn't about the possibility of beating the market; it's about the probability you'll meet your financial objectives by earning a fair payout for the risks you take. A portfolio of index funds dramatically increases that probability of meeting your bottom line.

For more information on fund selection and portfolio construction, read *All About Index Funds* (McGraw-Hill, 2006), *The ETF Book* (John Wiley & Sons, 2009), and *All About Asset Allocation* (McGraw-Hill, 2010). I provide several model portfolios in all three books. My books are available on Amazon.com and summaries of the books are available on my web site at www.RickFerri.com.

Summary

This chapter tells a very important story. Efficient investing is different from efficient markets. Investors should select the best way to manage their portfolio so as to have the highest probability for success.

Active fund investors have strong headwinds against them. The probability of selecting a winning fund is low; the average payout for those winning funds does not compensate them enough for the shortfall from being wrong; the addition of several active funds in a portfolio reduces the probability of success; and the longer that portfolio is held, the odds drop even more. That's a lot of headwind!

A portfolio of index funds and market tracking exchange-traded funds is superior to active management. It's the most efficient way to reach your financial goals; that's the bottom line!

PART

II

CHASING ALPHA AND CHANGING BEHAVIOR

CH A PTER 7

The Futility of Seeking Alpha

*The evidence powerfully confirms that, at least in the mutual fund
industry, the holy grail doesn't exist. But investors seem hell-bent on
carrying out the search for winning funds of the future, no matter
how futile the search has proven to be.*

—John C. Bogle

*How quickly investors flock to better-performing mutual funds, even
though financial researchers have shown that the "hot" funds in
one time period very often turn out to be the poorest performers in
another.*

—David Dreman

Advocates for active management frame their argument by
claiming that the markets are inefficient, and as such, there are
ways to outperform them without taking extra risk. This chapter
puts that argument to rest.

We have learned so far that about 1 in 3 active fund managers
are able to capitalize on this claimed inefficiency, which is no better than chance. In addition, the excess payout earned by the winning active fund managers is far below a fair payout given the large
shortfalls from the losing active funds. What's worse, the identities
of the 1 in 3 active managers who outperform the indexes change

from period to period. The winning active managers in one period are typically not the winning managers in the next.

There have been, and will continue to be, a handful of active fund managers who have earned a high enough excess return to compensate investors for the low probability of selecting them. The problem for investors is identifying these few managers in advance. If they can be identified in advance, then active management makes sense. But there is no known method for selecting winning fund managers of the future.

All That's Needed Is a Crystal Ball

The naysayers of index funds argue that there are ways to select winning active funds in advance, and this makes active management a winning bet. Seeking alpha with a winning mutual fund method would make sense if one existed, but it doesn't. And even if such a method did exist, it would stop working rather quickly as millions of investors pile into the same winning active fund and handcuff the manager with billions of new dollars to invest.

Investors who are seeking alpha are looking for skilled managers, and this assumes skill is identifiable. Is it? About one-third of managers beat the market over a five-year period, but are all these managers skillful? Are any skillful? Perhaps the winning managers just got lucky.

It takes many years to determine if a winning manager has skill or is lucky. Skilled managers have track records that are proven with time and over complete market cycles. They may not beat the market every year, but they're consistently close.

That's not how most winning funds perform. Often a manager has one or two big winning years and then their performance fizzles out. Where there's no consistency, there's no talent. It should be no surprise that most winning active managers don't have consistency, which means they don't have skill. They just got lucky.

If it's possible, as some claim, to select skilled fund managers in advance, then what's the methodology for doing so? It certainly would have been revealed in academic studies by now. Do such studies exist? If so, what's the secret?

By far, the two most popular factors used in fund selection by the public are past performance and fund ratings. Other factors are fee analysis, the amount of assets in a fund, and qualitative factors such as where the manager went to college.

Unfortunately, I was unsuccessful in identifying any comprehensive study on mutual fund selection that provided evidence that a successful fund selection method exists. There were a few studies that suggested ways of narrowing down the field by eliminating funds that had certain characteristics such as the highest fees, or only including funds that had certain qualitative features such as a large personal stake in the fund by the manager, but no single factor consistently worked.

Recall that the very reason academics began studying mutual funds in the 1960s was to discover managers who had skill. Their efforts were unsuccessful back then and new efforts remain unsuccessful today. If the Ph.D.s can't figure out how to pick winning managers, then it's not likely that an individual investor or investment advisor is going to do it.

Why, then, do financial magazines, newspapers, newsletters, web sites, and so on continually suggest that there are ways to select winning active funds? Because it makes money for these companies and the people who provide the advice! Investors will pay for the names of advertised winning funds, even though there's no demonstrated reason why those funds should outperform in the future.

There's another reason beat-the-market fund advice exists. Actively managed fund companies spend heavily to advertise in various media outlets. So, while the financial media is fair to the passive world by giving index funds and ETFs their due, it's the billions in advertising revenue from the active fund providers that feed the media outlets. Consequently, there will always be beat-the-market advice front-and-center in the public's eye.

Past Performance as a Way to Predict Future Returns

"Past performance is not an indication of future returns." That's what the SEC requires all mutual funds to disclose in their marketing material. We've all seen and heard this phase 1,000 times. But it might as well not exist, because most people ignore it.

An overwhelming percentage of investors and advisors select mutual funds based almost exclusively on past performance. Their underlying assumption for relying on past results is that it has predictive value. Not so. There's only scant evidence that past performance predicts future long-term returns, and most of that evidence rests in the worst performing funds.[1] While there's also been some evidence that top performing funds may persist, at least for a short while, these trends are unreliable and they don't appear to be large enough or long enough to capitalize on.

Persistence of Performance Academic Studies

Performance persistence studies began in the 1960s and grew in popularity during the 1990s as more mutual fund data became available. This coincided with a period when the survivorship-bias in mutual fund databases was being addressed and corrected.[*]

"Hot Hands in Mutual Funds; Short-Run Persistence of Relative Performance 1974–1988" was published in a 1993 issue of the *Journal of Finance,* written by Darryll Hendricks, Jayendu Patel, and Richard Zechhauser. The authors sampled 165 no-load growth equity funds to test for short-term persistence and came to several conclusions: (1) There was short-term persistence in the winning funds, but it didn't last beyond four quarters; (2) new money-flows into the winning funds bloated the asset base and detracted from future performance; (3) a manager's drive to outperform appears to diminish as fund assets increase; and (4) salaries and fees rose in response to investment success.[2]

The most important point of the "Hot Hands" study was the apparent persistence in some mutual fund returns. The second important point was that it didn't last.

Other academic studies conducted around the period came to similar conclusions: "We find evidence that differences in performance between funds persist over time and that this persistence is consistent with the ability of fund managers to earn returns," according to Mark Grinblatt and Sheridan Titman in their 1992 *Journal of Finance* article.[3] "Our sample, largely free of survivorship bias, indicates that relative risk-adjusted performance of mutual funds persists; however, persistence is mostly due to funds that lag

---

[*]Mutual fund databases were plagued by survivorship bias through the mid-1990s. As funds closed or merged, their entire historic performance was purged from the database. Most of these funds had poor performance leading up to their closures, so their purging the database artificially increased the return of the average fund because only the better performing surviving mutual funds were left. Most providers of fund databases have since fixed the survivorship biases by adding back the performance.

the S&P 500," according to Stephen Brown and William Goetzmann in their 1995 study.[4]

Carhart's Work   An exhaustive and widely quoted mutual fund persistence study was published in 1997 by Mark Carhart in the *Journal of Finance*. This study was entitled "On the Persistence of Mutual Fund Performance."[5] The report was so meticulously done that rather than relying on a standard mutual fund database provided by another party, Carhart created a new database, which later became known as the CRSP Survivor-Bias-Free U.S. Mutual Fund Database.

Carhart's study covered diversified equity mutual funds that existed from January 1962 to December 1993. There were 1,892 total funds in his study, although many had gone out of existence over that period. The closed and merged fund performance was included until the termination month to make the database survivorship bias free.

Each year, mutual funds were ranked in equal numbered groups from 1 to 10 based on annual performance. The first group held the top performing funds for that year, and the 10th group held the lowest performing funds. All others fell among the other eight groups. All the funds were then analyzed to determine why they fell into their deciles.

Carhart used two models to compare fund performance: a single-factor model that adjusted fund returns using only beta and a four-factor model that included beta, size, value, and price momentum (see Chapter 4 for an explanation). The results were illuminating.

Carhart found that a four-factor model best explained fund performance over the period. The two factors that explained most of a fund's return were size and momentum (size is related to the relative size of companies held in a fund and momentum compares fund performance from one year to the next). Figure 7.1 illustrates these two critical factors. Funds in the first decile had the highest second year returns and funds in the tenth decile had the lowest.

Keep in mind that Figure 7.1 shows results according to regression factors results, not fund performance. These numbers measure how much each risk factor influenced fund returns in each decile rather than the amount of actual return these factors contributed to those funds. Higher factor influence means funds were heavily

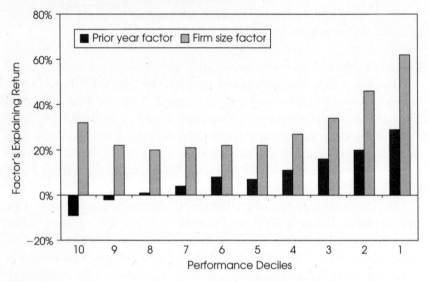

Figure 7.1   Carhart Factor Analysis Regressions of Mutual Fund Performance

affected by the factor regardless of how high or low the returns were. A negative number means that fund returns were negatively correlated with the factor.

Figure 7.1 shows that in all performance deciles, small cap stock exposure explained a large part of fund performance. The positive numbers mean that the fund managers positioned their portfolios to have a greater percentage in small cap stocks than the cap weighted index. Since small cap stocks outperformed large cap stocks by about 2 percent annually over the period of the study, mutual funds with an overweighting to small stocks should have outperformed the cap weighted market. The positive alpha from small cap stock across all deciles shows that the firm size effect influenced fund returns in all those deciles.

More interesting is how the previous year's performance of a fund influenced its current year return. Figure 7.1 shows that funds with high relative performance in the prior year tended to outperform again in the current year. This signals fund performance momentum. However, this positive momentum didn't persist beyond one year.

The exception was the bottom performing four deciles where prior year performance appeared to be a neutral to negative factor.

A negative factor means a reversal of fortune occurred from bad to better. However, some of the worst performing funds from the previous year did show the highest persistence with continued poor performance.

Fund momentum is caused by momentum in underlying stock holdings. According to Carhart, simply buying last year's winning stocks takes no manager skill and should not be counted as alpha. He concludes, "The results do not support the existence of skilled or informed mutual fund portfolio managers." The following is Carhart's conclusion:

> The evidence of the article suggests three important rules-of-thumb for wealth-maximizing mutual fund investors: (1) Avoid funds with persistently poor performance; (2) funds with high returns last year have higher-than-average expected returns next year, but not in the years thereafter; and (3) the investment costs of expense ratios, transaction costs, and load fees all have a direct, negative impact on performance. While the popular press will no doubt continue to glamorize the best-performance mutual fund managers, the mundane explanations of strategy and investment costs account for almost all of the important predictability in mutual fund returns.

One caveat of Carhart's study is transaction costs. His study was conducted with no penalty for the additional costs from sales loads or brokerage commissions. In addition, Carhart made no exception for funds closed to new investment. In the real world, these issues dilute portfolio returns and can eliminate any alpha derived from a mutual fund momentum trading strategy.

Fama and French   Eugene Fama and Kenneth French recently concluded a detailed study of 3,156 funds for the period January 1984 to September 2006. They wanted to find out if outperforming active managers were skillful or just lucky.

First, they quantified the number of funds that were expected to perform well by chance using a simulation model. Second, they compared actual funds to the model using a three-factor model. They found the top active funds performed roughly in line with the simulated results.[6] This suggested that, in aggregate, the number of winning active funds was no larger than what would be expected by chance; as a group, then, active managers exhibited no particular skill.

Fama and French did find that some managers who had sufficient alpha to cover costs using their three-factor model. Their conclusion was, "If we add back the costs in fund expense ratios, there is evidence of inferior and superior performance in the extreme tails of the cross section of mutual fund α [alpha] estimates." However, adjusting for fund momentum all but eliminated this apparent advantage. Consequently, skill was impossible to determine. It remains unknown if the top performing fund managers had skill or if they just got lucky.

Bond Funds   The persistence of top performing funds appears to extend to bond funds. The number of studies on bond fund persistence is relatively small compared to equity fund studies.

Jeroen Derwall and Joop Huij of the RSM Erasmus University in the Netherlands did find persistence in their 2007 study, "'Hot Hands' in Bond Funds."[7] The researchers concluded that there is performance persistence in the 3,549 bond mutual returns they analyzed for the period 1990 to 2003: "[we] . . . show that bond funds that display strong (weak) performance over a past period continue to do so in future periods. . . . We demonstrate that a strategy based on past fund returns earns an economically and statistically significant abnormal return, suggesting that bond fund investors can exploit the observed persistence."

Marlena Lee of Dimensional Fund Advisors disagrees with Derwall and Huij's conclusion. Lee analyzed the performance of 1,476 U.S. bond funds through 2008 and concluded that there is no evidence of positive after-cost expected alphas in bond funds in the top percentile. These results indicate that it's unlikely that investors can earn abnormal profits from investing in bond funds with superior past performance.

Lee notes, "In aggregate, bond funds underperform by an amount roughly equal to fees. Additionally, good past performance does not predict good future performance. The top decile of funds sorted on abnormal returns in the previous three years has insignificant alphas in the following six months. In contrast, the underperformance of loser funds persists for several years."[8]

It appears that the academics have different opinions about persistence of performance. Or perhaps the phenomenon is period-dependent; that is, it may exist during some periods and not others. What is clear from all the research is that chasing past performance is not a reliable way to select winning funds.

Continuous Persistence Studies

Standard & Poor's keeps a rolling count of mutual fund persistence. They provide this data free of charge through a semiannual report titled "The S&P Persistence Scorecard."* The Scorecard tracks the consistency of mutual funds over three- and five-year time periods. The University of Chicago's CRSP Survivorship-Bias-Free U.S. Mutual Fund Database provides the data for this analysis.

The ongoing S&P study separates U.S. equity mutual funds into groups based on four size categories: large cap, mid cap, small cap, and multi cap. Each group is then divided into four quartiles based on each fund's past three-year performance and the past five-year performance. These funds are re-ranked into quartiles after three and five years so that persistence is evident. Funds that closed or merged were placed in a separate category as were funds that had a style change.

Table 7.1 highlights the persistence results across 1,925 mutual funds for five years and 1,526 funds over three years ending in September 2009. The table is a composite report including all four size categories: large cap, mid cap, small cap, and multi cap. The three rows in each time period represent: (1) the actual second period fund dispersion across four quartiles by percentage including funds that have terminated or changed style; (2) the surviving funds and their quintile after eliminating terminated and changed funds; and (3) an equal fund distribution that occurs by chance.

Table 7.1 reveals the future performance to be completely random. The actual persistence numbers of surviving mutual funds (second row in each table) couldn't be closer to a random distribution (third row in each table) over both the three- and five-year periods. There is no persistence in mutual fund performance, at least during these three- and five-year periods.

S&P suggests in their study that screening for top-quartile funds may be an inappropriate method for fund selection, and I agree. For all practical purposes, the performance of mutual funds is not predictable based on past performance. What will happen in the future is independent from the past.

Morningstar Data   This discussion on persistence is capped off with actual performance data culled from the Morningstar database from 2007 to 2009. This is summarized in Table 7.2.

---

*The S&P Persistence Score Card is available at http://www.indexresearch .standardandpoors.com.

Table 7.1   Mutual Fund Persistence of Top Quartile Funds versus Random Selection

Three Year	# of Top Funds	1st Quartile	2nd Quartile	3rd Quartile	4th Quartile	Closed or Merged	Style Change
Actual	492	17.5%	17.4%	17.4%	17.4%	19.5%	10.7%
Surviving	337	25.1%	24.9%	25.0%	24.9%		
Random		25.0%	25.0%	25.0%	25.0%		

Five Year	# of Top Funds	1st Quartile	2nd Quartile	3rd Quartile	4th Quartile	Closed or Merged	Style Change
Actual	385	15.0%	14.9%	14.8%	14.9%	27.4%	13.0%
Surviving	230	25.1%	25.0%	24.9%	25.0%		
Random		25.0%	25.0%	25.0%	25.0%		

Source: S&P Persistence Scorecard, January 2010 (data through September 2009).

Table 7.2   A Lack of Fund Persistence in 2008 and 2009 (U.S. Domestic Stock Large-Blend[*])

2007 Top Funds	Average Rank in 2008	Average Percentile	Avg. 2008 Return	+(−) Cat Average
Top 10 Funds Average	368 of 527	70%	−40.2	−3.3
Top 25 Funds Average	343 of 527	65%	−38.8	−1.9
Top 10% 53 Fund Average	286 of 527	54%	−36.9	0.1

2008 Top Funds	Average Rank in 2009	Average Percentile	Avg. 2009 Return	+(−) Cat Average
Top 10 Funds Average	458 of 552	83%	18.1	−9.8
Top 25 Funds Average	434 of 552	79%	20.3	−7.6
Top 10% 55 Fund Average	424 of 552	77%	21.6	−6.3

[*]Blend means not value or growth.
Source: Morningstar Principia.

A simple screen for U.S. domestic stock large-blend mutual funds in 2007 turned up 527 funds. Had investors purchased any of the top funds at the beginning of 2008, they would have been disappointed by the end of the year. The top 10 funds from 2007 ranked on average 368 in 2008 and underperformed the category average by 3.3 percent.

If 2008 was a disappointment for momentum investors, then 2009 was catastrophic. There were 552 U.S. large-blend funds that met the screening criteria from 2008. The top 10 funds finished 458 out of 552 in 2009, underperforming the category average by 9.8 percent. The #1 fund in 2008 finished dead last in 2009.

Buying recent past performance is a tough-love way to seek alpha. Investors' love affair with last year's top funds often turns into a messy divorce just a few years later.

Former Federal Reserve chairman Alan Greenspan addressed manager persistence during testimony to Congress in 1998 in his Fed Speak way. Greenspan made this comment over the demise of Long-Term Capital Management, a failed hedge fund that threatened the entire financial system:

> This decade is strewn with examples of bright people who thought they had built a better mousetrap that could consistently extract an abnormal return from financial markets. Some succeed for a time. But while there may occasionally be misconfigurations among market prices that allow abnormal returns, they do not persist.[9]

Fund Termination Rates

One interesting side study from persistence reports is fund termination rates. These are the funds that don't survive from one period to the next. They're often referred to as dead funds, extinct funds, failed funds, or dropout funds. This group includes funds that merged with another fund or just closed and distributed cash to investors.

Investors who place money in a fund that ultimately closes will likely suffer a permanent loss. Cash is distributed to shareholders after termination, so there is no chance to recapture missed opportunities. Investors wishing to make up lost ground must reinvest their cash in another fund and hope for the best.

The next few paragraphs discuss two items of interest about terminated funds. One is the large number of funds that cease to exist over time and the second is the performance of these funds before they go away.

Carhart calculated that on average mutual funds terminated at a rate of 3.2 percent per year between 1962 and 1993. Of this figure, 2.2 percent per year disappear due to mergers and 1.0 percent was liquidated.

Carhart also found that one bad year rarely caused a fund to close or merge. He estimated that non-surviving funds underperformed by an average of 4.0 percent per year over a multiple number of years before closing.[10]

Other studies show that the number of funds that close or merge varies with market conditions. During bad markets, there are more closures than in good markets. The market turmoil from 2005 to 2009 caused the demise of 29 percent of domestic equity funds (almost 6 percent per year), 21 percent of international equity funds (more than 4 percent per year), and 10 percent of fixed income funds (about 2 percent per year). 2009 was a particularly bad year with over 10 percent of U.S. equity funds closing or merging. This information was derived from the S&P Persistence Score Card.

Fund closures also occur at a greater pace in the poor-performing quintiles, according to S&P. Their persistence studies show that funds in the 4th quintile closed at approximately four times the rate of funds in the 1st quintile. Table 7.3 shows the percentage of terminated funds over three- and five-year periods through September 2009.

Table 7.3   Terminated Funds by Performance over Three and Five Years through September 2009

Terminated Funds	Three Years	Five Years
1st Quintile (top)	8%	11%
2nd Quintile	17%	22%
3rd Quintile	19%	28%
4th Quintile (bottom)	32%	42%

Source: S&P Persistence Scorecard, January 2010

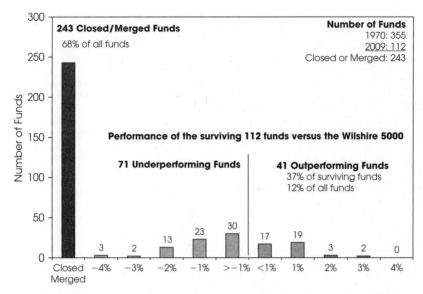

Figure 7.2   Mutual Fund Performance and Survivability since 1970
Source: Bogle Financial Markets Research Center.

John Bogle has kept track of the 355 general equity mutual funds that existed in 1970, which is a few years before the Vanguard 500 Index Fund was launched. Of the original 355 funds Bogle identified in 1970, 243 had closed or merged by the end of 2009. That's a 68 percent failure rate. Figure 7.2 visually represents those 355 funds and ranks the remaining 112 funds based on their long-term performance relative to the Wilshire 5000 index, a total U.S. market benchmark. The 1 to 2 win-loss ratio appears yet again!

Fund Expenses as a Predictor of Top Performance

We are continuously reminded by new academic studies and research from companies such as S&P and Morningstar that, as a group, actively managed funds underperform the market by close to their average costs. Accordingly, it might make sense to buy active funds that have low costs because they might have a better chance to be top performers. Unfortunately, it's not that easy.

Comparisons between fees and returns show that, as a group, actively managed funds with high fees tend to perform worse than the category average, but this isn't true for individual funds. Some of the best performing funds have the highest fees and some of the worst performing funds have low fees.

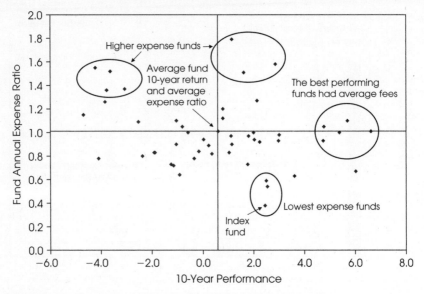

Figure 7.3   Comparing Large Cap Fund Returns to Fees

It also shows that, as a group, actively managed funds with low fees tend to perform better than the average active fund. However, a low fee does not increase the odds of beating an index fund. The data show the probability that a low fee fund will produce alpha is no higher than the probability an average fee fund will do the same.

Many of the lowest fee active funds tend to be closet index funds. A closet index fund is a fund that's purposely managed to deliver returns close to the index. The managers of such funds tend to hold a lot of stocks, and the sector makeup of a fund is close enough to an index to generate near index returns.

Figure 7.3 is a scatter plot of sampled U.S. large-cap stock fund performance over 10 years compared to fund expense ratios as reported by a fund's prospectus. As shown, the lowest fee funds performed admirably and close to the index, while the high fee funds performed less than average. The best performing funds, however, had neither very low nor very high fees. Their expense ratio was about average for the category.

Figure 7.4 illustrates the fee for top performing funds in a different way. The average of five funds was used for this illustration to smooth the data. U.S. small cap stock funds are depicted over

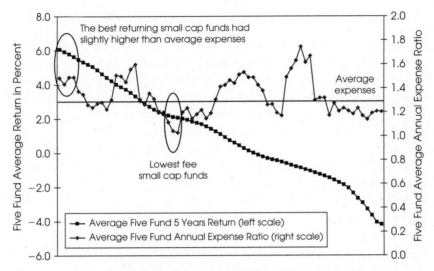

Figure 7.4 An Average of Five U.S. Small Cap Funds and Fees

a 10-year period ending in 2009. The best performing funds had expenses that were slightly higher than the 1.3 percent average fee. The lowest cost funds outperformed the average fund, but not by much.

Buying low cost active equity funds is a safe strategy for someone who doesn't wish to be off the market by much yet wishes to have a chance to outperform slightly. But this isn't the way to pick top performing funds. Investors who believe that buying low-cost actively managed funds will increase their odds for outperforming an index fund appear to be making a mistake.

Bond funds exhibited the same fee characteristics. The lowest fee bond funds had above average performance for the category, although not much different than an index fund. The best performing bond funds had fees about twice as high as those of the lowest fee funds.

Fund expenses are extremely important when purchasing an index fund, but not as important when seeking alpha. Neither low-cost nor high-cost actively managed funds were in the top deciles of performance. In every asset, and across every market sector and style, the top performing winning funds charged fees that were close to average for the asset class.

Ratings as a Predictor of Top Performance

Mutual funds have been sorted, ranked, and rated by independent companies for decades. The number of mutual fund rating agencies has grown over the years, with Morningstar, Lipper, and S&P being the most popular. Virtually every large brokerage firm has mutual fund analysts that sift through the funds they market in an effort to identify potential top performers. In addition, many magazines and web sites have mutual fund ratings, including *Forbes, U.S. News & World Report,* and even *Consumer Reports.* ETF rankings are a new sector of the industry with budding new companies, such as IndexUniverse.com competing against the big fund rating providers for this space.

Rating methods have been revised and enhanced over the years as more data on mutual funds become available and research methods improve. Consequently, the criticism of ranking methods leveled by older academic studies may no longer be applicable today because the methodology has changed.

We do know that investors care greatly about fund rankings. Morningstar's *star rating* has a significant effect on mutual fund sales. This makes rating agencies an important component in mutual fund sales and marketing. One study found that a fund's initial five-star rating produces inflows 53 percent above the normal flow.[11]

These high fund flows lead one to ask, "Are mutual fund rankings predictive?" Noël Amenc and Véronique Le Sourd of the EDHEC Risk and Asset Management Research Centre carried out an in-depth study of mutual fund rankings in 2007. The study, entitled "Rating the Ratings: A Critical Analysis of Fund Rating Systems," did a comparative analysis of the leading rating systems from Morningstar, Lipper, and Standard & Poor's.

Results of the study suggest that ratings don't deal adequately with three aspects of fund evaluation: risk, persistence, and category definitions. With the exception of Lipper, the rating systems didn't explicitly take into account or try to evaluate a fund's extreme loss risk, and they didn't have a performance persistence measurement.

Also, all the rating systems use relative rankings within each category, which makes the ratings attributed totally dependent on the definition of the categories. Only 46 percent of funds had investment attributes that were consistent with their rating category objective, while 54 percent of funds were misclassified. Over one-third of funds were severely misrepresented.[12]

Other studies also found issues with the rating agencies. One report implied that Morningstar's fund rating methodology introduced an age bias into its star ratings that made it difficult for older and larger funds to earn top marks. The studies suggested that the system favored new funds that held few assets. As these funds aged and grew, they became progressively less likely to exhibit top performance.[13] The implication is that the best opportunities for selecting top funds may be with new funds that hold few assets and don't yet have a rating.

Another study found similar problems with top ranked funds. Over 80 percent of top rated funds fell severely short of their expectations over the next 36 months.[14] One possible explanation is that the fund manager was lucky and not skillful. Another explanation may be the asset growth resulting from a five-star rating that drives so many new investors and so much new money into a fund. When that happens, it must be managed entirely differently and can't perform to the same level as it did prior to receiving the rating. This explanation is consistent with the age bias found in fund performance.

John Bogle spoke of the problems facing investors who buy into burgeoning hot funds during a 1997 speech entitled "Nothing Fails Like Success":

> There are three major reasons, I think, why large size inhibits the achievement of superior returns: (1) the universe of stocks available for a fund's portfolio declines; (2) transaction costs increase; and (3) portfolio management becomes increasingly structured and group-oriented, and less and less reliant on savvy individuals.[15]

In a 2010 article entitled "How Expense Ratios and Star Ratings Predict Success," Morningstar Director of Research Russell Kinnel explains that expenses were a better predictor of future performance than star ratings.[16] He confirmed that over every time period, the cheapest quintile funds in every asset class produced higher total returns than the most expensive quintile.

Kinnel pointed out that star ratings were successful at predicting fund survivability. He confirmed that the survival rate of 5-star funds is higher than 1-star funds by a considerable margin. Fully 53 percent of 5-star international equity funds survived and outperformed their category average, whereas a mere 13 percent of 1-star funds survived and performed better than the average fund in their category.

Perhaps the best use of fund ratings is to identify and avoid the chronic worst performing funds. The elimination of bottom ranked funds could help whittle down the universe somewhat. But then, who needs ratings for this? The task could be accomplished just as easily by avoiding chronically poor performing funds and funds with very high expenses.

I do believe the fund rating agencies deliver a vital service to investors. They're a good place to learn about funds. The agencies provide transparency and detailed information about funds and their managers, and also provide news and information about fund companies and structure.

Qualitative Factors as a Predictor of Top Performance

Qualitative factor studies go beyond past performance, ratings, and fees. They include background investigations of managers and the culture of fund companies and their owners. It's a belief that certain characteristics may have an influence on fund manager performance and the overall performance of fund companies.

Do certain qualitative traits lead to superior fund return for a manager and better overall performance for a fund company? Some academics believe so. They have worked for decades with limited success trying to detect unusual or unique characteristics in a manager in an attempt to find the next Warren Buffett.

Many consultants do this type of analysis for large institutional clients, and some even have had noteworthy results, but even they admit to making big mistakes. It appears the future great managers are not the typical fund managers that you'd find by screening a database superior past results or ratings.

Most of the great managers aren't for hire by the general public. The truly talented managers like to fly under the radar as long as possible to keep their assets manageable. If they become exposed, they tend to stop taking new clients. This isn't to say that it's impossible to find a good manager among the 5,000 plus actively managed fund marketplace; it's just extremely difficult to recognize true talent and invest in it before the superior returns occur.

Manager Education and Experience

All mutual fund managers are smart and educated. There's no shortage of folks in the financial industry with impressive academic degrees and high-level industry certifications competing for good paying mutual fund manager jobs. Arguably, the smartest and the brightest among them have a better chance of outperforming the market than their marginally brilliant brethren—that is before the best of the best quit the mutual fund industry to become grossly overpaid hedge fund managers.

Judith Chevalier and Glenn Ellison started their search for superior intellect among mutual fund managers using college entrance exam scores and undergraduate college choices. The two studied the relationship between performance and manager's SAT scores, the institution from which the managers received their undergraduate degrees, whether the managers had a master's of business administration degree (MBA), how long the managers have held their current positions, and the age of the managers. Their study looked at 492 managers responsible for managing growth funds for at least part of the period of 1988 to 1994.[17]

The study yielded some interesting results: (1) There was evidence that managers with MBAs outperformed managers without MBAs, but the only reason for this appeared to be that the higher educated took greater market risk as measured by beta; (2) younger managers tended to outperform older managers by a slight amount, which could be attributed to the extra hours they spent in the office trying to establish a name in the business and avoid being fired; (3) high SAT scores on college entrance exams were a positive contributing factor in return, perhaps because it allowed these managers to get into the best business schools, or perhaps because they made better contacts in business school, or perhaps because they are just smarter; (4) managers who graduated from Ivy League schools tended to outperform those from non–Ivy League schools, perhaps because they are more intelligent or perhaps because of the contacts they made.

Many fund managers have earned a financial analyst designation known as a CFA charter and offered by the CFA Institute in

Charlottesville, Virginia. Becoming a chartered financial analyst is a long and laborious three-year minimum self-study, graduate-level program for investment professionals that's particularly rigorous in investment analysis and portfolio management.

Does earning a CFA charter make any difference in the returns of fund managers? The answer appears to be a definite *maybe*. A recent CFA Institute article reported this observation:

> A growing body of empirical research focuses on the CFA designation and whether charterholders outperform other financial professionals. A review of the literature reveals a patchwork of studies that don't uniformly and unequivocally show outperformance by charterholders. . . . The studies finding that the charter produces demonstrably superior job performance so far outnumber the ones that don't. This may be a preponderance of the evidence but not clear and convincing evidence or proof beyond a reasonable doubt.[18]

There does appear to be some evidence that high SAT scores, an Ivy League diploma, and perhaps a CFA designation do have a positive influence on manager performance. Being young relative to peers may also be a slight advantage for growth stock managers, perhaps because they may understand the technology sector better. However, the evidence is inconclusive for value stock managers, fixed income managers, and managers of international funds.

Skin in the Game

Is there a positive impact on performance when managers of mutual funds hold a sizable ownership stake in the funds they manage? David F. Swensen, chief investment officer at Yale University, believes so. He makes the following observation in his popular book *Unconventional Success: A Fundamental Approach to Personal Investment*:

> The vast population of the fund industry contains a small subset of truly talented investors who deserve the trust associated with managing the assets of others. Within that small subset, a handful of mutual fund managers transcend the pure pursuit of profit, placing the selfless service of investors' needs above the selfish search for personal gain. In particular, in those rare instances in which mutual-fund managers own a significant

stake in the funds that they manage, the manager transmutes from agent to principal, dramatically increasing the odds of serving investor interests.[19]

There is academic data to reinforce Swensen's observation. The SEC passed a disclosure rule in 2004 regarding portfolio manager ownership in the funds they manage. Allison Evans was the first researcher to study this new disclosure information.[20] She spent six months hand-culling SEC documents to create a database of managerial ownership. The data was screened for multimanager funds and funds that changed managers during the period of 2003 to 2005. This left 273 single manager funds that existed for that period.

The data suggested that fund ownership levels for managers varied, and in a few instances were quite large. Evans studied this new data and published a paper on her findings in 2006.

The paper examined the association between a mutual fund manager's personal investment in a fund and that fund's performance before and after tax. The findings were as follows: (1) Mutual funds with a large ($1 million and over) managerial ownership interest outperformed funds with lower or no ownership interest; (2) security turnover in the funds with high managerial investment was lower than funds with low or no investment, and this increased after-tax returns; and (3) Evans cautioned that the single study period was short and that the database was small, thus recommending much more work be done in this area before any findings should be considered conclusive.

There does appear to be a correlation between a manager's stake and investment return. However, Swensen does caution that if investors begin placing too much value on manager ownership that fund companies may try to play this trend by increasing their stake in their own funds. This will make it appear that the managers are more committed when, in fact, the investment was made solely for the purpose of attracting more capital to the fund.

Summary

The probability of selecting winning active funds is low, the payout for success is low compared to the risk, and superior performance doesn't last long. Most people who seek alpha don't find it, especially when they use the three common methods of past performance, fund ratings, and low fees.

Winning with active funds appears to require a skill set that goes well beyond analyzing quantitative factors and deep into understanding qualitative factors. However, there's no guarantee these in-depth methods will work, and most investors and advisors don't have this information or the skill to analyze it. In addition, some of the best and brightest tend to get taken off the market as talented fund managers are scooped up by the hedge fund industry. A better solution is not to waste time trying to find talent when so little exists.

Warren Buffet is fond of saying that he would rather be certain of a good return than hopeful of a great one. This is certainly true when it comes to passively managed index fund portfolios. Passive investing is the most efficient investment solution for today's investor.

CHAPTER 8

Active and Passive Asset Allocation

People exaggerate their own skills. They are overoptimistic about their prospects and overconfident about their guesses, including which managers to pick.
—Richard Thaler, University of Chicago

It isn't what we know that gives us trouble. It's what we think we know that just ain't so.
—Will Rogers

The second part of the active versus passive debate goes beyond mutual fund selection into the timing of purchases and sales. Asset allocation is how and when an investor diversifies among different types of investments in a portfolio. An investor following a *tactical* asset allocation strategy attempts to beat the market by changing asset class weights using market valuation forecasts or price trends. In contrast, an investor following a passive or *strategic* asset allocation strategy holds a fixed allocation among several broad asset classes in their portfolio over the long-term. Passive asset allocation strategies have proven to be a more effective long-term solution for investors.

Tactical versus Strategic

Many investors try to achieve superior returns or reduce risk in their portfolios by varying the allocations among the asset classes at the right times. This method is commonly referred to as tactical asset allocation. To be successful, an investor must rotate money into mutual funds that represent asset classes or market sectors before the superior performance occurs and out of the sectors prior to poor performance. These tactical shifts in allocation can be large or small depending on an investor's strategy and conviction.

Market timing strategies are a zero-sum game in the marketplace. The financial markets don't earn any more or any less return just because one person is buying and another is selling. If one investor buys in at the right time it means another investor must have sold at the wrong time.

There is academic precedence that points to measurable losses for investors who frequently trade their accounts. Using recent findings from behavioral finance and survey data involving a large sample of online brokerage clients, Arvid Hoffmann, Hersh Shefrin, and Joost Pennings found that nearly all equity trading strategies produced lower returns than the markets. Trading based on technical analysis (or charting) was the worst strategy. The raw net results of using trends and other chart patterns to predict returns was negative 0.92 percent per month. Trading based on financial news, intuition, and professional advice was the second worse with a raw net return of negative 0.65 percent per month.[1]

Many mutual fund investors are also poor market timers. They have a long history of trend following behavior, similar to the trend following behavior that Hoffmann, Shefrin, and Pennings noted in their study. Fund investors shift money into asset classes that have recently gone up in value and take money out of asset classes that have recently gone down in value. Buying high and selling low has never been a good way to invest. I estimate these tactical asset allocation errors cost investors about 1 percent per year.

Strategic asset allocation is a better strategy. Asset class weightings are set based on investor's personal needs and only change when their circumstances change. This fixed allocation of asset classes is maintained religiously through regular rebalancing back to asset class targets regardless of market conditions.

Mutual Fund Flows Show Bad Timing

Mutual fund companies regularly report new purchases and sales of their funds, making it possible to track investors' buying and selling habits. This information is available to the public through a number of databases.

Studies of fund flow data over the decades suggest that fund investors are chronic trend followers. They invest more money in funds that have recently performed well and take money out of funds that have recently performed poorly. This behavior can be characterized as a buy-high sell-low mentality. These bad habits of fund investors show up in individual portfolios as a timing gap between what could have been earned in a strategic asset allocation strategy and what investors actually earned using a tactical asset allocation strategy. This gap represents a cost to active investors.

Mutual fund flow data is the subject of many articles in the financial media. The story of these articles is almost always the same: "Fund investors are poor market timers." They then quote a new study highlighting the knife wounds that fund investors inflict on themselves from their trend-following behavior. Some studies have concluded that fund investors lose several percent per year from poor market timing.

Mutual Fund Turnover Rates

We live in a rent-a-fund society. Investors typically hold onto their mutual funds for about the same time period as they hold onto a leased car or truck. That's about three years. They then tire of the funds or become dissatisfied with performance and follow the next bright idea. Mutual fund holding times tend to increase during a bull market and decrease during a bear market. Figure 8.1 illustrates the turnover rate for equity funds and bond funds for U.S. investors.

Exchange-traded fund (ETF) data isn't included in Figure 8.1, and for good reason. The ETF industry has astronomically high turnover rates because these products are used extensively by traders and institutional investors as hedge vehicles. Some funds average turnover rates of several hundred percent per year. There are also highly leveraged ETFs that are specifically designed to be held for only one day or less.

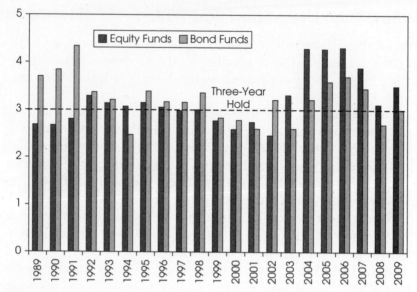

Figure 8.1   Average Investor Hold Periods for Stock and Bond Funds
Source: DALBAR, 2010.

High turnover among ETFs isn't necessarily a bad thing. It keeps hedge funds and active traders out of traditional open-end funds and away from long-term investors. They also create liquidity in the individual securities that lie inside open-end mutual funds and that lowers trading costs.

Flow of Funds Studies

Any analysis of mutual fund cash flows will uncover interesting information about how and when mutual fund investors make decisions. It provides a chronology of trading decisions made before the fact (ex-ante), which can then be compared to market outcomes (ex-post).

One use for fund flow data is a measurement of market timing skill among fund investors. This is done by studying changes in inflows and outflows among asset classes and then comparing this data to future moves in the markets. The overwhelming evidence shows from these analyses that people don't have timing skill. In fact, frequent changes in asset selection hurt portfolio performance by a significant amount.

Flow of funds studies go back several decades, with the early studies finding that investors chase top performing funds. One study from 1978 entitled "Is Fund Growth Related to Fund

Performance?" found that investors disproportionally added to top performing funds over a 10-year period from 1966 to 1975.[2] A similar study conduced in 1992 concluded that investors responded more strongly to high performance in aggressive actively managed funds by purchasing more of them than less aggressive funds.[3]

Fund ratings were also a factor in fund chasing decisions. The *Boston Globe* and the *Wall Street Journal* both reported in 1995 that about 97 percent of new investments that year went into mutual funds that had previously been awarded four or five stars by Morningstar. A 2001 study found that an initial Morningstar five-star rating results, on average, in six months of abnormal flows (53 percent above the normal expected flow). The authors of that study also found significant abnormal flow in the case of rating changes, with positive flow for rating upgrades and negative flow for downgrades.[4]

The Federal Reserve Bank of Atlanta conducted its own study and found that "mutual fund investors use raw return performance and flock disproportionately to recent winners but do not withdraw assets from recent losers." The Federal Reserve report noted that because of this behavior, "mutual fund managers have an implicit incentive to alter the risk of their portfolios to increase the chances that they are among the winners."[5]

ETFs tend to be used by people who are more active traders than traditional mutual fund investors, and this leads to more mistakes. Cash flow studies show extremely poor market-timing results by active ETF investors. TrimTabs Investment Research, a consolidator of mutual fund flow data, concluded that equity prices tend to fall after equity exchange-traded funds (ETFs) rake in large sums of money and rise after equity ETFs post heavy outflows. Regression analysis suggests the probability that equity ETF flows are a contrary leading indicator of equity prices is more than 99 percent. This means the flow of ETF money predicts market changes with high accuracy—in the opposite direction![6]

One mutual fund cash flow study after another has consistently shown the same performance chasing phenomenon. Fund styles with superior performance and high fund ratings raked in the most money, and this usually occurs close to the time when these investment styles peak in performance.

Institutions Are Also Trend Followers

Performance chasing isn't limited to individual investors. Pension fund committees exhibit similar behavior, although not to the same degree. Amit Goyal and Sunil Wahal examined the selection and termination of private investment managers by 3,400 pension plans between 1994 and 2003. Plan trustees showed a tendency to hire investment managers after they delivered positive excess returns. However, these new managers failed to deliver returns better than the managers who were terminated for poor performance.[7]

In a more recent study, Jeffrey Busse, Amit Goyal, and Sunil Wahalu used a new, survivorship bias-free database to examine the performance and persistence in performance of 4,617 active domestic equity institutional products managed by 1,448 investment management firms between 1991 and 2008. Controlling for the Fama–French three factors and momentum, the trio found no distinguishable alpha in the data.[8]

The previously mentioned study done by Federal Reserve Bank of Atlanta also looked at pension fund flows and found that trustees do act differently than individual investors in one regard. For pension funds, it is whether a manager beat a benchmark that's important. For individual investors, it's the magnitude of outperformance.[9]

Pension trustees who oversee employee-directed retirement accounts such as 401(k) and 403(b) plans are tasked with selecting funds for the plans. The investment committees for these plans exhibit a strong preference for past top performing mutual funds. One recent study shows that as trustees change fund options, they tend to choose funds that outperformed in the past, but after the change, the new funds performed no better than the underperforming dropped funds.[10]

Large university endowment investment committees also exhibit performance chasing behavior in their asset allocation decisions. Developed international markets posted equity returns of 24 percent over a three-year period ending in 2006 and emerging market posted returns of 36 percent while the U.S. equity markets posted returns of only 13 percent. In response, college endowments boosted their allocation to foreign markets from 14 percent in 2003 to 20 percent in 2006.[11]

Investors who jump on a trend expecting to see above market returns more often find themselves standing in the slow lane at the checkout counter. The consequences of this losing tactical allocation strategy are clearly evident in the portfolios of individual investors and many institutional investors.

Measuring the Timing Gap

The timing gap is consistent, predictable, and measurable. But before you can appreciate this, a brief explanation of performance calculation methods is required.

Flip through the mutual fund section of your local newspaper or look at any web site to find the performance of your favorite mutual fund. The result you see is a *time weighted* return of the fund. This is an internal rate of return number that assumes no cash flows into or out of the fund. It's used strictly for comparing the return of the fund to the return of an appropriate index.

Time-weighted returns assume that $100 is invested in a fund at the beginning of a period and remains invested throughout the period. The calculation is the same regardless of the time period. It doesn't matter if the returns are year-to-date, 1 year, 5 years, or 25 years.

A fund's time weighted return rarely reflects the actual return of an individual investor because it doesn't account for the money that investors add to the fund or deduct from the fund. These additions and withdrawals from a fund over time create real dollar profits and losses for investors. These real profits and losses are known as *dollar weighted* returns. The example on page 124 explains the difference between the two returns.

The shortfall in return caused by tactical asset allocation is a timing gap that can be measured by comparing mutual fund cash flows to the subsequent performance of sectors and markets. A negative return from timing occurs when money is shifted out of a poorly performing asset class that subsequently outperforms or flows into an asset class that subsequently underperforms.

DALBAR Studies the Performance Gap

Early attempts to measure the timing gap began in 1994 with DALBAR, Inc. The firm was commissioned by the active mutual fund industry to investigate the differences in holding times between load funds and no-load funds. The theory put forth by the fund companies was that investors stayed invested longer in load funds than they did in no-load funds, thus giving the load fund investor higher returns. The fund companies hoped to use this information to counter the criticism they were receiving for selling funds with high sales commissions.

The Timing Gap: Time Weighted and Dollar Weighted Returns

Assume you invest $1,000 in a stock mutual fund at the beginning of the year. At year end, the fund is up 15 percent and you made a $150 profit. Satisfied with this result, you place another $1,000 in the fund at the beginning of year two. Unfortunately, during the second year the fund lost 10 percent.

Question: Over the two-year period, what was the funds' reported time weighted return and what was your dollar weighted return?

Answer: The mutual fund had a reported 1.7 percent time weighted return over the two-year period. It earned 15 percent the first year and lost 10 percent the second. Thus, a $100 investment at the beginning of year one and reinvested in year two would have grown to $103.50 by the end. That's an annualized return of 1.7 percent.

However, you invested only $1,000 in the fund starting in year one and added the second $1,000 in year two. Since the fund gained 15 percent when you had $1,000 invested and then fell 10 percent after you added the second $1,000, your account finished year two with only $1,935. That's a $65 loss (not a 1.7 percent annualized gain).

Mathematically, your dollar weighted return was negative 2.2 percent annualized over the two-year period. The difference between the fund's time weighted return and your dollar weighted return was negative 3.9 percent annualized.

The DALBAR study did show that load fund investors held onto funds longer than no-load investors, but this finding wasn't what made this study famous. DALBAR revealed huge timing gaps for both load fund investors and no-load fund investors. These gaps were so large that they astonished the investment industry. Some people tried to discredit the study by pointing to flawed calculation methodologies. However, even when new calculation methods were used the gaps remained sizable. It appeared that the DALBAR was onto something important.

The most recent DALBAR study covering a 20-year period ending in 2009 found that equity mutual fund investors had average annual returns of only 3.2 percent while the S&P 500 averaged 8.2 percent, and fixed income fund investors had average annual returns of 1.0 percent, while the benchmark Barclays Capital Aggregate Bond Index averaged 7.0 percent.

DALBAR found a nearly 5 percentage point gap between equity funds and fund investors, and a 6 percentage point gap between bond funds and fund investors. These are extremely large shortfalls for investors. Are individual investors and advisors really that bad at timing the markets? The data complied to date suggests they are.

Market Timing Gaps

A bear market in stocks tends to happen about every five years and lasts about a year and a half. Studies on investor behavior show that people act very differently during down markets than they do in up markets. Basically, they're scared in bear markets and brave during bull markets.

The DALBAR Guess Right Ratio measures how often and when the average investor makes smart decisions to get in or out of the stock market in general. This ratio also shows how often the average investor realizes a short-term gain by either buying or selling mutual funds before a market rises or falls. A reading above 50 percent is positive and a reading below 50 percent is negative. Figure 8.2 illustrates the Guess Right Ratio through 2009.[12]

Ironically, investors are right about the stock market's direction in more years than they are wrong as shown by the disproportionate number of years when the ratio was over 50 percent. However, when investors are pessimistic, they dump stocks. The wrong years tend

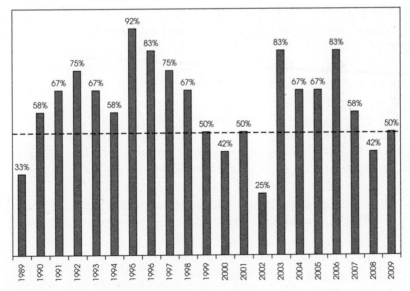

Figure 8.2   The Guess Right Ratio
Source: DALBAR, Inc. 2010

to occur in the recovery after a bear market, and investors miss the rebound.

In a Gallup Poll of investors taken on March 4, 2009, just a few days before the market bottom, only 18 percent of investors believed the stock market would show a sustained recovery by year end; 27 percent thought it would take two years, 25 percent said three years; 19 percent said longer. About 2 percent said the stock market would never recover.

Only 18 percent of the investors' surveyed in the Gallup Poll guessed right. The S&P 500 gained 67 percent from its intraday low on March 9 until year end.

Morningstar Studies

Morningstar weighed in with a comprehensive study on dollar weighted versus time weighted returns. They calculated the 1-, 3-, 5- and 10-year time weighted returns and dollar weighted returns through 2009 for open-end mutual funds based in the United States.

The Morningstar study found significant deficiencies in investor timing decisions. U.S. equity fund investors experienced a negative 1.4 percent gap in return over 10 years while bond fund investors experienced a negative 1.3 percent gap over the same period. In aggregate, the timing gap was negative 1.5 percent across all asset classes and sectors.[13] Figure 8.3 illustrates the difference in major asset class returns for the period.

Broad asset classes see higher cash inflows after the markets have performed well and outflows after markets have done poorly. A deeper analysis shows that the biggest contributor to these performance gaps likely comes from sector rotation within asset classes; in other words, market timing.

Morningstar divides mutual funds into dozens of sectors, styles, and industries to analyze dollar weighted performance across the spectrum of fund categories. Investors' fared poorly from their timing in most categories. Here are some 10-year results:

- Large cap growth funds had returns of negative 2.2 percent, while investors in those funds had returns of negative 2.7 percent.
- Small cap value funds earned 8.8 percent, while investors in those funds earned only 7.1 percent.
- Precious metals funds had the highest return of 18.6 percent, while investors in those funds earned only 15.9 percent.

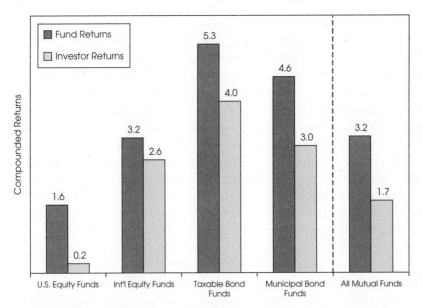

Figure 8.3 Morningstar Category Returns and Investors' Returns (10 years ending in 2009)
Source: Morningstar, news.morningstar.com/PDFs/avginvret.pdf

- Diversified emerging markets funds performed well with returns of 9.0 percent, while investors beat that average with a return of 9.9 percent.
- U.S. taxable bond funds outperformed investors by about 1.3 percentage points.
- Municipal bond funds beat investors by 1.6 percentage points.
- Emerging markets bond funds earned 2.8 percent more than investors did in these funds.

The returns of mutual funds outperformed the returns of investors in most categories. In aggregate, investors hurt their performance by more than 1 percent per year. This is the penalty that active investors incur by thinking they can be successful market timers.

Dumb Money versus Smart Money

Investors who chase past performance are referred to by academics as *dumb money*. This is a "quiet" term because no academic is going to say publicly that these investors are dumb. Yet, mention this term at an analyst conference and everyone in the room knows exactly what it means. There are many investors, both individuals and institutions, that herd into sectors, strategies, and asset classes based on the belief that past superior performance will continue into the future, and for no other reason.

An interesting paper by Andrea Frazzini and Owen Lamont outlines how smart money capitalizes on the way dumb money invests. First, the study explains why investors have a striking ability to do the wrong thing by sending their money to mutual funds that own stocks that do poorly over the subsequent years. Second, they develop a trading strategy based on this behavior to predict future stock returns. In a nutshell, doing the opposite of what most people believe will be profitable can lead to excess returns.[14]

Smart money attempts to take advantage of dumb money mistakes whenever possible. Recall the grilling of Goldman Sachs's trading desks by Congress in the spring of 2010. They decided to reduce their positions in subprime mortgages because they thought a lot of dumb money was buying. The firm is still in business today because they won that bet. However, this strategy doesn't always work.

There have been many occasions when betting against dumb money hasn't worked out. Long Term Capital Management thought they were betting against dumb money by purchasing Russian bonds as others were dumping them in 1998. Russia ultimately defaulted on its foreign debt obligations. This led to insolvency for Long Term Capital Management and put the country on the verge of a financial market meltdown. In order to avoid the crisis, the president of the New York Federal Reserve had to orchestrate a bailout by several leading Wall Street firms.

How the Dumb Money Gets Divided

Tactical asset allocation is a zero-sum game. When someone underperforms the market it means someone must have outperformed before fees and expenses. The grand total dollar-weighted for the average investor in all funds over the past 10 years was a 1.68 percent annualized return compared with a time-weighted 3.18 percent for the average fund according to the Morningstar study. So, where did this 1.50 percent go?

Much of it went to brokers, brokerage firms, and their trading desks. Another portion went to a handful of talented money managers who skillfully separate investors from their money. Finally, believe it or not, a portion went to investors who develop a passive strategic asset allocation strategy and rebalance asset classes annually.

Investors who lose with their tactical asset allocation strategies indirectly provide excess returns to investors who religiously rebalance their strategic allocation. This occurs because rebalancing naturally forces investors to sell some amount of their better-performing investments and buy more of their worse performing ones. Although it seems counter intuitive to do this, over time, rebalancing increases portfolio returns and lowers risk.

Strategic asset allocation and regular rebalancing provides what is widely referred to as the only free lunch on Wall Street. It's a nice thought, but every economics student knows there's no such thing as a free lunch, especially on Wall Street. Any extra gain in one person's account means a loss in someone else's.

The loser in this case is the investor who believes sector rotation strategies and market timing decisions can beat the market. That investor loses about 1.5 percent return annually according to Morningstar and a lot more according to DALBAR. This loss amount from trading mutual funds is controversial. My opinion is that investors lose at least 1 percent per year from these activities.

Assume three investors each start to invest in January 2000 with a portfolio of 45 percent in U.S. stocks as represented by the S&P 500, 15 percent in international stocks as represented by the MSCI EAFE Index, and 40 percent in bonds as represented by the Barclays Capital Aggregate Bond Index. One investor uses tactical asset allocation in an attempt to beat the markets and underperforms them by 1 percent annually. The second uses a buy-and-hold strategy and lets the portfolio sit over the 10-year period, thereby earning market returns. The third investor rebalances every year for 10 years and thereby outperforms the tactical asset allocator and the buy-and-hold investor. Figure 8.4 illustrates the outcomes.

The rebalanced portfolio in Figure 8.4 picked up an excess compounded return of 0.9 percentage points over the market portfolio that wasn't rebalanced during the last decade. This occurred because rebalancing is a natural way to sell high and buy low without having to make a market prediction.

The rebalancing benefit varies with market conditions. The benefit was high in the past decade because the markets were volatile. Over the long term, the benefit tends to be about 0.3 percentage points net of trading costs.[15]

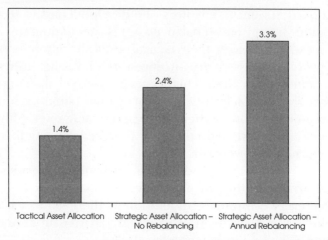

Figure 8.4 The Benefit from a Strategic Asset Allocation 2000–2009

This excess return earned from strategic asset allocation represents a real wealth transfer that takes place in the marketplace. This return is enough to make up all the fund fees and trading costs that index fund investors incur, leaving these investors with very close to market returns. You can't do much better than that.

Putting It All Together

Table 8.1 quantifies four portfolio management choices and is overly generous to active investors. Investors who use low-cost index funds and ETFs and strategic asset allocation earn market returns. Investors using actively managed mutual funds lose about 1 percent

Table 8.1 Quantifying Portfolio Management Choices

	Index Funds and Market Based ETFs	Actively Managed Mutual Funds and ETFs
Maintain a fixed strategic asset allocation	Passive/Passive Near market returns	Passive/Active 1.0 percent less
Employ a tactical active asset allocation	Active/Passive 1.0 percent less	Active/Active 2.0 percent less

over index funds, and investors who employ tactical timing strategies lose another 1 percent. Investors who use both active funds and a tactical asset allocation strategy are expected to underperform an all-index fund strategic allocation strategy by about 2 percentage points per year.

Disciplined passive investors are smart-money investors. They follow a long-term strategic asset allocation strategy based on their needs and fill their portfolios with low-cost index funds and ETFs to represent those asset classes. They don't mistakenly believe that they have the skill to pick outperforming funds and know they don't have the timing skill to rotate in and out of different asset classes and sectors.

Many investors use both a strategic allocation and a tactical allocation. This strategy has been called *core and explore, core and satellite, barbell, core plus,* and a variety of other names. The idea is to place part of the portfolio in a strategic asset allocation using index funds and ETFs, and then play with the remaining part of the portfolio using tactical asset allocation.

I call these combined strategies *core and pay more* because that best describes the outcome. The cost of the explore side is more expensive than the core side, and there's no reason to believe that the active management results will be any better simply because there is less of it. Investors will likely earn market returns for their passive positions in index funds and below market returns in that portion using tactical asset allocation.

Investment returns for a passive strategic asset allocation are much more likely to earn superior returns than those earned from tactical asset allocation strategies. The nuances of strategic and tactical asset allocation strategy go beyond the scope of this book. For an in-depth study of asset allocation techniques, read *All About Asset Allocation*, 2nd Edition, by Richard Ferri (McGraw-Hill, 2010). A summary of this book is on my web site at www.RickFerri.com.

Summary

A high percentage of new money flows into asset classes, sectors, and styles that have had recent high returns. This trend-following behavior likely results in a loss of more than 1 percent per year in investors' portfolios. For active fund investors, the timing gap loss is in addition to the shortfalls from the actively-managed funds they buy.

Passive investors outperform those who attempt tactical asset allocation. Through regular rebalancing, passive investors benefit from the mistakes of people who follow the crowd into past outperforming sectors. A passive strategy using index funds and ETFs that is followed religiously provides investors with the highest probability for investment success.

CHAPTER 9

Changing Investor Behavior

The costly game of active management guarantees failure for the casual participant.

—David F. Swensen

You don't need to beat the market to achieve your financial goals. Trying to beat the market creates a huge distraction that takes your mind off the mission of building wealth, and this lowers the probability of reaching those objectives. Avoid strategies that promise to deliver excess returns and you will earn higher returns.

The path to changing from an active strategy mindset to a successful passive one is based on exposure, education, understanding, belief, and commitment. People first must be exposed to the passive versus active debate, and then have the willingness to pursue the facts. The desire for more knowledge and understanding leads to a new set of investment beliefs and a financial commitment to the strategy. This leads to better portfolio performance.

This chapter is about changing behavior, and in a sense it's like changing religions. It's about discovering the vices of active management and making a life-style change into the indexing church. Once a person enters this house of clarity and transparency, they rarely leave. As worshippers gain more knowledge and understanding, many join the choir to sing their praise loud enough so that those walking around outside will hear. This is how the message of passive investing grows and spreads.

Helping People Go Passive

The evidence for passive investing is deep and broad. A passive fund strategy, coupled with a prudent strategic asset allocation, represents the best opportunity for meeting long-term financial goals.

Here's a quick review of mutual fund facts covered so far:

- Low-cost index funds and ETFs that track market benchmark funds beat most actively managed mutual funds.
- The probability that an active fund will beat an index fund drops over time.
- The excess return from winning active funds is well below a fair payout.
- The winning active funds of the future cannot be identified in advance.

In addition, here's a review of portfolio management facts:

- The more active funds in a portfolio, the lower the chance for portfolio outperformance.
- The longer those active funds are held, the lower the chance for portfolio outperformance.
- Tactical asset allocation, including market timing, lowers expected portfolio returns.

These facts are well documented in the studies covered throughout this book. So why doesn't every investor embrace passive investment strategies? The purpose of this chapter is to offer a few general thoughts about why more people don't go passive when the evidence is so clearly in favor of this way to invest.

Three Non-Indexers

Non-index investors can be divided into three categories: the uninformed, the naysayers, and the procrastinators. More specifically:

1. The Uniformed: investors who don't know about passive investing or don't understand it.
2. The Naysayers: investors who know about passive investing but think they know better.

3. The Procrastinators: investors who understand and accept passive investing but don't implement the strategy.

Not everyone takes the path or knows it exists. There are those who are never enlightened, those who refuse to be enlightened, and those who believe in the strategy but never finish the job.

The Uninformed

The evidence in favor of passive investing is wide and deep, and the media does talk about these benefits a fair amount, yet many investors aren't familiar with the concept or are unaware of the advantages. It's not their fault. Wall Street and the actively managed mutual fund industry spend an inordinate amount of money flooding the airways, print media, and Internet with messages about how their active strategies will either save you from calamity or make you rich. These messages are a disservice to investors because they aren't true. However, Wall Street knows that the more confused and off balance you are about investing, the more money they'll make.

It has been my personal experience that a majority of people who are using active strategies don't know about passive investing or they don't have a good understanding of the benefits. Once they do gain this knowledge, they are generally open to a good vetting about the methodology and will weigh the options.

Sometimes unknowing investors have money in an index fund through an employee pension fund such as a 401(k) and they don't realize it. They may have invested in it because someone at work told them to "buy this fund." It's typical for these people to say funny things about the index funds during market cycles, such as, "This fund is doing really well!" or "This fund is performing terribly!" They don't make the connection between what goes on in the market and what happens in the fund they own. But this can be easily fixed with a little education.

Not knowing about or understanding passive investing isn't a bad thing. People *are* interested in their money and want to learn. The concepts aren't hard; they're just different. We all learned that the world isn't flat even though it appears to be and that the Earth revolves around the Sun even though it appears to be the other way around. Anyone can learn that higher returns come from keeping costs low and not trying to beat the markets, even though Wall Street preaches otherwise.

Helping a Friend   The best way for an inexperienced investor to learn about passive investing is through a trusted relative, associate, or friend, and one of the best ways to reinforce this learning is to read an easy book on the subject. There are several beginners' books on passive investing. Consider Bill Schultheis's *The Coffeehouse Investor* (Penguin Group, 2009) or John Bogle's *The Little Book of Common Sense Investing* (John Wiley & Sons, 2007). I wrote a beginner book entitled *Serious Money* (self-published, 1999). It's available for free on my web site at www.RickFerri.com and my company's web site at www.PortfolioSolutions.com.

Short, easy to read books on index investing capture a person's interest and make them eager to learn more. When people see the light, they'll often collect a library of passive investing books. No doubt this collection will include *Common Sense on Mutual Funds*, 2nd Edition, by John Bogle (John Wiley & Sons, 2009) and *The Four Pillars of Investing* by William Bernstein (McGraw-Hill, 2002). In addition, I've written *All About Index Funds*, 2nd Edition (McGraw-Hill, 2007), *The ETF Book* (John Wiley & Sons, 2009), and *All About Asset Allocation*, 2nd Edition (McGraw-Hill, 2010).

The Internet is another great learning tool for passive investors. A premier web site is www.Bogleheads.org. This 20,000-member online community discusses and promotes the investment ideas and business philosophies of John C. Bogle, the founder and former Chairman and CEO of the Vanguard Group. This site is not solely about passive investing. It's also about all things financial from the best deals on life insurance to where to purchase good wine.

Speaking of the Bogleheads, you'll want to pick up a copy of *The Bogleheads' Guide to Investing* (John Wiley & Sons, 2006) by Taylor Larimore, Mel Lindauer, and Michael LeBoeuf. Taylor is the forum's founder. There's also a follow-up book titled *The Bogleheads' Guide to Retirement Planning* (John Wiley & Sons, 2009) that has many Boglehead contributors.

Another good place for people who want to learn about passive investing is Vanguard's web site at www.Vanguard.com. They can read about how fees affect returns, how index funds work, how to create an asset allocation, and a wide range of topics. It is a great place for unbiased education about investing.

Where Not to Get Passive Advice   Where you get your investment advice is a key to the quality of advice you receive. When someone tries to sell you an investment idea that they're compensated for in some way, they'll often wrap their advice around a trendy growth story such as alternative energy or smart phone technology. This isn't advice; it's sales. One way to ensure you're getting unbiased advice is to have an understanding of how advisors are paid in the investment industry. Ideally, the place or person where you get your advice isn't compensated to sell high fee products and services.

Wall Street is called the *sell side* of the business. Brokerage firms in particular earn revenue primarily by selling investment products. This revenue can be commissions or fees or both. Conflicts of interest occur when a broker earns a higher commission or fee by selling one product over a comparable lower-cost alternative.

Investment companies that earn fees directly from clients for managing portfolios or providing advice are called the *buy side* of the business. Conflicts of interest can still occur on the buy side when an advisor knowingly withholds information from a client that may have a material effect on how a portfolio is managed, such as misrepresenting passive strategies as being inferior to active, a strategy that pays the advisor a higher fee.

When you're discussing investments with someone in the business, ask them if their firm is on the sell side or the buy side. If it's the sell side, then you have to use some caution to ensure that the advice you're getting isn't tainted by commissions. If it's the buy side, then you have to be on the lookout for any withholding of information that may have an impact on their recommendations. If the advisor doesn't know the difference between the sell side and the buy side, then they haven't been in the business very long and that should raise a caution flag.

On both the sell side and the buy side, a typical sales strategy used to promote actively managed products is for an advisor to talk up the potential for earning a superior return. What's often left out of those conversations is the probability of achieving this return. Each investor is left to figure out the probability of success on their own.

You're setting yourself up for trouble if you don't assess the risk of an investment. Investment frauds lure in their prey by creating the illusion of safety and a high return. Think of Bernie Madoff. He told clients they would earn high returns in the 8 to 10 percent range every year regardless of market risks. Apparently, Madoff followers didn't ask how this return could be earned year after year with no risk of loss, or perhaps they didn't want to know.

The subprime mortgage meltdown in recent years is another example. The possibility of higher returns impeded the judgment of many institutional investors in that market. Brokerage firms repackaged low-quality mortgages and sold them as AAA rated securities to insurance companies, financial firms, pension plans, and even to foreign governments. Banks scooped up thousands of subprime loans like children scooping up candy thrown by clowns in a parade. The allure of high returns with low risk put these firms in peril when the assets failed. The taxpayers were left on the hook for billions of dollars because these too-big-to-fail firms needed to be rescued.

Wall Street Sells the Sizzle   I joined the investment industry as a rookie stockbroker in 1988. Like all rookies, I was sent to the firm's three-week boot camp in New York City to learn about the company and the industry. This school didn't have much to do with learning about investing. We were there primarily to learn to sell investment products.

The first thing we learned about selling investments was that greed and fear drive most decisions, and we were expected to use these emotions to influence client decisions. To hone this skill, part of the training was to make 20 cold calls each day to potential investors, and pitch them an idea or ask for a meeting. Stockbrokers call this *dialing for dollars.* Sales contests were common, even at boot camp. The trainees who had the most success dialing for dollars earned a free dinner at an expensive New York restaurant followed by a Broadway show.

I didn't win any free dinners or shows. My sales technique was too bland. This was frustrating to my instructors. They urged me to stop talking about facts and start talking about benefits. I remember to this day being repeatedly told to "sell the sizzle, not the steak!" The interpretation of that phrase is to sell the image of what the investment can do for an investor and leave out most facts and details.

Trainees were provided books to refine our sales technique. One book was *The Art of Selling Intangibles* by LeRoy Gross (Prentice Hall Press, 1988). Gross was a successful Merrill Lynch stockbroker during the 1970s and 1980s. In his book, he flat out states, "*Nothing* captures interest faster and keeps it at a higher level than the mouthwatering thought of a profit. If the potential gain is large, your prospect's interest focuses sharply on your next comment."[1] Gross was saying to sell the sizzle, not the steak.

You may be impressed with the communication skill of an advisor, but this doesn't mean they have investment skill. Make sure all the facts are disclosed. Of particular interest should be the probability that an active fund has for outperforming a comparable index fund, by how much, and why. Most advisors will become fidgety and defensive trying to answer these questions because they don't know.

Wall Street's Battle against Indexing During the late 1980s and early 1990s, when I was working as a stockbroker for Wall Street firms, index investing was not a large threat to my book of business. Few clients knew what an index fund was and rarely did they ask. If a client did inquire about index investing, our canned response was, "Index funds guarantee average performance. We know you can do better." That was a true statement. It is possible to do better; it's just not likely.

Index funds started encroaching on the brokerage business during the late 1990s. The Vanguard 500 Index Fund was easily beating the majority of active funds and other high cost products being sold by brokerage houses. This created a lot of good press for indexing and bad press for active management. Consequently, stockbrokers started losing thousands of clients and billions in assets to indexing giant Vanguard as well as other index fund providers.

As the stockbrokers watched their clients fly out the door, Wall Street fell back and retrenched. Some brokerage firms wrote papers citing the dangers of index fund investing because they weren't actively managed. Other firms pushed *core and explore* strategies that falsely implied that some markets were so inefficient that active managers could easily outperform index funds. None of this was true, of course, but it sounded plausible to many brokerage firm clients and that helped slow defections.

The brokerage firm I was with during the late 1990s started its own S&P 500 index fund that remarkably had low fees and no commissions. This fund wasn't advertised and had no marketing literature. Stockbrokers were instructed to recommend this fund only after a client mentioned that they might move their accounts elsewhere and buy index funds.

I had taken a keen interest in passive investing at the time and wanted to convert clients over to a portfolio of all low-cost index funds. There were a few ETFs available and that's where I invested my clients' money. But it wasn't possible to invest with Vanguard or other index fund providers because our firm had no sales relationships with companies that didn't pay commissions or fees to sell their products.

Attitudes have changed somewhat since I left the brokerage industry over a decade ago. Today, Wall Street firms reluctantly promote ETF portfolios in fee-based accounts. These portfolios aren't low-cost of course, but at least Wall Street now begrudgingly acknowledges that passive investing is an alternative to active management, at least with part of a portfolio.

The Naysayers

In early 2001, shortly after the bubble burst in technology stocks, Paine Webber together with Gallup conducted a survey of individual investors and their outlook for stock market returns. People were asked to give their 12-month market forecast as well as a forecast for their own personal account. The responders pegged the market return at 10.3 percent for the year and estimated that their personal return would be 11.7 percent.[2] These investors believed they were going to beat the market by a whopping 1.4 percent on average for the year.

Subsequent Gallup surveys over the years show similar results. Respondents to their surveys believe they'll earn about 1.5 percentage points over the market's return. We know that can't happen. People tend to be unrealistic about their investment skills. Behavioral finance helps explain why overconfidence exists.

Behavioral Finance   Behavioral finance is a branch of financial analysis that uses social, cognitive, and emotional factors to understand the economic beliefs and decisions of investors. Its beginnings stem from a revolutionary 1979 paper by Daniel Kahneman and Amos Tversky on investor behavior. Their paper proposed a new theory called prospect theory (*prospect* in this sense means "lottery"). Prospect theory describes how people make choices based on how they analyze potential losses and payouts.[3]

Prospect theory is very involved and beyond the scope of this book. However, a superbly written and easy to read synopsis of this theory and many other behavioral finance theories can be found in *Your Money & Your Brain* by Jason Zweig (Simon & Schuster, 2007). It is an excellent starting point for delving more deeply into this field. Zweig opens the book with this remark: "There may be nothing in the entire spectrum of human endeavor that makes so many smart people feel so stupid as investing does."[4] I would add, " . . . and they'll never admit it."

I make no claim to being a behavioral finance expert. The following sections of this chapter provide a brief description of cognitive issues that appear to me to be driving factors in the active versus passive debate. These factors are not presented in any particular order.

Everyone's Doing It   "With so many people beating the market, why shouldn't I try? It can't be that hard." Or so it seems. Skim through any issue of a popular financial magazine, and you will come away with the impression that many more people are beating the market than is actually the case. This is because only successful investors are interviewed in the media, and only the winning mutual funds are advertised, while the majority of those who are losers sit quietly in the background.

Not only does the hope of beating the market sell active management, it sells magazines, newsletters, web site subscriptions, books, and technical analysis trading programs. A search on the Barnes & Noble web site for books with "Beat the Market" in the title resulted in 68 recommendations. If any of these methods actually worked, why on earth would anyone give away this priceless secret in a book or a newsletter? That makes no sense.

"Confessions of a Former Mutual Funds Reporter" is a delightful article written in 1999 for *Fortune*. We don't know the author, but we do know it was a former mutual fund journalist from a large personal finance magazine. The opening paragraph tells all:

> Mutual funds reporters lead a secret investing life. By day we write "Six Funds to Buy NOW!" We seem to delight in dangerous sectors like technology. We appear fascinated with one-week returns. By night, however, we invest in sensible index funds.[5]

The anonymous journalist confessed that he or she worried about misdirecting readers with hot-fund advice but was assured by the magazine's editors that in personal finance journalism, it doesn't matter if the advice turns out to be right, as long as it appears plausible.

Speak No Evil   Active management dominates the investment marketplace. The companies behind active management spend billions in advertising dollars each year to maintain this dominance. These advertising dollars unquestionably drive some of what's said and written about in the media.

Jim Cramer is an accomplished hedge fund manager and a popular media figure. He's known for his occasional rants on television and in the press. Much of the time, his poison darts are thrown at company executives or government policies. Occasionally, Cramer takes aim at the mutual fund industry. But he has to be careful with what he says. The following is an unabashed commentary from Cramer that appeared online:

> I, personally, have been repeatedly told by important advertisers in the business that they don't want anything "critical" (read: negative) about mutual funds. Mutual funds pay too many bills in this business. . . . If you knew about the pressures that we in the media are under to ignore these terrible performances, you would know why so many people stick with these funds. They stick by them because everyone has bought into the notion of hear no losses and see no losses in order to keep the advertisers happy.[6]

The overexposure of winning funds and the hiding of losing funds creates the illusion that there are more winning funds than losing funds. For these reasons and others, the general public believes that the odds of beating the market are much higher than they are.

The Winner's Curse   Random results from investor decisions have an important impact on future decisions. If an investor makes excess returns from lucky stock picks, they often attribute their success to something other than luck. This is referred to as *the winner's curse.*

Roulette is a casino game of random numbers requiring no skill. A ball is spun in the roulette wheel and it randomly lands on 1 to 38 different numbers, including 0 and 00. Winners in the game correctly guess which numbers will come up; there's no skill involved. Imagine people who won money playing roulette for several days in a row. At some point, they'll begin to wonder if they do have some element of extraordinary insight. They may begin to believe there are patterns in the numbers and that somehow their subconscious brain is picking up on these patterns. They start rationalizing personal skill where none exists.

The popular television game show *Deal or No Deal* provided one group of researchers the opportunity to analyze how past actions affect future decisions. Their study observed thousands of contestants from three countries as they played the game and made choices.[7]

No skill is involved on the part of contestants on *Deal or No Deal*. A contestant is shown 26 briefcases that each contains a hidden amount of money ranging from one penny to one million dollars. The contestant picks one of the briefcases and then owns its unknown contents. Then the other 25 briefcases are opened one by one, with the game stopping occasionally for a bank offer—the opportunity to walk away with a sure amount of money. If the contestant says "no deal," more briefcases are opened, followed by a new bank offer. The game continues in this fashion until the contestant either accepts a bank offer or rejects all offers and receives the contents of the first briefcase picked.

Ironically, the order in which suitcases were opened affected future decisions. Attitudes towards risk changed depending on which suitcases were opened early in the game. The researchers found that early success in the game caused people to change their preference for risk later in the game. Contestants tended to increase their risk preferences by continuing to play (saying "no deal") when a disproportionate number of suitcases with smaller amounts were opened early or when a disproportionate number of suitcases with larger amounts were opened early. In contrast, their neutral counterparts who had a mix of high and low suitcases had a greater propensity to deal even though odds and payouts for winning for all participates were the same in every game.

Investor decisions are path dependent. Without having any particular skill, investors who have several winning bets in a row often misinterpret luck as skill, and this can lead them to act as though they had skill. If investors believe their perceived investment skill will shift the odds in their favor, then they are apt to use active management strategies even though no shift in the odds has actually occurred. This false belief of skill keeps many investors in active strategies and this reduces the probability of their success.

Bad Accounting   One reason many people believe their investment skills are superior is because their accounting skills are inferior. They think they're performing better than they actually are. In reality, most people have only a vague idea of how their investments are performing.

One famous case of poor accounting occurred during the 1990s with members of a local investment club in Beardstown, Illinois. The Beardstown Ladies became instant media celebrities in the mid-1990s after the club proclaimed fantastic investment results. The club reported a 23.4 percent compounded return versus 14.9 percent for the S&P 500 over a 10-year period ending in 1993. The ladies said their investment skill may have come from a homemaker's insight into companies whose products they regularly bought, such as McDonald's and Coca-Cola.

This success propelled the Beardstown Ladies investment club to national stardom. Members appeared on all the morning television shows, in commercials, and spoke on nationwide radio programs. Not to miss a moneymaking opportunity, the club published a bestselling book on personal finance and investing.

When something seems too good to be true, it probably is. In late 1997, a reporter from *Chicago* magazine noticed something peculiar about the club's investment results. After recalculating the numbers, he discovered that a gross error had been made. The ladies' actual return was only 9.1 percent, far below the 23.4 percent they reported, and almost 6 percentage points below the S&P 500. This error was so large that the accounting firm of Price Waterhouse was called in to carefully calculate the returns and clear the air. In the final tally, the club's worst fears were realized.

For years, the ladies deposited monthly dues into their portfolio account so they had more money to buy stocks. In error, the dues were added to the portfolio balance as if they were investment gains rather than contributions. This mistake made the investment performance appear much higher than the actual results. An embarrassed club treasurer blamed this error on her misunderstanding of their accounting software.[8]

It's very common for investors to make return calculation errors when attempting to determine investment results. Additions and withdrawals in an account have to be handled in a proper way. Improper accounting can quickly distort returns and give investors a false sense of accomplishment. These errors compound over time.

Today's investors can easily calculate accurate portfolio performance by purchasing a computer program or using one of the many web-based applications available. Many brokerage firms now provide this information for free to their clients. Keeping accurate performance results is one of the best ways to reveal the shortfalls of active management.

Improper Benchmarking   Calculating accurate investment performance is only half the battle. Once investors know their actual return, they'll want to compare their results to appropriate market benchmarks. This will determine if an account is performing in line with comparable indices.

Selecting a proper benchmark is often a difficult task. A relevant benchmark reflects the asset classes and investment strategy that a portfolio manager is following.

Often there's no single benchmark that mirrors an investment strategy or the asset classes in a portfolio. In that case, a custom index can be created using an appropriate blend of indices to match how an account is being managed. If an account is holding some bonds or bond funds, then the benchmark for the account includes a bond index. If an account has a foreign stock allocation, then the benchmark includes a percentage in a foreign stock index. If a manager is buying small cap stocks, then the benchmark includes a portion in small cap stocks.

An unfortunate practice that happens all too often in the advisor industry is the use of intentionally inappropriate benchmarks. This practice can dramatically distort the advisor's skill, or lack of it. Red flags should go up whenever advisors claim to be outperforming their stated benchmark by 4 or 5 percent per year because that just doesn't happen. No advisor is that good.

More often than not, an advisor who is showing high returns relative to a benchmark is using an inappropriate benchmark that they know is easy to beat. If this benchmark begins to perform better than the advisor, the advisor changes benchmarks. This makes the manager's otherwise mediocre returns look better than they really are and that impresses less informed clients and prospects.

Advisor performance reporting practices can be dreadful. There is no standardization. Advisor performance reporting is largely unregulated by the Securities and Exchange Commission (SEC). By design, many individual investors are kept underinformed by their advisors so that they never really know how their accounts are performing against proper benchmarks.

Here is a true story about one investment advisor who intentionally misleads prospects and clients by comparing their performance to an improper index. I was participating in a conference for retiring airline pilots in early 2010. There were several other investment advisor firms at the conference who were also soliciting the future retirees. I asked another advisor if his firm used a passive or active investment strategy. He said his firm was an active manager. Then we had this interesting exchange:

"How has your performance been?" I asked.

"Great! We beat the S&P 500 by 4 percent over the past decade."

"The S&P 500 is your benchmark? So you're a large cap U.S. stock manager?"

"No. We use lots of investments like Treasury bonds, commodities, and foreign stocks."

"Then why are you using the S&P 500 as a benchmark? You should be using a composite benchmark that includes bonds, commodities, and foreign stocks."

"Well . . . look . . . you and I both know the people at these conferences aren't sophisticated. They don't know one benchmark from another. So, we tell them what they want to hear. We tell them we beat the market."

"So, let me get this straight. You measure client performance against an inappropriate benchmark that was easy to beat over the past decade, which makes your performance look much better than it was, and then you justify it by saying this is what your clients want to hear. Did I get that right?"

With that, our conversation abruptly ended.

The S&P 500 is a fine benchmark for large cap U.S. equity managers. It can also be used in a composite index. However, it's not appropriate to measure the performance of a multi-asset class portfolio against the S&P 500. Nonetheless, this is the sole index that many advisors choose to show their performance against because over the past decade it was easy to beat.

Trying Hard to Forget   You don't like your returns this year? Wait a year and you'll think you did better. Ask any investor how their mutual funds performed last year and you are likely to get some surprising results. Most responses will be off by several percentage points and always in the direction that made their fund selections look better.

Researchers asked two distinct groups of investors to recall how their funds performed over the past year. The first group interviewed were architects. They were asked to estimate the fund returns of their 401(k) investment options. This group overestimated their past performance by 5.1 percentage points. The second group was composed of investors who belonged to the American Association of Individual Investors (AAII), an organization of mostly nonprofessional investors who enjoy learning about the markets. This group was deemed to be more knowledgeable about investment matters than the architects. They overestimated their past performance by 3.4 percentage points.[9]

The overall results are consistent with the theory of cognitive dissonance. Investors would rather alter the facts than admit they have no special investment skills. This makes it difficult to fix flawed investment strategies.

Selective Memory as a Profession   Wall Street has turned cognitive dissonance into a business model. Have you ever heard a brokerage firm ever say they were wrong about an investment recommendation? Their analysts say they were early or late on a call, but never wrong. And you'd be hard-pressed to find advisors who admit their mutual fund selections underperformed the markets over the years. Everyone thinks they're above average in the investment industry, or never admit they aren't.

Go to any advisor and ask for recommendations on finding a superior active manager. It's almost guaranteed that the mutual funds and private account managers you'll be shown have had high relative returns recently. You'll also be shown the combined return of a hypothetical portfolio using these funds. Hypothetical portfolio returns are quite popular in the industry. You'll rarely see the actual results of previously recommended portfolios because most didn't perform well.

Truth be told, the mutual funds and private portfolio managers being recommended by many advisors today are not the same ones that were recommended five years ago. Ask an advisor to show you their past mutual fund recommended list from 1999 or 2005 along with the subsequent results and you'll not likely get that information. By not showing past recommendations and actual returns, and by only presenting the past performance of a new set of managers who performed well, an advisor creates the illusion of skill in the minds of their clients.

The Procrastinators

There can be a lot of time and space between awareness, understanding, and commitment. People who are aware that index funds exist may never go the next step and educate themselves on why investing passively is in their best interest. And people with a good understanding of the issues and who are in agreement with indexing may never commit to the strategy.

Why do these failures to commit take place? Perhaps it's a lack of confidence, or perhaps it's procrastination, or perhaps it's hope that their current strategy will someday turn the corner. John Maynard Keynes stated that "The state of long-term expectation, upon which our decisions are based, does not solely depend on the most probable forecast we can make. It also depends on the confidence with which we make this forecast."[10] In Keynes's words, a lack of confidence among investors in the passive investment strategy may be a key reason for a failure to commit.

It takes time to build confidence in passive investing. I became aware of this methodology in the early 1980s. However, I didn't fully appreciate the strategy until the early-1990s after working on the sell side of the investment industry, and it still took me a few more years before I finally dropped all active investing entirely and switched to a fully passive approach. That was the wisest investment decision I ever made, and one of the most calming moments I recall in my investing career. As with more investors, I was completely at ease with my decision to implement a completely passive investment approach.

The Endowment Effect   The *endowment effect* occurs when an investor believes that what they own is superior to something they don't own even though that belief is demonstratively not true.[11] The owners of poorly performing actively managed mutual funds value them more than non-owners. Many people will cling to an actively managed mutual fund that has performed poorly because they see better performance down the road even though there's nothing relevant on which to base that prediction.[12]

There is a tendency of investors to hold losing investments too long and sell winning investments too soon. University of California professor Terrence Odean analyzed the trading records for 10,000 accounts at a large discount brokerage house and found investors demonstrated a strong preference for selling winners rather than losers. Their behavior did not appear to be motivated by a desire to rebalance portfolios or to avoid the higher trading costs of low-priced stocks. Nor was it justified by subsequent portfolio performance.[13]

Selling a loser is admitting an investment mistake. Many investors would rather hold their losing investments and wait for them to recover rather than take the loss and switch into a different strategy. I see the endowment effect at work in the investment management business. The number of new client inquiries declines sharply during a bear market as people reject the idea of changing strategies until they make up some of their loses. Taxable investors are handicapped by the endowment effect because a bear market is the ideal time to sell losing investments and switching their strategy. This period creates the lowest capital gains and generates the greatest amount of tax losses. Tax losses can be used to offset capital gains in the future and lower taxable ordinary income.

The Land of the Lost   Many investors start the conversion to a passive portfolio but never finish it. Half the portfolio is efficiently managed in low-cost index funds and the other half remains stuck in an inefficiently managed legacy of active funds. This creates nothing but a portfolio mess. It's the land of the lost.

David Swensen addresses this halfway point in his excellent book entitled *Pioneering Portfolio Management*: "No middle ground exists. Low-cost passive strategies suit the overwhelming number of individual and institutional investors without the time, resources, and ability to make high quality active management decisions."[14]

Everyone who investigates the passive management solution needs to eventually make a decision. Either they're going passive or not. Halfway isn't efficient. It doesn't work. Chances are you'll end up sliding back to the active side.

Veering Off Course   Advocates of passive portfolio management will tell you that the strategy is simple. The fund selections are straightforward, the asset allocation methodology isn't difficult to figure out, and a portfolio is easy to implement and maintain. But they often leave out the most difficult factor—*emotions*.

Adhering to a passive strategy is easier said than done because our human emotions can get the best of us. Going passive requires a leap of faith that the markets will take care of us in the long term. That may sound like a good plan in a bull market, but what about a bear market? It's in tough times when you'll hear the active side say that "this time it's different" and "indexing doesn't work in this environment." You have to dismiss this noise or it'll tear at you until you capitulate, and that will wreak your long-term plan.

"Stay the course" is a phrase used in the context of a war or battle meaning to pursue a goal regardless of any obstacle or criticism.

A modern usage of this term was popularized by John Bogle. During rough times in the market, don't waver in the face of adversity, "Stay the course!"

Passive investing will work for you if you can hold the vision. The following was adapted from an article that I wrote for Forbes.com in 2010 after a very volatile period in the markets. It illustrates how good intentions but a lack of commitment often degenerate into inferior performance.[15]

A Steady Hand Pays Off in Unsteady Markets

Each December, four of my friends gather at a coffee shop to exchange pleasantries and talk investments. The four then decide what changes, if any, they will make to their portfolios, and then go out and execute them.

My friends discussed modern portfolio theory in an intelligent fashion during their December 2007 meeting. This approach revolves around establishing a portfolio with a set ratio of stocks and bonds and then rebalancing once a year to maintain the original weightings. The idea is that this Steady Eddie investment process will maintain the integrity of the portfolio and potentially increase returns long-term.

All four friends decided to give modern portfolio theory a try. At the beginning of 2008, they independently invested $100,000 each in two exchange-traded funds that track stock and bond indices. This involved each putting $60,000 into the Vanguard U.S. Total Stock Market ETF and the other $40,000 into the Vanguard Total Bond Market Index ETF. The plan was then to rebalance annually to restore this 60/40 mix.

As we now know, 2008 was destined to be a brutal year for stocks. All four of my friends lost money, and by year's end their $100,000 portfolios had shrunk to $80,567 each.

The mood at the December 2008 gathering was somber. Talk centered on government bailouts, the ballooning federal deficit, and the generally depressed tone that had overtaken America. When the discussion turned to investments, there was grave concern about the future. Finally, the four friends questioned whether modern portfolio theory was the right strategy for the new investment environment.

In a sign of the lack of agreement, each of the four ultimately pursued different paths.

- Panicky Pete decided he couldn't take it anymore. He sold out of the Vanguard stock ETF entirely in early 2009 and put the money in his bond index fund.

- Nervous Nelly was also very concerned about the stock market and sold half her stock position around the same time. She also added the proceeds to her bond ETF.
- Wait-and-See Willie didn't know what to do, so he didn't do anything at all, except worry.
- Disciplined Diane stuck with the original plan and rebalanced at the beginning of 2009, as if oblivious to the stock market storm raging around her. She took about $10,000 out of her bond ETF and put it into the stock ETF, bringing her portfolio back to her original target allocation of 60 percent stocks and 40 percent bonds.

Diane had no better idea than anyone else what would happen to the stock market in the year ahead. She had, however, seen enough recessions to know that the stock market and economy eventually right themselves. That wasn't her main reason for hanging tough, though. Diane told me she was tired of following get-in get-out advice and wanted a plan that was more stable and long-term. Modern portfolio theory was that plan.

Earlier this year, I asked my friends how their $100,000 accounts had done during 2009. Here is a summary of their results:

	2009 Year-End Value	Total Return 2008–2009
Panicky Pete	$83,526	−16.5%
Nervous Nelly	90,320	−9.7%
Wait-and-See Willy	93,053	−6.9%
Disciplined Diane	95,706	−4.3%

Disciplined Diane was far ahead of Panicky Pete and Nervous Nelly, who'd sold into the downturn (see table below). She was also ahead of Wait-and-See Willie by about 2.6 percentage points. This excess return was earned because Diane rebalanced last year while Wait-and-See Willie didn't.

Diane's results provide a nice example of why a buy, hold, and rebalance strategy is more beneficial to long-term investors than a buy, hold, and do nothing strategy—and far more beneficial than a market timing strategy.

Source: Forbes.com, March 8, 2010.

Investing Is Serious Business

Investing your hard-earned money is serious business. This task should be approached with the same prudence, integrity, and discipline as you do with your chosen profession. Research must be thorough and accurate. Once the best solution is found, it should be implemented and maintained with the greatest discipline. It's your best chance for long-term success.

Being dedicated to an investment strategy is no different than being dedicated to a career. It takes years of training before becoming proficient at any profession. Yet many people manage their investment portfolios much differently than their careers. They either don't have a long-term plan or don't stick with it long enough for it to work.

Successful passive investors are disciplined. They make this strategy a long-term commitment. There'll always be years when an actively managed portfolio outperforms a passive portfolio, but the active funds won't outperform by much and not for long. Staying the course with passive investing will work in the future.

Make the Change and Stay the Course!

Often I am asked if investors should dump all their actively managed mutual funds at one time and buy all index funds or if they should gradually move "when the time seems right." In my opinion, the answer is to dump and jump. Just get it done.

I believe there's no practical reason to delay making the change. The odds that the old active funds are going to improve significantly are remote. Drag your feet once your decision is made and the transition may never get done. So, get it done. As the Nike ad says, *just do it!* Out with the old active strategy and in with the new passive approach. You'll feel relieved once the transition is made and your portfolio is set.

Summary

Passive investing is a simple solution to a complex problem. Maintaining a portfolio of index funds based on a sensible investment policy has the highest probability of meeting your financial goals.

Why, then, don't more people follow this approach? There are a variety of reasons, including a lack of awareness, a lack of understanding, a lack of belief, and simple procrastination. Those who don't know need a starting point and a support network of believers to help them move along in the process. Those still lacking commitment should look at their portfolio performance and benchmark the returns so they can see clearly that they are hurting themselves.

The procrastinators can become fully committed with a little push from reading another book or listening to a motivation speech by an indexing expert or by watching a video. This adds conviction and encouragement.

Passive investing works. Discover it; learn more about it; grow to believe in it; implement it; follow it; then tell others about it. You'll be in better financial shape for making the transition and so will those who follow you. Once you make the commitment to passive investing you're there for life. You won't go back to active management.

PART

III

THE CASE FOR PASSIVE INVESTING

10

The Passive Management Process

Passive investing is power investing. It's the winning solution for investors today. A few years ago it wasn't possible to build a passive portfolio of index funds and ETFs that covered all asset classes because most funds didn't exist. That's no longer the case today. Passive funds are available in every major asset class and investment style across the global marketplace.

This successful investment experience hinges on three key elements: the development of a prudent investment policy, full implementation of the policy, and the discipline to adhere to the plan in good times and bad. When a passive investment policy is prudently crafted, fully implemented, and rigorously maintained, the probability for financial success increases exponentially. This chapter is an overview on how this process takes place.

The Five Step Process

The process for creating and implementing a passive investment plan has five steps:

1. Determine a portfolio's objective by understanding the investor's income needs, time horizon, tax situation, ability to handle risk, and unique circumstances.
2. Analyze various asset classes to estimate their long-term risks and returns, correlations with other asset classes, and tax efficiency if applicable.
3. Create an appropriate strategic asset allocation that reflects the investment objectives.

4. Choose securities that best represent each asset class. Low-cost index funds and select ETFs make good choices because they offer broad diversification and closely track market indexes.
5. Implement the plan fully and maintain the strategic asset allocation through occasional rebalancing to control portfolio risk and enhance return.

These five steps also lead to a written Investment Policy Statement (IPS). An IPS documents structure and helps ensure fair and equitable investment results over the long term. IPS suggestions are provided at the end of the chapter.

Step 1: Understanding and Defining Needs

Investing has a purpose, which is to fill a financial need. Perhaps you're trying to provide adequate after-tax income to meet your monthly bills or perhaps you're trying to grow your assets to meet long-term obligations. Outlining the purposes for investing before committing capital to a strategy puts the horse squarely in front of the cart.

Investment strategy differs among investors depending on their needs. Individual investors are different from institutions. Individuals invest for themselves and their loved ones. The choices and actions that individual investors make will have a direct bearing on their wealth and the wealth they will transfer to their heirs. In contrast, institutional investors manage money for other people. The choices made and actions taken by trustees will affect the lives of others. Institutional investors have a fiduciary obligation to invest in the best interests of these asset owners and beneficiaries. These accounts include, but are not limited to, pension funds, endowments, and foundations.

Individual Investors   Individual investors will find it helpful to do some basic financial planning before making investment decisions. It is important to estimate your known current and future income sources and match them to your current and future obligations. How much income will be needed from your investment portfolio? Is the required investment cash flow high or low? The answer can make a big difference in an investment policy.

Individual investors generally face five big liabilities over a lifetime: education costs, home ownership, retirement funding, charitable giving, and a bequest to loved ones. The last two needs are typically considered later in life and only after the first three are adequately covered. The big five do not include daily living expenses for necessities such as food and clothing, or discretionary items such as vacations and recreation.

The income needed to match current and future liabilities will likely come from a variety of sources: earnings, investments, Social Security, and perhaps a pension. Inheritances can also be a future source of income. An inherited Individual Retirement Account pays a distribution each year based on the size of the account and the deceased's age at death. A year-by-year analysis of inflows and outflows provides a clear picture of how much cash will be needed from investments, which aids in the planning process. Chapter 11 sets out a detailed case for passive investing by individuals.

Institutional Investors   For the purpose of this book, institutional investors are defined as people who manage other people's money. It doesn't matter if a person is a trustee of a multibillion dollar pension plan or a $500,000 foundation.

The law states that making investment decisions for other people puts a person in position of a prudent expert, and this carries a legal responsibility to act responsibly and in the best interests of an account's beneficiaries. A pension fund trustee invests to provide retirement income for all eligible plan employees. An endowment invests to provide cash flow for an institution's operations. A foundation may invest to provide for various charities. In all these examples, individuals who are paid or volunteer their services are fiduciaries to the beneficiaries and must act prudently.

Many institutional accounts have an infinite life with liabilities existing into perpetuity. Accordingly, today's trustees must consider the plight of trustees who will take over from them. One small error today can turn into a black hole for future trustees.

401(k) plans, 403(b) plans, and other self-directed employer-sponsored retirement plans are special entities. The plan sponsor (the employer) sets up an account for tax-deferred savings according to legal mandates. One of the plan sponsor's fiduciary obligations is the prudent selection of investment options. The participants in turn make their investment selections from those options. The plan sponsor should have a well articulated policy for selecting investment options and a method for reviewing those options on an annual basis.

Later chapters make a detailed case for passive investing for institutional investors. Chapter 12 covers charities and private trusts, while Chapter 13 covers pension funds and self-directed employer-sponsored plans such as 401(k) plans.

Step 2: Study Market Risk and Estimate Returns

Asset classes are broad categories of investments such as stocks, bonds, real estate, commodities, and money market funds. Each asset class can be further divided into categories. For example, stocks can be categorized into U.S. stocks and foreign stocks. Bonds can be categorized into taxable bonds and tax-free bonds. Real estate investments can be divided into owner-occupied residential real estate, rental residential real estate, and commercial properties.

The subcategories can be further divided into investment styles and sectors. Examples of styles include growth and value stocks, large and small stocks, and investment-grade bonds and non-investment-grade bonds. Sectors can be of different types. Stocks can be divided by industry sectors into industrial stocks, technology stocks, bank stocks, and so on; or they can be geographically divided, such as Pacific Rim and European stocks. Bonds can be divided by issuer, such as mortgages, corporate bonds, and Treasury bonds. A well-diversified portfolio may very well hold a good number of asset classes, categories, styles, and sectors.

The asset allocation process among various investment choices begins with a risk and return assessment. Successful investors study all asset classes and their various components in order to understand the differences among them. They estimate the long-term expectations of risk and return, and study how the returns on one asset class may move in relation to the returns of other classes. Then they weigh the advantages and disadvantages of including each investment in their portfolio.

Investors expect to be paid for taking financial risks. Consequently, all financial assets are priced based on their perceived risk. The greater the perceived risk, the greater the expected return. When the perceived risk of an asset class is low, the expected return is also low relative to more risky asset classes.

Table 10.1 is a sample of long-term expected returns for various asset classes. Each year, I analyzed the primary drivers of asset class long-term returns, including risk as measured by implied volatility, expected earnings growth based on expected long-term GDP

Table 10.1   Asset Class Long-Term Expected Risk and Returns

Asset Class	Real Expected Return %	With 3% Inflation	Expected Risk %*
Cash Investments			
U.S. Treasury bills (one-month maturity)	0.5	3.5	1.5
Certificates of deposit (one-month maturity)	0.9	3.9	1.8
U.S. Government-Backed Fixed Income			
Intermediate-term U.S. Treasury notes	1.5	4.5	5.0
Long-term U.S. Treasury bonds	2.0	5.0	5.5
GNMA mortgages	2.0	5.0	8.0
Intermediate tax-free municipal (A rated)	1.5	4.5	5.0
Corporate and Foreign Fixed Income			
Intermediate-term high-grade corporate (AAA–BBB)	2.3	5.3	5.5
Long-term investment-grade bonds (AAA–BBB)	2.8	5.8	8.5
Intermediate-term high-yield corporate (BB–B)	4.0	7.0	15.0
Foreign government bonds (unhedged)	2.5	5.5	7.0
U.S. Common Equity and REITs			
U.S. large cap stocks	5.0	8.0	15.0
U.S. small cap stocks	6.0	9.0	20.0
U.S. micro cap stocks	7.0	10.0	25.0
U.S. small value stocks	8.0	11.0	25.0
REITs (real estate investment trusts)	5.0	8.0	15.0
International Equity (unhedged)			
Developed countries	5.0	8.0	17.0
Developed countries small company	6.0	9.0	22.0
Developed countries small value companies	8.0	11.0	27.0
All emerging markets including frontier markets	8.0	11.0	27.0

*The estimate of expected risk is the estimated standard deviation of annual returns.
Source: Portfolio Solutions, LLC, www.portfoliosolutions.com

and foreign sales growth, an implied 3 percent inflation rate, and current cash payouts from interest and dividends on bond and stock indexes. These factors plus others are used in a valuation model to create an estimate for risk premiums over the next 30 years.

The risk in each asset class tends to be fairly stable over time relative to other asset classes, and that means that the risk premium in asset classes should be fairly stable relative to each other as well. This implies that a capital markets line (CML) can be calculated based on these relative risks and expected returns. Table 10.1 reflects the CML estimate of fair long-term payments for each asset class relative to each other over inflation. These estimates are rough at best. No one knows what the exact returns for markets will be over the next 30 years.

In addition to creating expected risk and return estimates, investors should consider the potential correlations among asset classes going forward. Ideally, the investments selected for a portfolio will have diversified risks so that the correlations among these risks are not high. Low correlation among investments helps a portfolio hold its value in extremely poor market conditions. For example, U.S. Treasury bonds performed admirably in 2008, while most other asset classes suffered. A portfolio that had Treasury exposure was shielded to some extent by those holdings.

Tax efficiency is also a consideration if a portfolio is subject to income taxes. Investors should be aware of which asset classes, styles, and sectors are better placed in tax-advantaged accounts such as a tax-sheltered retirement account and those that are suitable for taxable accounts.

Asset allocation is the cornerstone of a prudent investment plan and is the single most important decision that an investor will make in regard to a portfolio. Many issues need to be considered when developing an investment plan. Getting this part of the investment policy right is of paramount importance. Investors would do well to study this subject intently and nail down an appropriate asset allocation that fits their needs.

Step 3: Select an Asset Allocation

The backbone of an investment plan is its asset allocation. At the 50,000-foot level, asset allocation is all about developing overall return goals while controlling risk. At the 5,000-foot level, it is about the expected risk and return of major asset classes and the correlations between those risks and returns. At the 500-foot level, asset allocation is about tweaking a portfolio using sub-asset classes to enhance the expected return of a portfolio.

Risk and return go hand in hand. Without risk, there is no expected portfolio return after taxes and inflation. A risk-free portfolio that distributes money annually will lose value every year net of taxes and inflation. The only way to distribute money and maintain portfolio value net of taxes and inflation is to accept some financial risk.

A good way to look at asset allocation is as if an investor has two portfolios: a short-term portfolio for current cash needs plus emergency money and a long-term portfolio that provides cash for long-term liabilities and builds wealth. This approach is no different than a corporate balance sheet where current assets and current liabilities are separate from long-term assets and long-term liabilities plus owner's equity.

The short-term portfolio should be in safe assets such as money market funds, certificates of deposit, and short-term bond funds. The return on these investments won't be high, but a high return is not the primary reason for investing this money. Safety is the most important objective. No investor should risk this capital because it's needed to pay bills over the next year.

The investments in the long-term portfolio should be more aggressive. Time is on the side of these assets, and it's appropriate to take some risk in equities and perhaps higher risk fixed income to potentially earn a higher return. The higher expected returns from long-term assets help add real after-tax purchasing power to a portfolio.

Some people call the two portfolio approach the *bucket approach.* One bucket holds cash-like investments for short-term needs and the other bucket has long-term investments that refill the short-term bucket when needed. Whatever this approach is called, it makes sense to have one pot of money in very safe investments to pay bills when they come due plus a cushion for unanticipated expenses, and another pot of money to fund long-term liabilities and grow wealth.

Tobin Separation Theorem   James Tobin was a pioneer in the area of risk budgeting, and he explained this real world asset allocation process with elegance and insight. Tobin realized that investors have a full range of investments preferences, and expanded potential investor choices to include low risk assets. Tobin earned the Sveriges Riskbank Prize in Economic Sciences in Memory of Alfred Nobel in 1981 for his work.

Tobin stated that investors should first determine their appetite for risk. This appetite should be satisfied from an equity allocation that is optimal for the asset classes in the allocation. Liquidity and safety needs are satisfied with a cash portfolio that has no price risk. In a sense, Tobin was saying that there are two portfolios, safe and risky, and each investor should own some risky assets, but only after taking care of their liquidity needs with no risk assets. He called this idea the *separation theorem*.[1]

Tobin believed that there are optimal allocations within the safe portfolio and the risky portfolio. These optimal allocations within the safe and risky portfolios are the same for everyone. The only thing that changes is the amount allocated to each bucket. In Tobin's view, "You would choose the same portfolio of nonsafe assets regardless of how risk-averse you were. Even if you wanted to change the amount of risk in the portfolio, you'd do it by changing the amount of the safe assets, relative to the nonsafe assets but not by changing the different proportions in which you held the nonsafe assets relative to each other."

Step 4: Investment Selection

Tobin explains asset allocation as risk diversification between risky assets and non-risky assets. In order to expand risk diversification, each investment in a portfolio could have some measure of fundamentally different risk than the other investments. At times the unique risk of one asset class will not be correlated with the return of another asset class, and this reduces overall portfolio risk. For example, during different periods the return of real estate doesn't move in the same direction as the return of stocks. This gives a portfolio diversification. Of course there will be unavoidable risk overlap in all risky assets during a crisis, which cannot be avoided.

The different investments selected for a portfolio have a number of characteristics. For example, asset classes to be included in a portfolio should have these traits:

1. The asset class is fundamentally different from other asset classes.
2. Each asset class expects to earn a return higher than the inflation rate over time.
3. The asset class must be accessible using a low-cost diversified fund or product.

The first criterion for asset class inclusion is that an investment under consideration be quantifiably different from all other investments. Sometimes the difference between investments is obvious, and sometimes it requires significant analysis. It is easy to isolate fundamental differences between major asset classes. Stocks and bonds are uniquely different. They have different obligations from the issuer, have different income streams, and are even taxed differently.

Differentiating between categories within an asset class can also be straightforward. A European equity index consists of companies with their headquarters in Europe. That makes it fundamentally different from a U.S. equity index, which consists of companies with their headquarters in the United States. By definition, European stocks and U.S. stocks are mutually exclusive. Membership in one index precludes membership in the other.

Finding unique investments among category styles is more complicated. Styles are segments within categories rather than separate categories. For instance, there is not much fundamental difference between large U.S. stocks and small U.S. stocks. The accounting is the same, the exchange they trade on is the same, and the taxes are the same. Nonetheless, U.S. stocks can be divided so that a large stock index is quite different than a small stock index. Then the two indexes can be analyzed to discover different risk-and-return characteristics.

The second criterion for asset class inclusion is that the expected return must be higher than the inflation rate. All investments have an inflation expectation built into the price. Bonds pay interest based on the expected inflation rate until maturity, plus a fair risk premium over inflation based on the riskiness of the bond. Stock prices have an inflation expectation built in and also grow above inflation as real earnings growth occurs and dividends are paid by the companies.

Commodities are a fundamentally different investment than stocks and bonds. However, commodities have no real expected return and pay no interest or dividends. A pound of copper today will be a pound of copper 100 years from now. It won't multiply into ten pounds of copper, and no dividends or interest will be paid by it during the period.

I'm not an advocate of commodities in a long-term investment portfolio because they don't grow and don't deliver any income. In fact, commodities have underperformed inflation over the long term, net of trading and storage costs. Nonetheless, there is a big push by the investment industry to add commodities to an asset allocation. Part of this push may have more to do with the high fees that commodity products carry for the product providers than enhancing diversification in a portfolio.

Finally, the third criterion for inclusion is that the asset class should be investible with low-cost index funds and ETFs, or a least a near-index type, broadly diversified actively managed fund. Most asset classes are available in an index fund or ETF so there is no need for active funds.

Some segments of the market are not as easy to invest in using index funds or ETFs because the indexes are difficult to replicate in a real portfolio. Municipal bonds are a good example. The market is highly segmented with limited trading in most issues. Funds that attempt to track municipal bond indexes don't have the diversification that's the hallmark of a good index fund investment. As an alternative, there are active funds that for all practical purposes can substitute for municipal bond index funds. Vanguard offers several municipal bond funds that hold hundreds of securities and charge very low fees.

Not All Index Funds Track Benchmarks   Be very selective when analyzing indexes and the funds that track them. Indexing may sound straightforward, but there are vast differences in costs and strategies among index funds and ETFs. One fund may follow the same index as another except that the fees are higher or dividends are handled differently. Another fund may say it tracks an index, but the index is actually an active investment strategy rather than a broad market benchmark.

Wall Street is very clever at marketing actively managed products disguised as index funds. For nearly 25 years, all index funds and ETFs brought to the market tracked well-known benchmark indexes. These were plain vanilla products that were easy to understand. Times have changed.

In 2003, Invesco PowerShares introduced ETFs that followed indexes that were far from plain vanilla. These indexes were based on highly active quantitative management strategies. The active management industry had figured out that anything can be called an index for marketing purposes provided that the security selection and weighting method can be defined, captured in a daily average, and publicly published.

In less than a decade, the actively managed "index" fund marketplace exploded with hundreds of these products. All of these funds have distinctly higher expenses than traditional index funds that track benchmarks. Many track indexes with witty names such as fundamental indexing, AlphaDEXes, and Intellidexes. The imagination of Wall Street to make and market products never ceases to amaze me.

The selection of index funds and ETFs to represent asset classes is no longer easy. Morningstar Principia lists nearly 2,000 index funds of various types, and more are launched every year. However, only a few dozen funds are truly of interest to a purely passive fund investor. The indexing marketplace is too involved for a detailed discussion in this book; however, I've taken on that task in two other books: *All About Index Funds*, 2nd Edition (McGraw-Hill, 2007) and *The ETF Book*, 2nd Edition (John Wiley & Sons, 2009). Book descriptions are available on my web site at www .RickFerri.com.

Low-cost passively managed index funds and ETFs that track market benchmarks are the only investments recommended for passive investors. These low-cost funds, coupled with a fixed strategic asset allocation based on needs, create a high probability solution for nearly every investor.

Step 5: Implementation and Maintenance

The best laid plans are useless if not implemented in full, which is more the norm rather than the exception. This inactivity is due to a host of excuses, including procrastination, distractions, laziness, lack of commitment, and the never-ending search for a perfect plan.

My estimate is that less than 50 percent of investment plans are actually fully put into practice, and less than 10 percent of all investment plans are fully implemented *and* maintained for more than five years. There are a lot of good intentions out there, but there is much more procrastination.

Regular maintenance is required after an investment plan is implemented in full. At a minimum, the owners or trustees should ensure that cash is invested when it is deposited and that dividends and interest are reinvested unless they are needed for withdrawals. In addition, asset allocation should be checked periodically to ensure that the portfolio is allocated close to the fixed allocation as outlined in the IPS. If the allocations are off by more than a certain percentage as outlined in the IPS, then rebalancing should take place to put the portfolio back in line with the IPS targets.

A good plan has long legs and should last several years without major modifications. Annual reviews and adjustments are appropriate, with major changes occurring only when something has changed in the personal lives of the owner or beneficiaries of the account. Aside from rebalancing, portfolio changes should never be made in reaction to poor market conditions.

Take the time to establish a prudent investment plan for your needs, implement that plan, and begin to maintain it. Putting a good plan into action today is much better than searching for a perfect plan whose outcomes cannot be known in advance.

Investment Monitoring   Performance monitoring is a science unto itself. It can be as complex as any field in the investment business. Appropriate indexes have to be selected as benchmarks to ensure an apples-to-apples comparison with a live portfolio, and deviations in returns from the benchmarks should be explained through detailed attribution analysis.

The bible for evaluating and presenting investment results is *Investment Performance Measurement* published by the CFA Institute through John Wiley & Sons.[2] It's a 1,000 page monster with small print and written by several notable Ph.D.s in the field. This book is not for the mathematically challenged.

The CFA Institute has a special designation for people who master performance monitoring. The Certificate in Investment Performance Measurement (CIPM) program offers the industry's only designation dedicated solely to the specialized field of investment performance evaluation and presentation. Written exams are required to earn the designation as well as several years' experience monitoring investment results.

Fortunately, monitoring a portfolio of passively managed index funds and ETFs is not nearly as complex or opaque as trying to monitor the performance of actively managed funds. The comparisons within asset classes are relatively straightforward because the index funds are intended to track the indexes.

That being said, there are many reasons why an index fund may go off track from an index. Performance mismatches occur due to fees, trading costs, index changes, restrictions on fund holdings, dividend cash flows that don't match the theoretical index dividend payments, and redemptions during market stress to name a few.

On the plus side, securities lending and arbitrage trading can increase the returns of the fund over the index.

Occasionally, an index fund will stray from its passive strategy. During 2002, Vanguard's Total Bond Market Index Fund (symbol: VBMFX) underperformed the Barclays Capital Aggregate Bond Index by a full 2.0 percentage points. That was an unheard of tracking error for an index fund, especially a Vanguard fund. The fund trustees admitted to allowing the fund managers to use their discretion in the fund by making a large bet on corporate bonds—at precisely the wrong time—and then instructed them to sell the position, again at precisely the wrong time. The net result was a huge hit to investor returns and well deserved embarrassment to Vanguard managers and the fund trustees.

Problems can also occur when a portfolio holds funds that are not quite index funds, but those funds offer the best representation for an asset class. Municipal bond funds were mentioned earlier. Often the bonds in a municipal bond index are illiquid, which means a fund manager is likely to hold different securities. When a fund is not performing as expected, it typically takes several calls to the fund company to get a straight answer as to why a fund is acting a certain way. Sometimes a good answer is never forthcoming. This makes it difficult for investors to decide if the fund's holdings are still acceptable as representative of that asset class.

Composite indexes should be created from individual asset class indexes using the same fixed weights as called for in the IPS. The composite index is compared to the overall portfolio to ensure that the performance is tracking as expected and that the risk in the portfolio continues to be within parameters. When a new asset class is added to the portfolio, or an asset class is eliminated, the composite index should also be adjusted as of the change date.

Policy Changes   Changing an investment policy is a major decision. Any change requires deep thinking and an evenhanded judgment and should not be made in a time of duress.

There are several good reasons to change an investment policy. The following are four prominent reasons.

1. The account owner's financial needs change.
2. Estate planning considerations change.
3. A bull market puts a portfolio close to its financial goal.
4. A bear market exposes more risk than an investor can handle.

Financial needs change for all of us during life's journey. There are periods when cash flow needs are high and periods when cash flow needs are low. In addition, unexpected things happen in our life (both good and bad) that may affect our need for cash. Starting a new business may prompt a person to become more conservative because they are now taking business risk or they need extra liquidity. A divorce could change both spouses' risk assessment and income needs as each party looks to their financial future as a single person rather than as a couple. A serious medical issue may change long-term goals, and that can affect investment decisions.

Financial needs also change for institutions. A large donation by an unexpected donor could change an investment policy. Restructuring a business could change the way a company manages its investment assets. Government changes in the way that companies calculate the discount rate used for pension valuation may affect the investment policy of pension funds.

When you realize that you have more than enough to live on for the rest of your life, are you still investing only for yourself? Perhaps you should consider, in part, the needs of your heirs. In that case, you are investing partly for yourself and partly for those who will receive a portion of your wealth, and the investment policy should change to reflect the needs of both parties. This goes against conventional thinking, which says you should be decreasing risk in the later stages of life. However, it often makes sense to increase risk later in life for the benefit of those who will inherit your money.

Market conditions generally should not affect asset allocation. However, there are a few exceptions.

A bull market will often propel a retirement portfolio to a value that's well ahead of its growth schedule and closer to its objective. This unexpected boost in return may afford the opportunity to reduce risk without jeopardizing a retirement goal. Granted, your future return may be lower by reducing risk, but the probability for reaching your goal will be higher even with a lower return.

Bear markets are never a good time to reduce risk, but sometimes it's the best course of action at that time. A bear market brings out the worst in us. There are some days during every bear market when we all wonder how far the market can fall. During those dog days, we can't flip on the television, a radio, or even check e-mail without in-your-face bad news about stock prices. The pressure can place people in a high anxiety situation.

Some people become so concerned during a bear market that they *must* do something with their portfolios. These people are in over their heads. They are investing beyond their tolerance for risk and it's affecting them emotionally. Their instincts tell them to get out. Before going to all cash in their portfolio, they should consider a small but permanent reduction in equity—perhaps a 10 percent reduction. This lowers portfolio risk, albeit it also lowers long-term expected portfolio return. However, selling a little stock in a bear market is better than panicking and selling it all.

Investment Policy Statements

All serious investors have a written investment policy statement (IPS). An IPS is the guidebook for an investment plan to follow over the long term. This document is all encompassing, discussing general needs both short-term and long-term; how the investment policy will provide for those needs; basic investment strategy; return expectations and risk limitations; asset allocation decisions; security selection methodology; and a process for portfolio implementation, maintenance, evaluation, and change as needed.

Investment strategy is an important component of the IPS. It outlines the portfolio's general investment approach, including how asset allocation decisions will be made and whether to use index funds or actively managed funds.

Asset allocation defines the fixed percent or percentage ranges committed to various asset classes such as stocks, bonds, real estate, cash, and so on. A strategic asset allocation would have a fixed allocation to asset classes, and often would subdivide these into styles and sectors. This slicing of asset classes into smaller sectors can aid a portfolio on occasion by reducing overall risk and potentially increasing return.

Investment selection methodology is also in the IPS. It outlines how securities will be selected for the portfolio. There may be a statement that defines the purpose of fund selection, such as to capture the return represented by a broadly diversified market benchmark. A passive investment approach would also mention why index funds and ETFs are to be used rather than actively managed funds.

Regular portfolio maintenance instructions should be included in the IPS to ensure that a portfolio stays on track. For example, instructions should outline when and how new cash will be invested as well as the reinvestment of dividends and interest can be in the instructions. How rebalancing will take place and when to ensure the portfolio is following its asset allocation strategy should also be included. For taxable portfolios, tax management using tax loss harvesting and tax swapping techniques lowers cost.

The investments in a portfolio should be evaluated at least annually to ensure they're performing in line with expectations and that they're still tracking their appropriate benchmarks. Perhaps new opportunities arise that warrant a change, such as when a new index fund is launched that better represents an asset class than the portfolio's current fund.

Finally, every few years the entire IPS should be reviewed to ensure that the asset allocation is still appropriate for the purpose it was set up. Perhaps an IPS was designed for accumulating assets before retirement and now there is a transition into retirement. Or perhaps an endowment requires a higher cash outflow than the policy was designed for. These changes in goals often lead to an asset allocation change that requires an IPS update.

This chapter covered the basics of investment policy decisions and writing an IPS, but it's by no means a definitive guide. I highly recommend *Winning the Loser's Game* by Charles D. Ellis for further reference. Here's one thought from Ellis's book:

> The principal reason you should articulate your long-term investment policies explicitly and in writing is to protect your portfolio from yourself—helping you adhere to long-term policy when Mr. Market makes current markets most distressing and your long-term investment policy suddenly seems most seriously in doubt. . . . The best shields against Mr. Market's short-term data and distress are knowledge and understanding, particularly of yourself and your own goals and priorities. . . . Don't trust yourself to be completely rational when all those around you are driven by emotion.[3]

At its core, Ellis's book is all about investment policy and even includes a sample IPS. Now in its fifth edition, his book is well written, widely acclaimed, and remains a favorite reference for many advisors.

Summary

This chapter provides a short introduction to portfolio management processes as well as references to books, articles, and studies to further your education on the passive management process. This works for all portfolios, including individual accounts, trust accounts, pension funds, endowments, and foundations. It is the highest probability solution to investment management.

The five step process for passive portfolio management provides a sound, effective, and efficient path to investment design, implementation, and maintenance. Following these steps religiously helps ensure that a portfolio remains purpose driven and provides the greatest probability for its success.

CHAPTER 11

The Passive Case for
Individual Investors

Most individuals make hash of their portfolios.
                                        —John M. Hartwell

It's commendable that you're reading this book on passive investing because it places you in the informed minority of all individual investors. You have the desire to learn about this strategy and why it's the best way to manage money for your benefit and the benefit of your loved ones. A passive investment strategy is the most reliable way to meet your family's financial goals.

Money is important to us. Not only does it provide financial security, it gives us a sense of well-being and self-worth and allows us to help our families and community. Getting money is typically accomplished by exchanging human capital (work) for monetary capital (money). Over our lifetime, we trade work for money, and money for goods and services. Most of the money we earn in a given year is spent that year. The rest is saved for future spending. The money that's saved needs to be invested prudently and with maximum efficiency so that it provides the most goods and services in the future.

Passive investing is the ideal solution for investment money because it has the highest probability for providing the most monetary value in the future. It ensures superior returns over what people would have earned if they had followed actively managed strategies. When investment expenses are reduced and market timing mistakes are eliminated, portfolio returns *must* go up! It's basic arithmetic.

Begin at the End

An investment policy should be put in place by every investor before one dollar is invested. The best place for individuals to begin forming an investment policy is with a clear vision of their personal long-term financial goals and objectives. Consider the following questions:

- What do you expect money to do for you and when?
- How much money is needed to accomplish this goal?
- What would you do with extra money if you have it?
- Who will inherit your wealth when you're gone?
- How wealthy do you want your children to be?

These questions relate to the meaning of money and how it affects you and your family. These may not be typical questions when forming an investment policy, but they are a starting point because the answers do ultimately drive investment decisions. For example, if you only have enough money to take care of your needs, then your portfolio should be invested for that purpose only. However, if you have more money than you need, the excess money will likely be invested for different purposes. You may wish to set up trusts for the benefit of your children or college savings accounts for grandchildren, or establish a charitable account. All these accounts could be managed differently because they have different investment objectives.

To assist in identifying major financial obligations, consider the following list. They are the six most common large expenses we face and are listed in the sequence in which they occur:

1. Personal education expenses
2. Home purchase and upkeep
3. Family expenses including college savings for children
4. Achieving adequate retirement income
5. Charitable giving
6. Bequests to loved ones

These life obligations become investment objectives for which an individual investment policy statement (IPS) is designed. They specify precisely the financial goals that the policy should address.

The following second set of questions helps quantify financial obligations. They involve traditional financial planning and budgeting issues such as living expenses, retirement planning, health insurance, long-term care, travel, and so on.

- How much money are you currently spending each year?
- How much is needed for necessities, how much for discretionary spending, and how much is for children's college and other time-specific expenses?
- Are there special circumstances such as a child with special needs or parents who may need assistance?
- How much do you anticipate spending in retirement each year?
- What is the amount of retirement income you expect from Social Security, pensions, inheritance, investments, and other sources?
- Will your house be paid off by the time you retire?
- Is your health insurance coverage adequate?
- Do you or a loved one have a serious health issue that isn't covered by insurance?
- Do you have or need long-term care insurance or will you self-insure?
- Are you planning to pay for your grandchildren's education?

The preceding questions are raised to identify potential financial obligations and liabilities. No doubt, your IPS will change and change again over your lifetime, partly because your obligations change and partly because your priorities change. The payments for each obligation can be over a short period, such as college tuition, or they can be over decades, such as retirement income. Some obligations extend beyond life itself, such as bequests to heirs and charities upon death.

For a young person, education is the top priority because it is an investment in human capital. This is the value of potential earnings power over one's lifetime. The next step is generally the purchase of a home, which often coincides with starting a family and all the costs associated with raising children. Sometime during middle age, focus shifts to securing adequate retirement income.

During retirement, focus can shift again to a policy of giving. This is the distribution of wealth to family members and loved ones as well as favored charities. Estate planning takes care of the rest upon our demise. Accordingly, an investment policy review during different stages of life ensures that it is up to date with these changing priorities.

Estimating Future Obligations

We all have a limited time on Earth, and the government is kind enough to tell us about how much time that is. The Internal Revenue Service (IRS) publishes mortality tables for singles and married couples.[1] The IRS table currently shows that a 21-year-old should expect to live another 62 years until age 83. The Social Security Administration expects 43 of those years will be spent working full-time and the remaining 20 years will spent working part-time or not working.

In a sense, the government is saying that the typical 21-year-old will work full-time for two years to pay for one year of retirement or semiretirement. That's not a lot of time to accumulate assets. A serious savings and investment policy needs to be in place during those 43 working years to reach a retirement goal.

Estimating the cost of future obligations is probably the most important part of investment planning because it quantifies how much money is needed. This process is also the most difficult part of investment planning because so many assumptions are made. We don't know precisely how much a particular obligation will cost, let alone the changes that may occur in our lives from now until the day the obligation comes due. Inflation also complicates the issue. There is no telling what things will cost in the years ahead after inflation.

I recommend making cost estimates in today's dollars and hold inflation off for a later adjustment. This method makes the process easier because thinking about costs in today's dollars is much easier than thinking about inflated costs in the future. For example, how much does a college education cost today, and how much income will you need in retirement in current dollars?

Obligations are paid with cash from several sources. The amount you'll need to withdraw from savings in retirement is the amount not covered by a pension, Social Security, or other income sources. This withdrawal amount will determine your savings and investment target amount at retirement.

Examples of Savings Goals

The following is an example of a retirement savings goal calculation. The example assumes a 2 percent real rate of return on a portfolio during retirement, which is a 5 percent nominal return assuming 3 percent inflation. This return is appropriate for a conservative portfolio that has about 30 percent in stocks and 70 percent in fixed income.

Assume you're withdrawing $48,000 per year from your savings to cover living expenses in retirement that aren't covered by other income sources. If you're not concerned with leaving any money to your heirs, then your target retirement amount is 16 times $48,000, which is $768,000. This money will last 33 years before running out. If you're planning to leave heirs the full retirement amount in today's dollars, then multiply $48,000 times 20 because you'll be able to deduct $48,000 per year and still leave your heirs a sizable estate. The result is a retirement target of $960,000.

Since you're not retiring today, a discount is applied to the retirement target to find today's required value. This discount rate is based on time and a real rate of return (see Chapter 10 for real return estimates on various asset classes).

Assume you're retiring in 10 years and wish to have $768,000 upon retirement. Also assume you'll be adding $12,000 per year into your account. Finally, assume that the portfolio will earn 3 percent real return (a pre-inflation return). How much do you need today to have $768,000 in 10 years? I'll spare you the math. You should have $466,000 already saved today.

The above calculation was done inflation-free. So, let's assume there's a 3 percent inflation rate over the next 10 years. The $768,000 target less inflation grows to a $992,760 target with inflation. That sounds bad. However, inflation is also part of investment return, so a real 3 percent return becomes a nominal 6 percent return. That alone makes up the difference in ending values. More good news is that your $48,000 withdrawal rate is also inflated up to a $64,500 annual withdrawal amount, although it doesn't buy any more goods or services.

It's not easy to calculate future obligations, but it's not impossible either. Doing obligation calculations helps us understand what our actual investment goals are. These numbers go on the liability side of a personal balance sheet. The asset side is where the money comes from to meet those liabilities.

The Asset Side

The future obligations are daunting and you're rightfully concerned. Where is the money going to come from to meet these liabilities? Have no fear. You probably have more equity than you think. The following sections are a laundry list of assets that most people have or eventually accumulate.

Human Capital

Assets are more than just material objects and paper. Human capital is our ability to earn income. It is the most valuable asset that people have early in their careers. Over time, human capital is converted into monetary capital, which is used to pay current and future obligations. This money buys goods and services, as well as real estate and investments.

Human capital is critical to our long-term financial well-being and it needs to be insured. There are three types of insurance that relate to human capital: life insurance, disability insurance, and health insurance. In case of our early demise, life insurance helps cover family obligations that otherwise would have been covered by human capital. Disability insurance also plays the same role in that it replaces human capital when we are unable to work. Health insurance protects people from costly health bills that may wipe out their savings.

Government insurance programs provide minimal assistance through death and disability insurance as part of the Social Security program. In addition, minimum government healthcare standards go into effect soon, and that could help some investors protect their personal savings. As with any government program, it is not known how much coverage will be available in the future, or the limits of this coverage. Insurance reviews are an important part of a regular financial review, particularly for a younger person who has a family to support.

Real Estate

It's common for people to buy a home early in life with their monetary capital. Real estate is a good use of capital because it has a dual purpose. A home provides shelter as well as an inflation and tax hedge. It is the only investment where the government lets you deduct the financing cost and property taxes each year, and then lets you earn a generous tax-free profit when you sell.

Home equity can also be converted into tax-free income during retirement through a reverse mortgage. In its simplest form, a reverse mortgage creates monthly payments from a financial institution to a homeowner who is over 62 years of age and owns their home that is their primary residence. Homeowners can receive monthly income from a reverse mortgage as long as they live in the home as a primary residence. A homeowner could potentially continue to receive monthly payments even after the loan balance is higher than the amount that the house is worth.

Pensions and Social Security

Many employers offer pensions to long-term employees. This is a valuable asset if you are lucky enough to have one. A pension pays you a fixed amount each month in retirement after a certain number of years of service. Pensions used to be more popular with private industry, until they became too expensive and regulatory intensive. Today, pensions are fading in private industry, although they are still popular in government and union jobs.

Many private employers offer pension funds to employees that pay a lump sum at retirement or termination. The value of the lump sum payout upon retirement or termination depends on the contribution amounts and the investment performance. These defined contribution plans can be employer funded, employee funded, or both.

The government mandates that all employees and business owners pay into the Social Security system (there are a few limited exceptions). This money is theoretically invested for our benefit and then is to be paid back to us in the form of a quasi-government pension in retirement. The amount we receive depends on how much we pay in and the age we start taking it out.

While Social Security in its current form will likely remain unchanged for people born before 1955, it is realistic to assume that people born sometime during the 1950s and beyond will get less than they were promised. Since I was born at the height of the baby-boomer generation in 1958, I am discounting the benefit amount on my annual Social Security Statement by 20 percent, and I don't expect to see annual inflation adjustments that keep pace with the actual inflation rate.

Inheritances

Some people will receive an inheritance from their friends or loved ones. These assets go on the asset side of your balance sheet and can be a great help in mitigating liabilities.

Most people who are in line for an inheritance don't consider its value in an investment plan because they don't feel it's their money. However, this money is as good as the rest. The person who is giving the inheritance to you wants you to have it. The best way to honor this person is to invest it prudently and spend it wisely.

Savings and Investments

Money not spent today is invested for another day. This is the capital used in the formulation of investment policy and should be addressed in an IPS. I categorize investments as four types: cash for immediate needs and emergencies, liquid long-term investments, illiquid investments, and speculative investments.

Figure 11.1 illustrates this hierarchy in an investment pyramid. The least risky are on the bottom and the most risky are on the top.

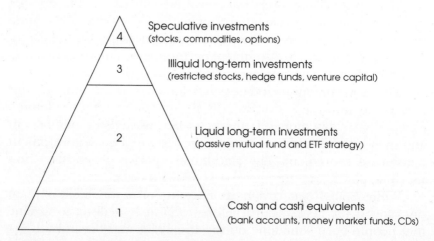

Figure 11.1   The Investment Pyramid

Here is a brief summary of the four investment types from the bottom up:

- **Cash and cash equivalents:** This money will be used to pay living expenses in the short-term in addition to major expenditures over the next 12 months. These include money in bank checking and savings accounts, money market funds, short-term certificates of deposit, and so on. Most people should strive to build 12 months in living expenses in cash so they can weather adverse situations such as job loss or health issues without liquidating long-term investments.

- **Long-term liquid investments:** This level represents the bulk of most investor's assets. These include long-term holdings in mutual funds, ETFs, and managed accounts. Passive investing in index funds and ETFs should be the strategy used in this core part of investment policy.

- **Illiquid long-term investments:** Many investors commit capital to private enterprises and partnerships where they have no management role. Often money placed in a private placement is tied up for many years. The potential reward for illiquidity is an expected higher return over the public markets. Often the early termination of a partnership agreement results in a significant price discount.

- **Speculative investments:** The greatest risk investments rely on timing to make a profit. The hold time on these investments can be from one minute to a few years. Their purpose is to take advantage of what appears to be mispricing in the market. The risk is if the investor is wrong. These investments include, but are not limited to, the trading of stocks, options, commodities, and leveraged or inverse ETFs as well as sector ETFs that are held for speculative purposes.

Passive investing covers the long-term liquid investments in the pyramid. This should be the major portion of an investment portfolio. In fact, in my opinion a vast majority of individual investors should avoid illiquid long-term investments and speculative investments.

Trying to make money in illiquid long-term limited partnerships including hedge funds and venture capital funds requires considerable skill in sorting out a few profitable opportunities from the rest. For every successful limited partnership there are at least 10 poor to mediocre ones, including Bernie Madoff–type scams.

Most individuals simply do not have access to top private management or have the expertise in selecting private funds. Highly skilled institutional investors pick off the attractive offerings long before the public is invited in.

David Swensen, CIO of the Yale endowment fund, eloquently sums up the prospective results from private partnerships in his highly praised book, *Unconventional Success.* Swensen strongly believes individual investors should stay with core passive investments:

> Non-core asset classes provide investors with a broad range of superficially appealing but ultimately performance-damaging investment alternatives. . . . Investors require unusual self-confidence to ignore the widely hyped non-core investments and to embrace the quietly effective core investments.[2]

Speculative investments in stocks, commodities, and high-turnover ETFs should also be avoided, or at least kept to an absolute minimum. These activities tend to undermine the prospects for reaching financial goals. Any money committed to speculative investing should be considered dead money in that it isn't expected to perform well relative to a passive strategy and could easily lead to substantial losses.

Matching Assets to Obligations

How much should you allocate to stocks and bonds? The answer depends on the timing of liabilities, the duration of liabilities, and the income from all other sources to meet these obligations before investments are considered. Knowing the amount of capital per year that investments need to provide to cover liabilities is a critical part of investment decision making.

It helps to create a cash flow analysis going out several years to link income sources to outflows. This will pinpoint critical times when more money may be needed from an investment portfolio. While you are working, most liabilities are covered by employment income. When you are retired, liabilities are covered by a combination of income sources including invested capital. Once cash flow analysis is accomplished, an investment plan can be created to match investment assets to liabilities.

An investment plan provides the road map to fair and equitable investment results over the portfolio's life. The objective is to provide the capital needed to cover liabilities that are not covered by other income sources. Asset allocation is probably the most important step in the planning process. It largely determines the growth path of your money and level of risk in the portfolio.

Asset Allocation

At its core, asset allocation is about dividing your wealth into different investments to reduce the risk of a large loss while targeting a specific return. Reducing the chance of a large loss increases the likelihood that an investor will maintain their investment plan during times of market duress. A failed investment plan occurs when people sell their risky investments at temporarily depressed prices, thereby locking in losses and throwing their financial future into disarray.

Successful investors study all asset classes and their various components in order to understand the differences among them. They estimate the long-term expectations of risk and return, and study how the returns on one asset class may move in relation to other classes. Then they weigh the advantages and disadvantages of including each investment in their portfolio as part of a total portfolio package.

The objective of portfolio management is to create and follow an investment policy that provides the resources required to meet current and future obligations. At its core, the portfolio management process relies on a prudent mix of asset classes that's based on research and reasonable assumptions about future risks, returns, and correlation with each other.

Strict adherence to an asset allocation strategy is required for the investment policy to have its desired effect and avoid unwanted drift. This requires the regular monitoring of asset class levels since the markets are constantly moving. Occasional rebalancing back to the target asset allocation ensures that the portfolio stays on track.

Risk control through asset allocation and rebalancing can't protect a portfolio every year. There will be times when all risky assets go down together, such as in 2008. However, when money flows out of risky assets, it typically flows to safer assets such as bonds. Treasury bonds had a very strong year in 2008. Everything reversed in 2009. Risky assets performed well while Treasury bonds didn't. Once you grasp the mechanics behind asset allocation and accumulate information on how different investments work with one another, you'll be ready to design a passive portfolio that has an expected return and an acceptable level of risk for your needs.

Tax efficiency may also be a consideration if the investment is going in a taxable account. Investors should be aware of which asset classes, styles, and sectors are better placed in tax-advantaged accounts, such as a retirement account, and which ones are suitable for taxable accounts.

Asset allocation is the cornerstone of a prudent investment plan and is the single most important decision that an investor will make in regard to a portfolio. For more information, read my book *All About Asset Allocation*, 2nd Edition (McGraw-Hill, 2010). The book is a detailed study of asset allocation and includes a wealth of information for individual investors.

Risk!

Risk is in the mind of the investor. Definitions of risk depend on who you are. Portfolio managers view risk as market volatility and measure it in standard deviation of returns. Institutional investors define risk as not having enough money to pay liabilities. Individual investors have a different and more direct definition of risk. It's the prospect of losing money. People don't like to see their portfolios go down in value, and when they do, they are more likely to make emotional decisions to sell than a portfolio manager or institutional investor.

In its pure form, risk is the probability a permanent loss will occur in a portfolio. A permanent loss occurs when an asset value cannot return to its purchase price because the assets are sold at a loss or become worthless. The only time market volatility creates a permanent loss in a passive portfolio is when an investor decides to sell at a loss because the markets will eventually recover.

Individual investors are more susceptible to selling in a down market than institutional investors. There is a good reason for this. Bear markets typically occur when the economy is in a downturn, which can affect individual investors in many ways. Economic weakness can cause job security concerns, potential pay cuts and benefits reductions, a drop in home equity value, and the risk that scholarship money will be cut or postponed for a child in college to name a few. These concerns weigh heavily on individuals and often cause enough stress for investors to reduce pressure where they can reduce it, which is often in their investment portfolio.

One method used to determine the maximum level of risk an investor can handle is to use a risk questionnaire. These tools are available for free on several web sites including www.Vanguard.com. How you answer the questions will give you a glimpse of your tolerance for risk, and this can help when designing a portfolio risk level.

Risk questionnaires can yield useful information if the questions are worded well. However, the questions typically address only one specific area: the maximum risk a person might be able to handle. Even this question cannot possibly be determined by a computer model alone. The questionnaire approach probably works better on young investors, who have a lot more in common with one another than people in their 50s and 60s.

More established investors should not rely solely on questionnaires for determining their risk level. More thought and attention should be given to their unique situation. Finding a person's maximum tolerance for risk requires soul-searching. We tend to feel brave when prices are going up, which means that it's not the ideal time to decide our risk tolerance level. Perhaps the best time to decide is after the market has dropped 20 or 30 percent when we're likely to be more honest with ourselves.

No one can guarantee that any investment strategy will achieve its stated objective. However, emotionally-charged selling in a bear market will almost guarantee that an investment plan will be derailed. The level of risk in an investment plan needs to be at a low enough level so that the plan will be diligently followed in all market conditions.

Investment Decisions

Investors create workable portfolios by first putting an asset allocation together that best suits their needs and ability to handle risk, and second, by selecting individual investments that best represent those asset classes. In general, you are looking for investments that have broad asset class representation and low fees.

The data from market indexes are the backbone for study and design of asset allocation strategies. This makes passively-managed index funds and ETFs an excellent choice for portfolio selection. Their overall higher return than actively managed funds, broad diversification, low cost, low tracking error with the markets, and high tax efficiency make these funds ideally suited to an asset allocation strategy. In addition, there are a large and growing number of index funds and ETFs on the market today that track most asset classes, styles, and sectors.

On the surface, it appears that selecting a few passive funds in different asset classes would be an easy task. In practice, there are vast differences among index methodologies and in the cost structures of index funds and ETFs that track indexes. Two funds may track an identical index and have different performance results due to differences in fees and fund structure. In addition, many funds are promoted as passive index funds while they actually follow highly sophisticated active strategies. It's a confusing marketplace that takes time and study to sort out.

Taxes are also a major consideration for individual investors. The best way to compound returns is to delay the payment of income taxes as long as possible and to pay taxes at a lower tax rate whenever possible. Traditional open-end index funds offer a significant tax advantage over actively-managed mutual funds. The turnover within indexes is very low in comparison to actively-managed funds of the same investment category. This results in fewer realized capital gains distributions to investors each year. ETFs have a greater advantage over active funds and index funds in that their structure allows the equity fund managers to rid the ETF itself of stocks that have unrealized capital gains. This reduces capital gains distributions by the fund and in many cases has completely eliminated them.

The detailed methodologies used by index fund and ETF managers to reduce taxes are beyond the scope of this book, although I do discuss these benefits in other books. For further reference, see *All About Index Funds*, 2nd Edition (McGraw-Hill, 2009) and *The ETF Book*, 2nd Edition (John Wiley & Sons, 2009).

Selecting index funds can be far more complex than it appears and further study is highly recommended. There are several fine books, articles, and web sites devoted to index funds and ETFs. All books by John Bogle and William Bernstein are excellent references. In addition, the www.bogleheads.org web site is an ideal place to ask anonymous questions about index funds, ETFs, and asset allocation.

Hired Help

The investment planning and implementation process can be an unwelcome chore for investors. The design, fund selection, implementation, monitoring, rebalancing, tax management, and occasional reassessment of strategy takes time, and that is not how many people want to spend their free time. In addition, many do-it-yourself investors tend to procrastinate or suffer from analysis paralysis, and this hurts portfolio performance. One way to fix these shortcomings is to hire professional help.

Advice seekers beware! The barriers of entry into the investment advisory business are woefully low, and easy money dreams attract all types. This leads to a broad range of competence levels. The biggest challenge when hiring an advisor is finding one who is truly knowledgeable about passive investing and committed to the strategy. I can tell you from firsthand knowledge that there aren't many. The big payout for advisors is on the active management side, and that's the level to which most advisors sink.

You'll likely be satisfied with your advisor if they are of like mind and charge reasonable fees for service. First, find one that is a die-hard believer in index investing using a passive asset allocation strategy. Next, ask exactly how the advisor is paid and what those fees are. Advisors' fees should be fair, and there should be no conflicts of interest with the investments they recommend.

An advisor should be willing to put all cost information in writing. Are you buying investment services? How much is that? What are the mutual fund costs? What are the trading costs? Is financial planning part of the fee or extra? Is tax preparation part of the fee? Advisors who are confident in their own ability will provide costs upfront and in plain sight for all to see and judge.

Compliance and legal issues plague some advisors. Make sure you check the background information of a potential advisor on the Securities and Exchange Commission web site at www.SEC.gov. If there is any question as to what a particular advisor's competence level is, move on and check out another advisor.

Some advisors promote hypothetical portfolio returns on their web sites. These returns aren't real. They're simulations. The advisor did not actually earn them. The advisor is claiming that by managing money in a certain way, these simulated returns may have been close to an actual return, but no one knows. I don't trust these returns, and no experienced investor would seriously consider them.

Once you go through the difficult search to find an advisor who believes wholeheartedly in passive investing and who you feel comfortable with, then your chances for a successful experience increases substantially. The following are some of the benefits provided by top advisors:

1. **Planning and implementation.** Advisors help clients understand their cash flow needs, then design, implement, and maintain a specific asset allocation to meet those needs. As a person's situation changes, the manager will suggest appropriate changes in the asset allocation.
2. **Consistency of strategy.** Discipline is critical to investment success. Investors need to follow their plan and rebalance their passive portfolios on a regular basis. It is the job of an advisor to ensure that this process happens.
3. **Create a circuit breaker.** During uncertain market conditions, some investors need to talk with someone about their concerns. A call to an advisor usually calms an investor's nerves and stops the investor from making an emotionally incorrect decision.
4. **Place someone on duty 365 days per year.** There are times when all investors get sidetracked. An advisor is there to do the investment chores for you all day every day.

Investment advisors are a luxury if you can afford one. Spend whatever time is needed to find the right advisor. A good advisor choice gives you peace of mind in knowing that your portfolio is being well maintained so you can enjoy your days doing other things.

Summary

Individual investors can increase their return and reduce costs with a prudently selected portfolio of passively managed index funds and ETFs. Creating a portfolio begins with critically analyzing current and future obligations and matching those obligations to an asset allocation strategy through proper fund selection.

There is a long-standing relationship between risk and return in any financial market. The markets with higher expected return have the greatest uncertainly that this return will occur in the short term. This knowledge can be used to build a portfolio using different asset classes with different risk and return characteristics. The goal is to design a portfolio that has the expected return and acceptable risk level so that you have a high probability of meeting your unique financial needs and future obligations.

The mechanics for prudent asset allocation and investment selection are more involved than how they are presented in this book. More reading is required to fully grasp these concepts. In addition, applying passive investing to a portfolio is much easier said than done. Do-it-yourself investors often do not complete the process or maintain it well. This is when a paid advisor can help.

Investing for the rest of your life and the lives of your loved ones is serious business. The passive strategy outlined in this book may not be a glamorous solution, but it does work. Calculate your future assets and liabilities, create a viable investment policy, implement your plan, diligently follow the plan, and grind out investment gains as they come. This no-nonsense, businesslike approach to portfolio management has the highest probability of reaching your long-term financial goals.

CHAPTER 12

The Passive Case for Charities and Personal Trusts

Worldly wisdom teaches that it is better for reputation to fail conventionally than to succeed unconventionally.

—John Maynard Keynes

Trustees who oversee other people's money are under strict legal requirements to act in the best interest of the beneficiaries to which they are responsible. Part of the trustee's responsibility is to make prudent decisions on investment policy. A passive investment strategy fits hand in glove with prudent fiduciary principles because it's efficient, effective, low cost, and this method has a high probability of achieving the goals of the trust and its beneficiaries over the long term.

A trustee's personal belief about the best way to invest may differ from passive investment approaches. However, being a trustee is about taking the right course of action for a trust, and this means making decisions as a prudent investor would. Low-cost, low-tax, and low-risk investing has been written about extensively in trust law and would likely be widely accepted by judges as a prudent investment strategy. It's an ideal choice for trusts and for trustees who are liable for their investment decisions.

Your Role as a Trustee

At some point in your life, you may be asked to oversee the assets of a charitable foundation or endowment, or the assets of a friend, relative, client, or a personal trust set up for another reason. Agreeing to oversee someone else's assets places you in a position of responsibility that goes well beyond how you manage your own affairs. Whether or not you're paid for this position, you're legally obligated to act in the best interest of the trust owners and beneficiaries.

There are many laws governing trust investments, depending on the type of trust and the state you live in. However, none of these laws restrict investments to government bonds, a list of securities, or an approved strategy. Rather, the regulations create a framework for making prudent investment decisions. The rules mostly pertain to adequate diversification, liquidity, and cost controls.

Every trustee has biases and beliefs about how investments should be managed. Trustees may believe that they're talented mutual fund pickers or good market forecasters, or that they have an uncanny knack for selecting big winners in micro cap stocks. However, what trustees believe about themselves as experienced investors and what's the right strategy for the trusts they oversee may be two completely different things. If a trustee ventures into active management, the courts may place the onus on the trustee to prove that this is a prudent decision and in the best interest of the trust and its beneficiaries. That would be difficult to prove given the overwhelming evidence against active management compiled in this book.

Managing someone else's money isn't about proving that a trustee has superior investment skill and can outmaneuver the markets. It's not about the trustee. The law cares only about the beneficiaries of the trust whose assets should be prudently managed by the trustee. If you're a trustee, the law cares that you're following an investment strategy that has the highest probability of meeting the needs of a trust and its beneficiaries. For all but a handful of very experienced and talented people, acting prudently means using a passive asset allocation strategy and selecting low-cost passively managed index funds and ETFs.

This chapter is all about why passive investment management is a suitable and prudent choice for managing other people's money. Two different types of trust accounts are discussed: personal trusts and charitable trusts. In the opinion of top fiduciary experts on the law of investment of trust assets, a low-cost and low-tax passively managed strategy is the default standard of modern prudent fiduciary investing.[*]

Laws Governing Trusts

Trustees have certain legal obligations. These include, but are not limited to, carrying out the express terms of a trust instrument, prudently investing trust assets, being impartial to all the trust beneficiaries, keeping settlors (those creating the trust) and beneficiaries informed about the trust and any actions taken with respect to it, staying loyal to the trust beneficiaries, and avoiding personal conflicts of interest. These various duties of a trustee may be expanded or narrowed by the terms of the trust, but in most instances cannot be eliminated completely.

The duties of a trustee that pertain to investment decisions place the trustee in a position as a fiduciary. This means that the trustee must act within the highest standards of care according to the law. The word fiduciary originally comes from the Latin *fides*, meaning "faith," and *fiducia*, or "trust." The law states that a fiduciary must act at all times for the sole benefit and interests of the beneficiaries of the trust, with loyalty to those interests, and must not put its own personal interests before this paramount duty of loyalty.

Managing investments for other people as a fiduciary isn't an easy task, especially for a layman. The financial markets are complex, and decisions can overwhelm even a trained professional. To make matters worse, there are confusing and often opaque legal guidelines found in legislation, case law, and regulatory opinion letters that must be followed. People with limited knowledge should be extra careful when implementing investment decisions to ensure that they follow important guidelines such as diversification, liquidity, and cost control.

---

[*] For a comprehensive treatment of trust law as it pertains to passive investing see the extensive writings of W. Scott Simon, an expert on the Uniform Prudent Investor Act and the *Restatement Third of Trusts*. He is the author of *The Prudent Investor Act: A Guide to Understanding* (Namborn, 2003) and a regular contributor to *Morningstar* publications on fiduciary standards for trustees, investment committees, advisors, brokers, bankers, and money managers. Simon's Morningstar columns may be accessed at http://advisor.morningstar.com.

There are two legal model acts that primarily govern the management of trust assets, depending on the type of account under management and the particular state. Trustees should be familiar with them both and the peculiarities in the state where the trust is resident:

- UPIA (Uniform Prudent Investor Act): addresses personal trusts.
- UPMIFA (Uniform Prudent Management of Institutional Funds Act): addresses foundations, endowments, and government-sponsored charitable institutions.

These model acts have many similarities in managing trust assets. They generally ring in harmony in that a trustee must invest and manage trust assets as a prudent investor would, by considering the purposes, terms, distribution requirements, and other circumstances of the trust. In satisfying this standard, the trustee must exercise reasonable care, skill, diligence, and caution.

Fiduciary 360 and its affiliate the Foundation for Fiduciary Studies are two of many private organizations dedicated to investment fiduciary education, practice management, and support. These organizations have identified similar characteristics of both model acts. There are seven *Global Fiduciary Precepts.*[1]

1. Know standards, laws, and trust provisions.
2. Diversify assets to specific risk/return profile of the trust.
3. Prepare investment policy statement.
4. Use prudent experts (for example, an investment advisor) and document due diligence when selecting experts.
5. Monitor the activity of the prudent experts.
6. Control and account for investment expenses.
7. Avoid conflicts of interests and prohibited transactions.

All trustees involved in different fields of investing including foundations and endowments, private family trusts, and pension plans (see Chapter 13) have one thing in common: they're required to live up to the standards of trust law, which are the highest known in the law.

Trusts and Passive Investing

Being a trustee can be a rewarding experience because it places you in a position to help other people. But, it can also be frustrating, confusing, and time-consuming. If you accept this position of responsibility, you must make a commitment to understanding the workings of trust law. At times, this means interpreting arcane legal language that only an attorney could love.

In addition, you'll need to understand the benefits and drawbacks of different investment strategies before implementing an investment policy. This means making a reasonable effort to verify all facts, costs, probabilities, and potential payouts for each strategy.

Passive investing strategies should be at the top of the list for all trustees because they offer a low cost, transparent, high probability investment option. Passive investment strategies fit the guidelines in the model acts perfectly because they place great emphasis on the duty to diversify, contain costs, and avoid speculation. There's no strategy that diversifies a portfolio, keeps costs and taxes low, and has a high probability of achieving trust objectives than a well-thought-out portfolio of passively managed investments.

There is overwhelming evidence that the continued high cost of active management will result in a low probability of success in the future. Trustees should know the odds against active management beating the markets when making investment decisions for trust beneficiaries. The data in this book has identified active management as having unnecessarily high costs and uncompensated risks that trustees should avoid.

Private Trust Management

By definition, private trusts hold personal assets. Typically, a settlor titles money or property in the name of a trust and appoints a person or legal entity such as a trust company to oversee these assets. The trustee is legally obliged to hold these assets and manage them for the benefit of one or more beneficiaries who are usually named by the settlor in the trust instrument.

There are two broad categories of private trusts: testamentary and living. Testamentary trusts are established in a will and take effect upon the death of the settlor (the person who established the trust). Living trusts are started during the life of the settlor and may continue after death. Trusts can be revocable, meaning that the settler can make changes at any time, or irrevocable, when the settlor permanently relinquishes the right to make changes in the trust instrument.

There are literally dozens of variations of private trusts depending on the wishes and goals of the settlor. There are special needs trusts, generation-skipping trusts, credit shelter trusts, and spendthrift trusts, to name a few. A personal charitable trust can also be established where some benefits go to a charity immediately and others go to the trust beneficiaries upon the death of the settlor.

Naming a trustee requires special consideration. According to the Uniform Prudent Investor Act (UPIA), the requirements of trusteeship should be "neither excessively demanding nor monolithic" and should "neither effectively preclude service by conscientious family members and friends nor permit casual, inattentive behavior by trustees who can, because of their expertise, meet a higher than ordinary standard of conduct and competence."[2] Every trustee must be willing and able to participate and diligent in their duties.

Often settlors appoint themselves as the trustees or co-trustees of a private trust. This self-appointment doesn't excuse the settlor from following trust law in any way, including prudent investment decision-making, and doesn't reduce or eliminate in any way the fiduciary duties the trustee owes to the trust beneficiaries.

(Third) Restatement of Trusts

The UPIA was promulgated in 1994 by the National Conference of Commissioners on Uniform State Laws. The 23 pages codify the essential principles of the more comprehensive *Restatement, Third, of Trusts* drafted by American Law Institute's in 1992 that stretched for more than 300 pages. The reporter for the Restatement is Edward C. Halbach, Jr., the Walter Perry Johnson professor of law emeritus at the University of California Berkeley School of Law.

The UPIA sets forth prudent fiduciary standards that regulate the investment conduct of trustees overseeing private trusts. Although UPIA, the model act, is not law, virtually every state has enacted UPIA into law while the remaining handful of states have enacted most of it.

At the heart of UPIA is the Prudent Investor Rule, which revised and updated the Prudent Man Rule established in 1830. Under the Prudent Man Rule, trustees were directed to "observe how men of prudence, discretion and intelligence manage their own affairs, not in regard to speculation, but in regard to the permanent disposition of their funds, considering the probable income, as well as the probable safety of the capital to be invested."[3]

The UPIA makes five fundamental alterations to the Prudent Man Rule, while retaining most of the prudent standards of fiduciary conduct. All changes were derived from the Restatement. The following comes directly from the UPIA[4]:

1. The standard of prudence is applied to any investment as part of the total portfolio, rather than to individual investments. In the trust setting the term "portfolio" embraces all the trust's assets.
2. The tradeoff in all investing between risk and return is identified as the fiduciary's central consideration.
3. All categoric restrictions on types of investments have been abrogated; the trustee can invest in anything that plays an appropriate role in achieving the risk/return objectives of the trust and that meets the other requirements of prudent investing.
4. The long familiar requirement that fiduciaries diversify their investments has been integrated into the definition of prudent investing.
5. The much criticized former rule of trust law forbidding the trustee to delegate investment and management functions has been reversed. Delegation is now permitted, subject to safeguards.

The Restatement treats diversification as one of the fundamental elements of prudent investing, and the committee drafting the Restatement incorporated modern portfolio theory (MPT) into the general language of the Prudent Investor Rule. This underscores MPT's influence in shaping investment practice since the 1960s.

Restatement commentary goes beyond stating that a trust account must be diversified by citing a fiduciary breach of duty if a trustee does not diversify an account: "Failure to diversify on a reasonable basis in order to reduce uncompensated risk is ordinarily a violation of both the duty of caution and the duties of care and skill."[5] These three duties—caution, care, and skill—comprise the essential elements of prudence.

No category or type of investment for a trust portfolio is deemed inherently imprudent under the Restatement. Rather, suitability is based on the trust's purposes and the needs of its beneficiaries. However, speculation and outright risk-taking is not sanctioned, and a trustee remains subject to possible liability for such conduct.

The UPIA recognized the benefits of mutual funds and other pooled accounts to aid in diversification. It is difficult for a small trust fund to diversify thoroughly by constructing its own portfolio of individually selected investments. Buying individual securities can be relatively expensive when a small investor attempts to assemble a portfolio broad enough to minimize uncompensated risk. For this reason, mutual funds and other pooled investment vehicles have become the main mechanism for facilitating diversification for the investment needs of smaller trusts.

The duty to minimize costs is addressed in the UPIA. This duty applies to delegation of investment duties as well as to other aspects of investment management. In deciding whether to delegate invest-ment activities to an advisor or money manager, the trustee must balance the projected benefits against the likely costs. The trustee must be alert to protect the trust beneficiaries from "double dip-ping." If, for example, the trustee's regular compensation schedule supposes that the trustee will conduct the investment management function, it should ordinarily follow that the trustee will lower its fee when delegating the investment function to an outside manager.

The main themes of the UPIA that appear throughout the act include using broad diversification unless there are special circum-stances, employing cost containment measures including tax con-trol in taxable trusts, avoiding speculation and outright risk-taking, and using mutual funds or other pooled accounts to achieve diver-sification at a low cost. These themes are very familiar to passive investors because they're the main reason why passively managed funds outperform actively managed investments.

UPIA and Passive Investing

The UPIA specifically avoids endorsing passive investing as the only prudent way to incorporate the lessons of modern portfolio theory and research. However, Edward C. Halbach, Jr., the Reporter for the Restatement and the person who stands alone at the apex of modern prudent fiduciary investing, has his own opinion about the benefit of index funds and passive investing as the preferred method of trust investing:

> Current assessments of the degree of market efficiency sup-port the adoption of various forms of passive strategies by pru-dent investors, including the widespread reliance on index funds. Assessments also tend to discourage incurring heavy investigative and transaction costs, including taxation of gains,

in pursuit of strategies designed to beat the market through "timing" or "stock picking" in major central markets.

On the other hand, these assessments have not prevented all intelligent and careful investors from including active management strategies in the investment programs for which they are responsible. Likewise, these assessments would not justify a legal rule that would bar fiduciaries from including active management strategies in investing funds for which they are responsible.[6]

Halbach elaborates on the cost of various strategies in relation to return, which points to a passive bias: "To the extent an investment strategy may demand extra management, tax and transaction costs or a departure from an efficiently diversified portfolio, or both, that strategy should be justifiable in terms of special circumstances or opportunities involved, or in terms of a realistically evaluated prospect of enhanced return."[7]

The key words for active fund investors are the *realistically evaluated prospect of enhanced return.* When the low probability of an enhanced return from active funds is coupled with the low payout of winning active funds relative to the underperformance from losing funds, there is no realistic prospect of an enhanced return. Halbach appears to agree:

> Active management involves new or increased expenses of investigation, analysis, and transaction costs, including capital gains taxation, *plus additional risks* that may result from the challenging judgments involved and from carrying a relatively high degree of diversifiable risk. [italics added][8]

There are clearly additional risks in active management when compared to passive investing. The odds of beating index funds are low and the average payout for being right does not adequately compensate for the risk of being wrong. When multiple active funds are used, the risk increases and costs go up, thus lowering the probability of outperformance. Active management just isn't worth the effort, and the prudence of using this strategy is very tenuous.

Scott Simon addresses passive investing at length in his exceptional book, *The Prudent Investor Act: A Guide to Understanding.* The following quotes from the book were included by Simon in an article he wrote entitled "In Indexing We Trust," published in the *Journal of Indexes* in 2004:

> During the course of drafting the Restatement, there was discussion about making passive investing the only way to invest and manage trust portfolios prudently. . . . In one of their articles, they [law professors] observed that "when market funds have become available in sufficient variety and their experience bears out their prospects, courts may one day conclude that it is imprudent for trustees to fail to use such vehicles."
>
> The drafters of the Restatement decided that requiring a passive-investing-only approach would be contrary to the notions of generality and flexibility that they intended to restore to trust investment law. Nonetheless, the two-part test suggested by Restatement Commentary, as well as the overall tenor of the Restatement, makes clear that trustees have the affirmative duty to justify proposed active investment strategies. A commentator notes that trustees have this burden.

It isn't worth the risk for a trustee to engage in any investment strategy other than a passive investment strategy. No trustee wants to become personally responsible for the failures of active management. Trustees who opt for active management over passive management may one day have to justify their actions by proving that they possess an unusually high degree of investment skill and can select an active strategy or active managers that have a high probability for outperformance in the future. If unable to do so, then the trustee would be at a higher risk of being in breach of their fiduciary duty.

Some trustees may believe they have the skill to select superior active management. However, that would be easy to disprove in court. There are only a handful of trustees in the country that have the level of knowledge needed to at least have a chance of selecting active managers that outperform. You are not likely to be in that group, and unless you sit on some of the largest endowments or foundations in the country, the members of this group aren't likely to be anyone you know. Accordingly, do what is in the best interest of the trust and in your best interest as a trustee—use a passive investment strategy.

Taxes and Personal Trusts

Personal trusts are different from pension and charitable trusts in that personal trusts are subject to annual income taxes. In some personal trusts, income and realized gains flow through to the income beneficiaries who personally become responsible for paying the tax. In other trusts the income is retained by the trust and the trust pays the tax at a special rate.

The UPIA reflects a *total return* approach to managing trust portfolios and tax considerations are a big part of total return. Taxable trusts and the income beneficiaries are in general best served by an investment strategy that minimizes portfolio turnover and other factors that can increase taxation.

Index funds, and particularly ETFs with their special tax treatment, are ideal investments for a private trust. The low turnover of securities in an index fund provides low distribution of capital gains. Combining index products with a strategic asset allocation keeps the turnover of the investments in index funds low, which helps keep taxes low.

UPIA and Active Management

The Restatement explains that the duty of prudence doesn't look to a universal standard of risk or cost, but calls for the trustee to examine and weigh numerous factors concerning an asset or activity and characteristics of the trust. All of this is to be done with due care and skill and with an eye towards the trust purposes and an overall degree of caution or conservatism reasonably appropriate to the trust at the time the particular investment decision is made.[9]

This leaves the door open for active management of private trusts. If trustees are convinced that high-cost active management is in the best interest of a trust and its beneficiaries, and they can adequately justify in writing such reasoning, then they may proceed. Passive investing is the answer in all other cases.

Nonprofit Organizations

The Uniform Prudent Management of Institutional Funds Act (UPMIFA) regulates the investment and expenditure of funds held by charitable institutions.[10] UPMIFA incorporates all the principles of the UPIA nearly verbatim. The UPIA is an excellent guide for the investment responsibilities of all fiduciaries who are involved with foundations, endowments, charities, and other nonprofit organizations.

A major goal of UPMIFA is the application of consistent standards for the management and investment of charitable funds so that the same standards apply regardless of whether a charitable organization is organized as a trust, a nonprofit corporation, or another type of entity. The model act has been enacted by most states.[11]

Nonprofit investing differs from investing in private trusts in a number of ways: (1) the nonprofit is often perpetual or nearly perpetual; (2) there's typically a constant need for cash outflows, while inflows from donations and other sources are erratic and the amounts tend to be uncertain; (3) most nonprofit organizations have a committee that sets investment policy and oversees investing activities; and (4) the committee members today will not likely be the same people years from now.

The decisions the investment committee makes today will affect those who take over in the future. Accordingly, the arguments for and against every action should be vetted and documented.

The Management of Nonprofit Accounts

An investment committee has many tasks, not the least of which is getting new members up to speed on what is going on in the organization and in the committee. These tasks of the committee can be generalized in six areas:

1. Understand the needs of the organization. This is the committee's foremost job, which includes identifying short-term and long-term funding requirements as well as any major projects under consideration.
2. Understand the needs of specific donors. This requires committee members to consider and follow the intent of a donor as expressed in the gift instrument.
3. Set investment policy so that it has the highest probability of meeting the organization's needs while considering the special needs of donors when applicable. This generally results in an allocation to liquid investments for current obligations and long-term assets for funding future obligations.

4. Decide on an investment strategy for all of the cumulative parts of the plan. This involves a review of different options, including the decision to be active or passive, or a combination in different accounts.
5. Interview and select one or more investment managers to implement the investment strategy across accounts.
6. Thoroughly review the investment policy annually to ensure it still meets the needs of the organization and donors, and review the investment managers' actions and results to ensure that they're performing in line with expectations.

The duty to minimize costs is described in UPMIFA, explained as "All costs or fees associated with an endowment fund are factors that prudent decision makers consider. High costs or fees of investment management could be considered imprudent . . ."[12] Commentary in Section 7 of the UPIA is blunt regarding the importance of maintaining low investment costs in modern prudent fiduciary investing: "Wasting beneficiaries' money is imprudent. In devising and implementing strategies for the investment and management of trust assets, trustees are obliged to minimize costs."[13]

Passive versus Active Investing

An investment committee will need to be thorough in its investigations and discuss the pros and cons of various investment strategies before selecting the best option for their organization. This requires detailed data gathering and an exhaustive analysis. The process should include new members of the committee who may have limited investment experience.

The UPMIFA authorizes the delegation of management and investment decisions to outside investment managers to the extent that such delegation is prudent under the circumstances. The act provides guidance with respect to the standards applicable to institutions and managers when investment authority is delegated. An organization must act in good faith, with the care that an ordinarily prudent person in a like position would exercise under similar circumstances, in (1) selecting a manager; (2) establishing the scope and terms of the delegation; and (3) periodically reviewing the manager's actions in order to monitor performance and compliance with the investment policy. If an organization complies with the standard set forth in UPMIFA, the organization should not be held liable for a manager's decisions or actions.

If every investment committee member were required to read two books on the selection of managers for nonprofit assets, they should be *Winning the Loser's Game,* 5th Edition by Charles Ellis (McGraw-Hill, 2010) and *Pioneering Portfolio Management,* 2nd Edition by David Swensen (Free Press, 2009). Peter Drucker called Ellis's book the best book on investment policy and management ever written, and Swensen's book is considered by most in the industry to be the bible for managing nonprofit portfolios.

Ellis and Swensen are thoroughly familiar with nonprofit account management, having served on investment committees for many years. As a result of their experiences, both are strong advocates of passive investment strategies for all but the most skillful investment committees. Passive investing will generate better performance at lower cost and is in keeping with UPMIFA principles on prudence.

I have been interviewed by many small nonprofit investment committees over the years and will candidly say that most people who sit on these committees don't have enough experience to select a skilled active manager. They don't know which questions to ask, what answers are truthful, or when a manager is leading them astray. Consequently, committee members tend to make manager decisions based on local reputation, gut feeling, or simply following the votes of other committee members. Those of us in the business call these interviews beauty pageants because they're not about the best process for managing money; they're about singing a sweet song and looking good in a business suit.

Here's one thought that every investment committee member of a small endowment or foundation should keep in mind when hiring active managers—the truly talented ones who may be able to beat the market *aren't interested in your business.* Why? Because your organization is too small. The best and brightest don't have time for a $2 million or $20 million foundation. They're too busy managing money for the $5 billion dollar endowment funds. Paraphrasing Charles Ellis, it's easy to tell a good manager from a mediocre one; the mediocre one wants to manage *your* money! If an active manager were talented, chances are you've never heard of him or her, and if you did, you'd never be able to hire them.

It is a tragedy when poor investment decisions cripple the ability of a nonprofit organization to help others. Bernie Madoff had almost everyone fooled that he was a top hedge fund manager. He took everyone's money, literally, and his high reported returns kept rolling in regardless of the amount he managed. Many nonprofits lost millions of dollars when Madoff's Ponzi scheme collapsed. Other organizations lost a large portion of their assets during the global recession because the investment committees made ill-timed asset allocation decisions. These mistakes didn't happen to organizations that adopted and maintained a prudent passive management strategy.

Your organization is important. It does good things for people and has an important moral message for society. That's why it's important for your organization to manage its assets efficiently and effectively. An adverse investment outcome affects too many people. Be prudent—be passive—and be disciplined about it.

Watch Out for Conflicts of Interest

Conflicts of interest run rampant in the trust investment industry. All the professionals who provide advice to trustees say they're fiduciaries, but very few are legally trustees, so they have a different level of responsibility. Unfortunately, some fiduciaries don't act like one when their paycheck is on the line.

It's common for trust attorneys who advise trustees to be financially tied to brokerage firms, insurance agencies, banks, and trust companies where they are compensated in some way for the business they refer. This compensation may be reciprocating referrals, referral fees, and even fee sharing arrangements. The law states that these business relationships must be disclosed. Nevertheless, when an attorney refers you to an investment advisor or an insurance agent or trust company, it's always prudent to ask, "What's in this for you?"

Many people hire a professional trustee to oversee and administer a trust or to sit on the investment committee. This person could be an individual such as an attorney, a trust officer at a bank, or some other professional. These people help decide how a trust account will be invested and where it will be managed.

Often, a professional trustee will decide to place the accounts they have under advisement with their own investment firm or an affiliate. The trustee may then earn fees from the management of these assets. It's illegal for a trustee to double dip by collecting both a trustee fee and investment fees from an account. The fee paid to a trustee should be reduced by the fees earned from the investment side.

What happens when trustees' investment fees dwarf their trustee fee? The excess revenue from investment fees still goes to the trustee as extra compensation or to some business relationship they have. This is a problem. It's difficult for professional trustees to be unbiased about investment options when they're being compensated in some way to be biased.

The Restatement emphasizes that trustee prudence is tested by the reasonableness of the trustee's conduct and not by the performance of the investments selected.[14] It's generally not prudent for a trustee to have any conflict of interest in the management of trust assets, but it's not illegal to have a conflict provided it's disclosed fully. It is illegal if a fiduciary is recommending an investment action solely because it pays them to do so (i.e., a quid pro quo or pay-to-pay situation) or they receive some benefit or favor from the people who are managing the money.

Separate Roles for Lawyers and Advisors

There are a number of prominent trust experts who write books for trustees. These books have great value in teaching people about trust law and trustee responsibility. However, they have limited use as investment guides.

Good lawyers write good books on trust law, and that's where it should end. For some strange reason, many experts on trust law feel compelled to provide detailed investment advice as well. Much of this advice is far from professional. The following are a couple of examples.

One popular book by two noted trust attorneys had this piece of advice: "As markets are inefficient, active management will pay off in the long run. Because not all stocks in the index have good fundamentals, a trustee who pursues a passive investment strategy by gathering into a portfolio 'hundreds of issues' may well be imprudently overdiversifying a portfolio."[15]

This passage is complete and utter nonsense. There's no academic evidence supporting the notion that active management has paid off in the long run, no way of telling which stocks have good fundamentals for investment purposes, and no research supporting the ridiculous notion that more diversification is imprudent overdiversification!

But it doesn't stop there. The same attorneys then say that "if you blindly throw money at index funds, then you should at least hold more than the 500 stocks in the S&P 500. . . . A trustee, for example, might consider a long-term buy and hold investment strategy using two index funds, one that tracks the Standard and Poor's 500 Index and the other that tracks the Nasdaq-100 Index."[16]

This advice shows poor knowledge of indexing methods. The S&P 500 primarily holds large U.S. stocks from all U.S. exchanges and NASDAQ-100 represents the largest 100 companies that trade mainly on the Nasdaq market, excluding financial firms. Adding a NASDAQ-100 index fund can't diversify the S&P 500 because essentially every stock in the NASDAQ-100 Index is already in the S&P 500 Index! Clearly, the attorneys who wrote the passage did no research into the construction of the S&P 500 and the NASDAQ-100.

The UPIA states that delegation to professionals is permitted by trustees, subject to safeguards. One safeguard is to use professionals who are experts in their field. Don't rely on investment advisors for legal opinions and don't rely on trust lawyers for investment recommendations. If you need trust work, by all means go to a trust lawyer. If you want investment advice, seek out a competent investment advisor who has strong academic credentials in the field and has many years' experience working with people who have similar situations.

Barring special circumstances, passive investing using a strategic asset allocation in low-cost, low-tax, and lower risk index funds and ETFs is the prudent choice for personal trusts. This portfolio management method has the highest probability for reaching the trust's objective.

Summary

Trustees who oversee other people's money and make investment decisions on their behalf have important responsibilities. The law places a heavy burden on trustees to ensure they are acting in the best interest of the trust. Trustees have a legal obligation to carry out the express terms of a trust, to prudently invest assets, to be impartial to the trust beneficiaries, to stay loyal to the interests of the beneficiaries, and to avoid personal conflicts of interest.

There are model acts of trust law that govern different types of trusts and how these assets should be managed. All of the model acts require that trustees have a high level of prudence, integrity, and expertise. Trustees should know which model acts govern the

CHAPTER

13

The Passive Case for Pension Funds

Managing pension money isn't an easy task for trustees. Most people who are asked to be a trustee on a pension committee are employees of the company or organization and have little experience or training in the laws that govern pensions. They also come to the job with a level of investment experience considerably below the prudent expert level of knowledge required by law.

Pension trustees make investment decisions that include, but are not limited to, prudently selecting investment options for the benefit of plan participants, and monitoring these choices to ensure that they're sticking to the investment objectives of the plan. In addition, trustees must avoid personal conflicts of interest when making decisions for the plan such as selecting companies to service the plan that provide a personal benefit to the trustee in some way.

Managing pension assets is all about providing plan participants with their earned benefits while effectively managing risk. This makes passive investment strategies an ideal choice for pension fund trustees because it has the highest probability of meeting a plan's long-range objectives for a given amount of risk. A passive approach is the most prudent choice for pension trustees.

Legal Acts Governing Pensions

Two different sets of laws primarily govern the management of retirement assets. Pension trustees should be knowledgeable about the law that pertains to the funds they oversee. In addition, familiarity with the Uniform Prudent Investor Act (UPIA) is a wise idea:

- ERISA (Employee Retirement Income Security Act): addresses qualified retirement plans such as profit sharing and 401(k) plans.
- UMPERSA (Uniform Management of Public Employee Retirement Systems Act): addresses state, county, and municipal retirement plans.

The Employee Retirement Income Security Act of 1974 (ERISA) is a federal law that sets minimum standards for pensions in private industry such as profit sharing and 401(k) plans. The purpose of ERISA is to provide protection for individuals and their beneficiaries who are participants in these plans.

The Uniform Management of Public Employee Retirement Systems Act (UMPERSA) covers state and local retirement plans for the benefit of participants and beneficiaries. ERISA does not apply to these plans. Instead, public employee retirement plans are regulated by laws in each state, and these laws vary considerably across the states. UMPERSA clarifies and makes uniform the rules governing the management of public retirement systems.

Both ERISA and UMPERSA require all plan assets to be held in trust, excluding insurance contracts. Plan fiduciaries are responsible for investing and managing plan assets according to the standards of trust law. In addition, trustees must follow the terms of pension plan documents to the extent that those terms are consistent with the laws governing a particular plan. Trustees and other fiduciaries are held to the highest standards of being a prudent investment expert, even though most trustees are far from being experts in these matters.

The primary responsibility of trustees is to run a plan solely in the interest of participants and their beneficiaries for the exclusive purpose of providing benefits to them. The law outlines the fiduciary responsibilities for those who manage plan assets including investment strategy, investment selection policy, monitoring and replacement of investments, and paying reasonable plan expenses. By law, all pension plans are required to be diversified in order to minimize the risk of large losses, although the law doesn't state what that level of diversification should be.

Breaches under ERISA Lead to Litigation

ERISA gives plan participants and their beneficiaries the right to sue for breaches of fiduciary duty. Courts are free to take whatever action is appropriate against fiduciaries that breach their duties under ERISA, including their removal.[1] Fiduciaries who don't follow the investment principles as outlined in ERISA may be liable, and if so, may be ordered to personally restore any losses to the plan or to restore any profits made through improper use of plan assets.

There were over 2,400 cases filed against ERISA fiduciaries during a 44-month period from January 2005 to August 2008. Almost every case involved a breach a fiduciary duty. Many cases cite violations of the Prudent Man Rule, which points to the possibility of poor investment decision-making by plan trustees.[2]

In my opinion, the number of ERISA cases litigated each year represents only a small fraction of the fiduciary breaches that actually occur. Unfortunately, most employees who are in poorly managed plans don't know their rights under ERISA and wouldn't have the financial resources to bring legal action even if they did know. Employees in small plans are particularly vulnerable because attorneys don't have a large financial incentive to pursue small plan trustees. That could change in the years ahead as employees become aware of their rights and seek damages for mismanaged plans in large class action lawsuits.

Delegation of Responsibility under ERISA

Trustees subject to ERISA can mitigate some of their fiduciary responsibilities and potential liabilities by retaining an investment advisor who accepts responsibility and any associated liability for the selection, monitoring, and replacement of plan investment options. This is achieved through a written contract between the trustees and an advisor, in which the advisor becomes a legally bound ERISA section 3(38) defined Investment Manager.

A 3(38) Investment Manager must be a bank, insurance company, or a registered investment advisor (RIA) subject to the Investment Advisers Act of 1940. Brokerage firms and the stock-brokers that they employ cannot be a 3(38) Investment Manager, that is unless a firm is also registered as an RIA and contracted under these services with a plan provider.

Upon becoming an ERISA section 3(38) Investment Manager, the advisor is an Independent Fiduciary to the plan as defined under ERISA section 405(d)(1). This makes the advisor solely responsible and liable for investment decisions with respect to the plan assets under their control. Plan trustees retain the responsibility to prudently select, monitor, and replace a 3(38) Investment Manager as needed.

The Plight of the Small Plan

In most small businesses, the owners are typically ERISA plan trustees. This is a dangerous situation for business owners. It's been my experience working with hundreds of small business plans that many owners/trustees have no idea and only a few have a vague idea of their significant fiduciary responsibilities and liabilities with respect to the plans they oversee. I have seen small business owners lose most of their wealth because they made bad decisions in their company pension plan and decided to make their employees whole rather than face litigation.

Many small business owners rely on the guidance of financial consultants from brokerage firms and insurance companies when they select investments for their retirement plans. Some business owners believe that these consultants provide a layer of protection in the event something goes wrong with the plan and they're sued by their employees. This is not correct. As mentioned previously, stockbrokers and insurance agents are considered product sales representatives. Consequently, they're not considered fiduciaries under ERISA and therefore have no fiduciary responsibility or liability with respect to ERISA plans.

An ERISA retirement plan is no place for a small business owner to play the market or try to extract excess returns from exotic investments. This misguided conviction has bankrupt many small business owners. ERISA attorneys make quick work of small business owners who claim to be prudent investment experts.

Being a steward of other people's retirement money is a huge responsibility, and ERISA demands accountability. If you're a trustee under ERISA who is overseeing a small retirement plan, even if most of the money is your own, for your sake and the sake of your business, select only passively managed low-cost index funds and ETFs for the plan. A well-managed and prudently invested retirement plan is a wonderful benefit for you and your employees. It helps create employee loyalty, provides good tax benefits, and helps you and your employees retire in dignity.

Self-Directed Retirement Plans

Self-directed retirement plans such as 401(k) plans are a large and growing part of retirement savings in the United States. Over 650,000 self-directed retirement plans exist of all sizes covering nearly 50 million American workers as active participants. About 47 percent of plan assets were held in mutual funds with the remainder of assets held at other institutions such as insurance companies and banks.[3]

A self-directed retirement plan such as a 401(k) allows employees to select their own investments from a preselected list of investment options. Plan trustees and other designated fiduciaries are ordinarily responsible for selecting, monitoring, and replacing investment options in the plan. In addition, these fiduciaries are responsible for containing costs and must ensure all charges are reasonable, given the services rendered.

Section 404(c) of ERISA provides a safe harbor to 401(k) trustees from the investment decisions made by plan participants within the plan investment options. For an example, if a participant was attempting to time the stock market and lost money, the trustees are not liable for the loss. However, trustees remain responsible for selecting and monitoring the investment options offered to participants in the plan. They remain legally responsible for ensuring that investment options are prudently selected, monitored against the proper benchmarks, and replaced when prudent to do so. Imprudent selection, inadequate monitoring, and lack of replacement by the trustees of a 401(k) plan can put them in the crosshairs of ERISA litigation attorneys.

One of the largest alleged imprudent investment option selection lawsuits involves Wal-Mart's $10 billion 401(k) plan. For more than a decade, the Wal-Mart employee 401(k) plan was advised by Merrill Lynch. The lawsuit claims that Merrill Lynch chose mutual funds with high fees that made payments to Merrill Lynch. The mutual fund investment options in the Wal-Mart 401(k) plan provided only retail class shares that charged significantly higher fees than institutional shares for the same fund. Seven of the ten funds charged 12b-1 sales fees from which participants derive no benefit. In addition, Wal-Mart trustees didn't change the investment options in the 401(k) plan despite the fact that they knew most of the funds underperformed. The lawsuit alleged that Wal-Mart employees who are plan participants paid $140 million in excess fees as a result of these infractions over a six-year period through 2007.[4] Merrill Lynch was not named in the case because in their role as a broker-age firm, they're not a fiduciary to the plan.

A U.S. District Court trial judge dismissed the case in late 2008, but that decision was unanimously overruled in 2009 by the 8th U.S. Circuit Court of Appeals. This sent the case to U.S. District Court where it is pending. In related news, Wal-Mart has made changes to its 401(k) plan that reduces costs to employees who are participants.

The Wal-Mart case highlights the need for trustees to prudently select, monitor, and replace investment options as needed in self-directed retirement plans. It also highlights the need to review costs and ensure that plan participants are not overpaying for participa-tion in a self-directed plan. Finally, the case shows that brokerage firms take no responsibly for their poor investment selections and bear no liability for the extra expenses incurred by plan participants.

Misguided Fund Selection

401(k) trustees suffer from the same biases as other investors when selecting investment options for the plans they oversee. On average, these administrators select funds that are recommended to them by consultants, which tend to be funds that recently outperformed randomly selected funds of the same type or style. However, when trustees change 401(k) investment options, the new funds perform no better than the dropped funds.

In 2006, Edwin Elton, Martin Gruber, and Christopher Blake published an enlightening research paper on 401(k) invest-ment options.[5] The major source of data for their study was 11-K filings for 401(k) plans with the U.S. Securities and Exchange Commission. 11-K filings are required to be filed every year for all 401(k) plans that offer company stock as an investment option for plan participants. The team gathered data on all 401(k) plans that filed 11-K reports in 1994 and traced the sample through 1999.

The authors selected 43 plans to study. These plans started with 116 funds, but during the course of the seven-year period, 215 funds were added and 45 were dropped. This is close to one addi-tional investment option for each plan per year during the period and as many dropped options as there were plans.

The trustees showed no skill in adding funds or replacing poor performing funds. The new funds tended to be the outperforming ones in a category that was already in the plan. Trustees also added funds from hot sectors and investment styles. Although the study found, on average, that the plan trustees chose actively managed funds that had recently performed well, these funds underperformed passive index funds. To make matters worse, the preponderance of evidence showed that the dropped funds performed better than the new funds in subsequent years.

Another interesting finding by the authors was the chronic lack of skill by certain plan trustees when selecting new investment options. In these plans, the past poor performance of investment options predicted future poor performance of new investment options. It seems that trustees who are bad at selecting mutual funds for their employees are not just randomly bad, they are chronically bad!

Turn-key Plans

Another reason why many self-directed retirement plans have poor investment options is because they are heavily influenced by advisors who work for brokerage firms and insurance companies. These individuals tend to recommend turn-key packages that are easy for the plan fiduciaries to administer, but carry high costs.

The costs in turn-key plans typically include recordkeeping, plan and participant servicing, compliance and legal, tax reporting, education, and investment management services to name a few. A business may see this bundled product as an attractive offering because (1) it is a new benefit for employees; (2) the owners or other trustees don't believe they have to do very much; and (3) the plan participants pay for most of the costs through investment fund fees, not the employer.

Often the investment options recommended in turn-key plans are expensive proprietary mutual funds managed by the brokerage firms selling the package. This offers the highest payout to the brokerage firm because they are keeping the entire management fee and any administrative costs.

Stockbrokers and insurance representatives selling turn-key plans may not want to appear as though they are completely arrogant or greedy. So, they often recommend a few funds from other companies and perhaps even an index fund. This doesn't mean they're not getting paid for recommending those funds. You can bet the brokerage firm has a revenue sharing arrangement with the outside fund companies whose funds they recommend, including the providers of index funds. Although the brokerage company makes less revenue under this arrangement than they would if money flowed solely into their proprietary funds, they're still not giving up that much.

Turn-key plans may be an attractive option for a start-up plan because it keeps the employer costs low; however, as assets build up in the plan, the turn-key self-directed retirement plan packages tend to become extremely expensive. The fees in the funds never go down regardless of the amount invested (case in point, the Wal-Mart lawsuit).

A better option for a growing plan is to separate the record-keeping services from the investment options. The trustees of a plan should hire a recordkeeping company and pay a negligible fee per year per participant for this service. This separation allows trustees to offer better investment options centered on low-cost and well diversified index funds and ETFs.

The Government Thrift Savings Plan

The Thrift Savings Plan (TSP) is a defined contribution retirement savings and investment plan for federal employees and military personnel. The TSP offers federal employees the same type of savings and tax benefits that many private corporations offer their employees under 401(k) plans. The retirement income received from a TSP account will depend on how much an employee contributed to their account during their working years and the earnings on those contributions.

The unique element of the TSP is its investment options. They are very low-cost passively managed index funds. Each fund is managed at only 0.028 percent per year. That's less than 3/100ths of one percent!

There are five core funds and five balanced fund investment options. The five balanced funds are an appropriate mix of the five core funds given different employee retirement dates. These are called target retirement funds. The fund options are:

1. Government Securities Investment (G) Fund: short-term U.S. Treasury securities
2. Fixed Income Index Investment (F) Fund: Barclays Capital U.S. Aggregate Bond Index
3. Common Stock Index Investment (C) Fund: S&P 500 Index
4. Small Cap Stock Index Investment (S) Fund: Dow Jones U.S. Completion Total Stock Market Index

5. International Stock Index Investment (I) Fund: MSCI EAFE
6. Five Lifecycle (L) Funds: L 2040, L 2030, L 2020, L 2010, and L Income Fund.

The Lifecycle funds are balanced funds that have varying asset allocations among the G, F, C, S, and I Funds tailored to different retirement time horizons. The L Funds are rebalanced to their target allocations each business day. The investment mix of each fund adjusts quarterly to become more conservative investments as the fund's time horizon shortens. The L 2010 fund is for participants who will withdraw their money between now and 2014, according to the TSP web site.[6]

In my opinion, the TSP is a very good model for a 401(k) plan. All the investment options are very low-cost index funds (core funds) and the balanced funds are composed of those same funds. The TSP has all the investment options that any plan sponsor could wish for: short-term government fund, bond market index fund, U.S. large cap fund index fund, U.S. small cap fund index fund, international index fund, and balanced funds that provide participants with various allocations to their low-cost core funds.

Granted, some of the investment options in the TSP may not be the ideal ones for exposure to various markets. For example, the EAFE index used by TSP only includes developed markets in Europe and the Far East including Australia. I would have preferred the FTSE All-World ex-US Index fund for an international fund because a fund tracking that index includes emerging markets, South and Central American markets, and North American markets not including the U.S. 401(k) trustees will decide what indexes and fund options are the most appropriate for the plans they oversee.

Summary

Pension trustees who oversee retirement money are fiduciaries. The law requires that they act in the best interest of plan participants and their beneficiaries. Plan trustees have a legal obligation to carry out the express terms of the plan document, to prudently select investments, and to avoid personal conflicts of interest.

ERISA is the federal law that governs all private pension funds including self-directed plans such as 401(k) plans. Relevant state laws and UMPERSA direct state, county, and municipal retirement plans. Trustees should know which law governs the particular trust they manage and be familiar with the law. Since all pension trustees are fiduciaries, they should be familiar with the Uniform Prudent Investor Act because it sets forth in a very concise way the prudent fiduciary standards that regulate their investment conduct.

Passive investing is an ideal choice for pension plans, especially small plans. The trustees of these plans typically are not professional investors, yet they have tremendous responsibilities in regard to selecting investments for a plan. Trustees who select investment options for 401(k) and similar plans should study the federal government's TSP and attempt to emulate those investment options. It's the prudent choice.

14

The Passive Case for Advisors

Advisors play an important role in their clients' lives. They guide investors by helping to form investment policy, implementing the policy, and maintaining the policy in an efficient and disciplined manner.

Advisors spend much of their time consulting with clients rather than conducting in-depth investment analysis. Consequently, a realistic advisor who tries to find active management strategies that beat the market will eventually conclude that their efforts have a low probability for success. If an advisor does beat the market, chances are they got lucky. However, getting lucky isn't a good business plan. Active management isn't a good long-term solution for advisors or their clients..

A passive investment philosophy is an ideal strategy for an advisor's long-term business needs. It's low cost, tax efficient, non-speculative, and provides clients with the highest probability for success.

Given that passive management is the ideal solution for most advisors, why do so many cling to active management strategies that detract from their primary job as a consultant? I am convinced they do this because they believe it's what their clients want. Most advisors know active strategies don't work well, and will admit privately that they don't, yet many continue to use them because they believe that this is why their clients have hired them. Nothing could be further from the truth.

Individuals who go to an advisor aren't looking to beat the markets. They're looking for prudent investment advice that's appropriate for their needs. They may say they would like to beat the market, but that's where education comes in. Advising isn't about betting the markets. It's about providing portfolio solutions for important client needs such as achieving financial security.

This chapter is an attempt to persuade those advisors who are using active management to change their methods. Rather than continuing to have revolving door clientele by selling the sizzle of active management strategies that have little chance for success, foster long-term client relationships by educating clients on the many benefits of passive investing. This is a win-win situation.

More Risk Means More Fees

Higher portfolio returns are earned only as a result of taking higher risks. Thus, by default, advisors who use active management strategies are taking more risks with their clients' money. But who benefits most from this extra risk taking? I argue that advisors benefit most. First, they demand a high fee for the hope of market beating returns. Second, if by luck or skill they're successful for a while, an advisor will aggressively promote their good fortune by seeking new business from investors who chase past performance. This can lead to a success providing luck doesn't change, but it's not a reliable business model.

Advisors who use active management promote the hope of market beating performance to sell their services to prospective clients. The glitter of potential higher returns works on prospective clients because people like to believe they're going to win. Chances are they won't win, but until the clients figure that out, the advisor collects their hefty fee.

In contrast, advisors using passive strategies grow their business slowly by educating prospective clients. This isn't an easy task. There's a lot of lead time in the education process because passive concepts are counterintuitive. Many people have difficultly conceptualizing that market returns are the best returns for most investors in the long-term.

Passive investing as a business model isn't a hot-money approach, and the people who hire passive advisors aren't looking for that. They're a more educated clientele. They want a sensible strategy that's rooted in logic and disciplined in its implementation.

Passive investing is a win-win business model that creates better relationships and greater client loyalty. This helps clients stay on course in poor market conditions, which leads to better client returns in the long run.

Types of Advisors

Advisors come in two types: registered investment advisors (RIA) who are legal fiduciaries, and brokerage firm representatives who aren't. A broker is a licensed representative of a securities firm and shares in the fees and commissions collected by that securities firm. An RIA is paid a fee directly from their clients for managing portfolios and providing other financial services.

Different government regulators oversee brokers and RIAs. Brokers are regulated by the Financial Industry Regulatory Authority (FINRA). RIAs are regulated by the SEC or their home state depending on the size of the advisory firm. To research information about a broker or an RIA, including past grievances, go to www.SEC.gov/investor/brokers.htm.

How do you tell the difference between an RIA and broker? Brokers are indentified by the words "Securities offered through (name of firm)" on business cards, web sites, and all stationery. Securities law requires this disclosure.

As mentioned previously, only RIAs are fiduciaries by law while stockbrokers are currently exempt. The law considers stockbrokers to be product sales representatives rather than advisors. However, they do have a suitability standard, which isn't as stringent as a fiduciary standard.

This difference between suitability and fiduciary care can be explained using an analogy. If you walk into a Chevrolet dealership, a salesperson is going to try to sell you a suitable vehicle that fits your needs. The salesperson isn't going to recommend a vehicle made by Ford or any other competitor even if they believe a different brand than a Chevrolet would be perfect for you. In contrast, if you personally paid a car-buying consultant to help you select a vehicle, then they would be obligated to recommend the best vehicle for your needs regardless of the make or model. The dealer is a salesperson who is recommending something suitable their firm sells while the car buying consultant is a fiduciary who is obligated to recommend the best vehicle.

Many government elected officials in Washington want all stockbrokers to be fiduciaries regardless of their product affiliations. Included in the Restoring American Financial Stability Act of 2010 is a provision for the SEC to study this idea and to make changes as appropriate. Thus, the law could change in the future to include stockbrokers, insurance agents, and other sales oriented professionals who render financial advice as part of their job to act as a fiduciary.

Brokerage Use of Passive Has Expanded

Access to low-cost index funds was very limited at brokerage firms during the 1990s. Most index fund providers didn't sell through the brokerage firms because they didn't want to pay the hefty fees that those firms wanted for access to their distribution channels.

I was a broker for more than 10 years from the late 1980s until the late 1990s before starting an investment advisory firm. Brokers like me who came to believe in low-cost index investing had to leave the business and form RIAs to pursue what we believed was in the best interest of clients.

Today, the world is different. Advisors of every type have access to a wide variety of index products through index funds and ETFs. It's no longer necessary for brokers to leave the industry to pursue a prudent passive strategy for their clients. In particular, the growth of ETFs provides low-cost index products covering almost every asset class and style. It is now possible for all advisors to build a client-centered business using low-cost passive strategies.

The Role of the Fiduciary Advisor

An advisor in the context of this chapter is considered a fiduciary. Even though brokers are not fiduciaries, I'm including them in this role because they should act as a fiduciary when advising clients and may be fiduciaries by law in the future.

A fiduciary advisor is required to prudently recommend an investment strategy that best serves the client. A fiduciary advisor must avoid conflicts of interest that put the advisor's business dealings ahead of a client's needs.

Fiduciary advisors are subject to the same legal acts, case law, and regularity opinions as other fiduciaries as covered in trust law in Chapter 12 and pension law in Chapter 13. Advisors who manage the investment process are held to a prudent expert standard in private retirement plans and a prudent investor standard in private trusts, charitable accounts, and public pension funds. Knowledge of legal acts and standards governing fiduciary duty is good practice for any advisor.

There are also different types of fiduciary advisors. For example, under the Employee Retirement Income Security Act (ERISA), there is a section 3(38) fiduciary and a section 3(21) fiduciary. An ERISA section 3(38) fiduciary is an investment manager who has discretion over account assets by contract with a plan sponsor. They are responsible for buying and selling securities in an investment portfolio and are legally accountable for their decisions. In contrast, a section 3(21) fiduciary refers to a person or firm who doesn't manage assets directly. Rather, they provide nondiscretionary advice or services such as administrative tasks and performance monitoring.

Fiduciary advisors are paid a fee for their service. The fee is typically an hourly rate or periodic retainer for a nondiscretionary advisor or a percentage of assets under management (AUM) for a discretionary asset manager. Brokers can also be held to a fiduciary standard when they place a client's assets in a fee-based managed account program.

Being a fiduciary advisor can be complicated. Even so, it's necessary for a fiduciary advisor to stay current with, and diligently conform to, the best practices as outlined in the legal and regulatory requirements. There are several sources of information for fiduciary advisors to keep up with the latest changes. These include regulatory releases, legal opinions, and private educational sources that explain it all such as Fiduciary360 and the Foundation for Fiduciary Studies.

What Clients Expect from Advisors

In a perfect world, all investors are knowledgeable and rational. They form their own investment ideas after diligent study and then seek like-minded advisors to help implement these ideas.

In the real world, many investors who go to advisors are not very knowledgeable. They don't know the intricacies of goal setting, risk assessment, asset allocation, and investment selection. That's why they're seeking the help of a professional.

People seek financial advisors to help them achieve their financial goals. They expect the advice they'll receive will be thoughtful, honest, and analytically sound. They're looking for advisors who'll listen to their needs, analyze their situation, and present solutions in a straightforward and efficient manner.

Clients are interested in an investment strategy that meets their goals. They want to know how much risk is appropriate for their situation, and they'll want to know what return to expect in the long term. They typically don't want to know or need to know all the details behind an investment strategy because that's going to be the advisor's job. While everyone is interested in the total cost of investing including taxes, most investors are not overly concerned about paying advisors their fee.

The Advisor as Educator

Investment strategy can be a confusing part of the education process. Most laymen don't know the difference between passive index funds and actively managed funds or strategic asset allocation and tactical asset allocation. It is up to the advisor to explain these differences and the pros and cons of each.

The advisor's role as an educator places them in a position of responsibility that often transcends their role as an investment manager. This teacher-student relationship goes beyond the implementation of an investment policy. Most people place great trust in their advisors, who they expect are providing unbiased information.

Table 14.1 provides an overview of four portfolio strategy options using mutual funds and ETFs. This table is a good start for educating a client on different investment strategies that are available to them, and the comparable cost of each strategy.

At the core, there are two dimensions to investment management. The first dimension is asset allocation decisions and the second is security selection. Investors should first decide which asset

Table 14.1   Four Portfolio Strategy Options

	Passive Funds index funds and some index based ETFs)	Active Funds (including actively managed ETFs)
Maintain a Passive Strategic Asset Allocation	#1 Passive allocation using passively managed funds	#2 Passive allocation using actively managed funds
Employ an Active Tactical Asset Allocation	#3 Active allocation using passively managed funds	#4 Active allocation using actively managed funds

classes they will invest in and then decide how to invest in those asset classes.

We'll make two assumptions when reviewing the four investment strategies in Table 14.1. First, the client is agnostic about using any particular strategy. Second, the advisor is paid the same fee regardless of the strategy.

- **Strategy #1:** Passive allocation using passively managed funds.
  - A long-term strategic asset allocation is formed based on client needs.
  - The investments selected to represent asset classes are low-cost index funds and ETFs.
  - Asset classes are rebalanced as needed to maintain the target allocation.
  - This strategy has the lowest mutual fund fees and trading costs, and has the lowest tax bite for taxable investors.
- **Strategy #2:** Passive allocation using actively managed funds.
  - A long-term strategic asset allocation is formed based on client needs.
  - Actively managed funds are selected with the intent to outperform the asset classes they represent on a risk-adjusted basis.
  - Asset classes are rebalanced as needed to maintain the target allocation.
  - This strategy has a higher mutual fund costs due to actively managed fund fees and a high tax bite due to the capital gain distributions from those funds.
- **Strategy #3:** Active asset allocation using passively managed funds.
  - A tactical allocation is formed based the advisor's comparative valuation of asset classes.
  - The investments selected to represent asset classes are low-cost index funds and ETFs.
  - Asset class allocations are changed when the advisor determines relative valuations have changed or the advisor's perception changes.
  - This strategy has low mutual fund fees and marginal trading costs due to trading from asset allocation shifts and a potentially high tax bite due to realized capital gains from tactical shifts that are assumed to be profitable.

- **Strategy #4:** Active asset allocation using actively managed funds.
  - A tactical allocation is formed based the advisor's comparative valuation of asset classes.
  - Actively managed funds are selected with the intent to outperform the asset classes they represent on a risk-adjusted basis.
  - Asset class allocations are changed when the advisor determines relative valuations have changed or the advisor's perception changes.
  - This strategy has the highest costs due to the expensive actively managed fund fees and trading costs from asset allocation shifts. It also has the highest tax bite due to capital gains distributions from active funds and a portfolio's realized capital gain from tactical shifts

Table 14.1 is a simple way to map out different strategies and costs to investors. Once clients understand these basic decisions, they will most certainly start asking questions. This is a good sign because it means the client is learning.

Strategy and the Fiduciary Advisor

All fiduciaries have certain duties with respect to investment management. Among them are the duty to diversify, the duty to control costs and taxes when applicable, the duty to avoid unnecessary risk, and the duty to loyalty by avoiding conflicts of interest. Let's look at the four investment strategies from a fiduciary's standpoint:

- **The duty to diversify**. There is no definitive statement in trust law that says how much a portfolio should be diversified, although there is wording that states, "Risk that can be eliminated by adding different stocks (or bonds) is uncompensated risk. The object of diversification is to minimize this uncompensated risk of having too few investments."[1] By definition, index funds provide the most diversification in each asset class and eliminate all uncompensated risk. In contrast, active fund managers rely on less diversification to beat the index. The managers either limit their holdings to a few favorable securities or they avoid unfavorable sectors. In addition, strategic asset allocation maintains broad diversification to many asset classes while tactical asset allocation may have no exposure or limited exposure to one or more major asset classes.

- **The duty to control cost and taxes when applicable.** There is no statement in trust law as to what the cost of investing should be, only that "it is important for trustees to make careful cost comparisons, particularly among similar products of a specific type being considered for a trust portfolio."[2] Index funds have much lower expenses than active funds that invest in the same class of securities. They also have low capital gain distributions each year, which lowers the tax cost in taxable accounts. In addition, a strategic asset allocation has limited trading that is generally associated with rebalancing. Tactical asset allocation strategies have higher turnover, and this increases trading costs and potentially creates higher capital gains for taxable accounts.

- **The duty to loyalty by avoiding conflicts of interest.** The law is very explicit in regard to loyalty: "The duty of loyalty is perhaps the most characteristic rule of trust law, requiring the trustee to act exclusively for the beneficiaries, as opposed to acting for the trustee's own interest or that of third parties."[3] If an advisor is an investment manager who is paid for managing assets but is viewed by the client as an unbiased consultant, that advisor has a fiduciary responsibility to disclose investment alternatives. The duty to loyalty is often breached by financial advisors and financial planners who act as a consultant first, and then refer clients to their own money management services. When advisors are viewed by their clients as an unbiased source of investment information, and those advisors ultimately recommend that clients use their money management services or the money management services of their firm or an affiliate, and does not recommend other unaffiliated alternatives with equal confidence, advisors are in breach of their fiduciary duty.

A fiduciary advisor is an ethical advisor starting from the moment they make initial contact with a potential new client. This means acting as a fiduciary before a legal contract is signed.

When an inexperienced person visits an advisor for advice and councel, it is the responsibility of the advisor to disclose how they are paid up front. It's also prudent to explain to a potential client that any advice given could be biased toward a particular investment strategy. Even a passive advisor should make this clear. If an advisor doesn't make these discloses, it could be viewed as a breach of their fiduciary responsibility.

What Advisors Present

Here is a real irony in the advisor business. Despite the fact that passive strategies are the most prudent choice for almost all investment advisors, a majority recommend something else.

Why do more advisors recommend active strategies over passive even though they are supposed to be acting in a fiduciary capacity? My belief is that they incorrectly assume a person wouldn't hire them otherwise. Many advisors falsely believe that competing on returns is the only way they'll attract new clients.

Here are a few reasons why I believe that advisors consistently recommend active strategies even though it's not in the best interest of their clients or their business:

"Clients don't need me if I just buy a few index funds and let the portfolio sit."

This is an unfounded excuse. Most investors won't implement a passive strategy on their own even if they know which funds to buy and how much to buy. People go to advisors for leadership, discipline, and guidance. That's what you provide.

"My fee isn't justified by following a simple passive strategy."

Advisor fees can be lower for a passive strategy but not always. Your fee is your fee. It keeps you in business so that you'll be there for clients when they really need you. That's a service worth paying for.

"My clients will expect me to do something in a bear market."

Yes, they expect you to act rationally and follow a disciplined strategy. They'll expect you to stay true to the investment policy. They expect you to do nothing when nothing is the right thing to do!

"I have always done active management. If I change, I'll look stupid."

Clients admire and respect advisors who fess-up and are willing to change when they find a better solution. It shows honesty and integrity.

"I'll never get new business because other advisors are going to outperform."

Recruitment is slower. Educating potential clients takes time. On the other hand, retention is considerably higher because passive advisors have a better understanding of their client's financial needs and the strategy better satisfies those needs.

These are all wrong assumptions. It's not about beating the market. Clients don't care to hear sound bites on how a proprietary trading model added 100 basis points of return over the last 30 days. That's setting them up for disappointment and ultimately terminating the agreement with an advisor.

There is an expression in the Gospel that sums up advisors who practice active management: "Live by the sword, die by the sword." The Chinese also have a saying that if you sit by the river long enough, the dead body of your enemy will float by. The clients of active advisors will eventually become the clients of passive advisors because the active advisors will eventually fall on their swords.

What clients want to hear is sound advice on how they can meet their financial objectives. Vanguard became one of the largest global investment managers over the past 35 years because people realized on their own that seeking alpha in mutual funds doesn't work. They realize that passive management works on a portfolio level better than active management. Advisors who use passive strategies and foster this ideal, are in an ideal position to capture more clients and keep them longer.

Passive Benefits to Advisors

There are many benefits to advisors who switch to passive investing for their clients. Here is a partial list of the benefits:

1. Easy to explain investment performance.
2. No more excuses for poor active performance.
3. No more frustrating market guessing or playing mutual fund roulette.
4. High retention from spending more time with current clients.
5. Creates more time to look for new long-term clients.

A passive strategy is best for investors and best for advisors. Passive investing based on a long-term strategic allocation represented by index funds and ETFs is the ideal option for client success and for building a healthy, long-lasting advisor business. Every advisor has access to these funds today through ETFs, even brokers, making this a win-win proposition for everyone.

Summary

A passive advisory practice reflects on an advisor's intellect and integrity. A passive advisor doesn't take more risk in client accounts for the sake of earning higher fees and potentially promoting the returns to other potential investors. Passive advisors gain new business by educating potential clients, by sitting on the same side of the table as their clients, and by being brutally honest about investment decisions. In turn, the strategy becomes the best long-term business model for investment advisors. It's a win-win strategy.

Glossary

active management   An investment strategy that seeks to outperform the average return of a financial market. Active managers rely on research, market forecasts, and their own judgment and experience in selecting securities to buy and sell.

annualize   To make a figure for a period of less than a year apply to a full year, usually for purposes of comparison. For instance, a portfolio turnover rate of 36 percent over a six-month period could be converted to an annualized rate of 72 percent.

ask price   The price at which a security is offered for sale. For a no-load mutual fund, the ask price is the same as the fund's net asset value per share. Also called offering price.

automatic reinvestment   An arrangement by which the dividends or other earnings from an investment vehicle are used to buy additional shares in the investment vehicle.

average coupon   The average interest rate (coupon rate) on all the bonds in a portfolio.

average effective maturity   A weighted average of the maturity dates for all securities in a money market or bond fund. (The maturity date is the date when the buyer of a money market instrument or a bond will be repaid by the security's issuer.) The longer the average maturity, the more a fund's share price will move up or down in response to changes in interest rates.

back-end load   A sales fee charged by some mutual funds when an investor sells fund shares. Also called a contingent deferred sales charge.

benchmark index   An index that correlates with a fund; used to measure a fund manager's performance.

beta   A measure of the magnitude of a portfolio's past share-price fluctuations in relation to the ups and downs of the overall market (or an appropriate market index). The market (or index) is assigned a beta of 1.00, so a portfolio with a beta of 1.20 would have seen its share price rise or fall by 12 percent when the overall market rose or fell by 10 percent.

bid-ask spread The difference between what a buyer is willing to bid (pay) for a security and the seller's asking (offer) price.

book value A company's assets, minus any liabilities and intangible assets.

book-to-market value (BtM) The book value of a company divided by its market value.

broker/broker-dealer An individual or firm that buys or sells mutual funds or other securities for the public.

capital gain/loss The difference between the sale price of an asset—such as a mutual fund, stock, or bond—and the original cost of the asset.

capital gains distributions Payments to mutual fund shareholders of gains realized during the year on securities that the fund has sold at a profit, minus any realized losses.

cash investments Short-term debt instruments—such as commercial paper, banker's acceptances, and Treasury bills—that mature in less than one year. Also known as money market instruments or cash reserves.

certified financial planner (CFP) An investment professional who has passed exams administered by the CFP Board of Standards on subjects such as taxes, securities, insurance, and estate planning.

certified public accountant (CPA) An investment professional who is licensed by a state to practice public accounting.

chartered financial analyst (CFA) An investment professional who has met competency standards in economics, securities, portfolio management, and financial accounting as determined by the Institute of Chartered Financial Analysts.

closed-end fund A mutual fund that has a fixed number of shares, usually listed on a major stock exchange.

commodities Unprocessed goods, such as grains, metals, and minerals, traded in large amounts on a commodities exchange.

consumer price index (CPI) A measure of the price change in consumer goods and services. The CPI is used to track the pace of inflation.

correlation coefficient A number between −1 and 1 that measures the degree to which two variables are linearly related.

cost basis The original cost of an investment. For tax purposes, the cost basis is subtracted from the sale price to determine any capital gain or loss.

country risk The possibility that political events (e.g., a war, national elections); financial problems (e.g., rising inflation, government default);

or natural disasters (e.g., an earthquake, a poor harvest) will weaken a country's economy and cause investments in that country to decline.

coupon/coupon rate   The interest rate that a bond issuer promises to pay the bondholder until the bond matures.

credit rating   A published ranking, based on careful financial analysis, of a creditor's ability to pay the interest or principal owed on a debt.

credit risk   The possibility that a bond issuer will fail to repay interest and principal in a timely manner. Also called default risk.

currency risk   The possibility that returns from investments in foreign securities could be reduced because of a rise in the value of one's own currency compared to foreign currencies. Also called exchange-rate risk.

custodian   Either (1) a bank, agent, trust company, or other organization responsible for safeguarding financial assets or (2) the individual who oversees the mutual fund assets of a minor's custodial account.

derivative   A financial contract whose value is based on, or derived from, a traditional security (such as a stock or bond), an asset (such as a commodity), or a market index (such as the S&P 500 index).

discount broker   A brokerage firm that executes orders to buy and sell securities at commission rates lower than those of a full-service brokerage.

distributions   Either (1) withdrawals made by the owner from an individual retirement account (IRA) or (2) payments of dividends and/or capital gains by a mutual fund.

dividend reinvestment plan   The automatic reinvestment of shareholder dividends in more shares of the company's stock.

dividend yield   The annual rate of return on a share of stock, determined by dividing the annual dividend by the current share price. In a stock mutual fund, this figure represents the average dividend yield of the stocks held by the fund.

dollar cost averaging   Investing equal amounts of money at regular intervals on an ongoing basis. This technique ensures that an investor buys fewer shares when prices are high and more shares when prices are low.

earnings per share   A company's earnings divided by the number of common shares outstanding.

efficient market   The theory that stock prices reflect all market information that is known by all investors.

enhanced index fund   A mutual fund designed to generally track an index, but may also use leverage, futures, and trading strategies to outperform the index. Also referred to as a strategy index and an alpha-seeking index.

exchange-traded fund (ETF) A mutual fund that trades like a stock on a stock exchange. The fund's approximate net asset value (NAV) is calculated every 15 seconds by the exchange it trades on. ETF shares trade close to the calculated price because of an arbitrage process that involves a third party called an authorized participant.

exchange-traded note An unsecured debt security issued by a bank or finance company that acts like an exchange-traded fund in that it tracks an index and also has the credit risk of the issuer.

ex-dividend date The date when a distribution of dividends and/or capital gains is deducted from a mutual fund's assets or set aside for payment to shareholders. On the ex-dividend date, the fund's share price drops by the amount of the distribution (plus or minus any market activity). Also known as the reinvestment date.

expense ratio The percentage of a portfolio's average net assets used to pay its annual expenses. The expense ratio, which includes management fees, administrative fees, and any 12b-1 fees, directly reduces returns to investors.

factors Specific risks in a portfolio, such as market risk, size risk, value risk, political risk, interest-rate risk, and credit risk.

Federal Reserve The central bank that regulates the supply of money and credit throughout the United States. The Fed's seven-member board of governors, appointed by the president, has significant influence on U.S. monetary and economic policy.

fee-only advisor An arrangement in which a financial advisor charges a set hourly rate or an agreed-upon percentage of assets under management for a financial plan.

Financial Industry Regulatory Authority (FINRA) Formerly the National Association of Securities Dealers (NASD), an organization of brokers and dealers designed to protect the investing public from fraudulent acts.

front-end load A sales commission charged at the time of purchase by some mutual funds and other investment vehicles.

fund family A group of mutual funds sponsored by the same organization, often offering exchange privileges between funds and combined account statements for multiple funds.

fundamental analysis Examining a company's financial statements and operations as a means of forecasting stock price movements.

futures/futures contracts Derivatives used to buy or sell specific amounts of a specific investment (such as grain or foreign currency) for an agreed-upon price at a certain time in the future.

global fund A mutual fund that invests in stocks of companies in both the United States and foreign countries.

gross domestic product (GDP) The value of all goods and services provided by U.S. labor in a given year. One of the primary measures of the U.S. economy, the GDP is issued quarterly by the Department of Commerce.

hedge A strategy in which one investment is used to offset the risk of another.

high-yield fund A mutual fund that invests primarily in bonds with a credit rating of BB or lower. Because of the speculative nature of high-yield bonds, high-yield funds are subject to greater share price volatility and greater credit risk than other types of bond funds.

index provider A company that constructs and maintains stock and bond indexes. The main providers are Standard & Poor's, Citigroup, Dow Jones, Barclays Capital, Morgan Stanley, Russell, and Wilshire.

indexing An investment strategy designed to match the average performance of a market and sectors of that market, usually at a very low cost compared to active funds.

inflation risk The possibility that increases in the cost of living will reduce or eliminate the returns on a particular investment.

interest-rate risk The possibility that a security or mutual fund will decline in value because of an increase in interest rates.

international fund A mutual fund that invests in securities traded in markets outside of the United States. Foreign markets present additional risks, including currency fluctuation and political instability.

investment advisor A person or organization that makes the day-to-day decisions regarding the investments in a portfolio. Also called a portfolio manager.

investment-grade bond A bond whose credit quality is considered to be among the highest by independent bond-rating agencies.

Jensen's alpha A ratio created by Michael Jensen that measures the return earned in excess of the risk free rate on a portfolio to the portfolio's total risk as measured by the standard deviation in its returns over the measurement period.

junk bond A bond with a credit rating of BB or lower. Also known as a high-yield bond because of the potential rewards offered to those who are willing to take on the additional risk of a lower-quality bond.

large cap A company whose stock market value is generally in excess of $10 billion, although the amount varies among index providers.

liquidity The degree of marketability of a security; that is, how quickly the security can be sold at a fair price and converted to cash.

load fund A mutual fund that levies a sales charge, when shares are bought (a front-end load) or when they are sold (a back-end load).

long-term capital gain A profit on the sale of a security or mutual fund share that has been held for more than one year.

management fee The amount a mutual fund pays to its investment advisor for the work of overseeing the fund's holdings. Also called an advisory fee.

market capitalization A determination of a company's value, calculated by multiplying the total number of shares of the company's stock outstanding by the price per share. Also called capitalization.

maturity/maturity date The date when the issuer of a money market instrument or bond agrees to repay the principal, or face value, to the buyer.

median market cap The midpoint of the market capitalization (market price multiplied by the number of shares outstanding) of the stocks in a portfolio. Half the stocks in the portfolio will have a higher market capitalization and half will have a lower market capitalization.

mid cap A company whose stock market value is between $2 billion and $10 billion, although the range varies among index providers.

momentum The tendency for a security's price to trend in one direction or another for a period of time.

municipal bonds Tax-exempt bonds issued by state, city, or local governments. The interest obtained from these bonds is generally free of federal income taxes, and sometimes state and local income taxes.

mutually exclusive The occurrence of one event excludes the possibility of another event. If an investment is a member of one index, this precludes membership in others.

negative correlation A situation in which the value of one of two investments moves opposite to the value of the other.

net asset value (NAV) The market value of a mutual fund or ETF's total assets minus liabilities, divided by the number of shares outstanding.

no-load fund A mutual fund that charges no sales commission or load.

nominal return The return on an investment before adjustment for inflation.

noncorrelation A situation in which the changes in the value of two different investments are completely independent of each other.

open-end fund An investment entity that has the ability to issue or redeem the number of shares outstanding on a daily basis.

operating expenses The amount paid for asset maintenance or the cost of doing business. Earnings are distributed after operating expenses are deducted.

option A derivatives contract in which a seller gives a buyer the right, but not the obligation, to buy or sell securities at a specified price on or before a given date.

overlap The situation that arises when two indexes or mutual funds are not mutually exclusive. The degree to which two funds or indexes have similar holdings, as measured in percentage of market value.

payable date The date when dividends or capital gains are paid to shareholders. For mutual funds, the payable date is usually within two to four days of the record date. The payable date also refers to the date on which a declared stock dividend or bond interest payment is scheduled to be paid.

portfolio transaction costs The expenses associated with buying and selling securities, including commissions, purchase and redemption fees, exchange fees, and other miscellaneous costs. In a mutual fund prospectus, these expenses would be listed separately from the fund's expense ratio. They do not include the bid-ask spread.

positive correlation A situation in which the value of one of two investments moves in unison with the value of the other.

premium An amount by which the price of a security exceeds the face value or redemption value of that security or the price of a comparable security or group of investments. It may indicate that a security is highly favored by investors. Also refers to a fee for obtaining insurance coverage.

price-to-book ratio (P/B) The price per share of a stock divided by the stock's book value (i.e., its net worth) per share. For a portfolio, the ratio is the weighted average price-to-book ratio of the stocks it holds.

price-to-earnings ratio (P/E) The share price of a stock divided by its per-share earnings over the past year. For a portfolio, the weighted-average

P/E ratio of the stocks in the portfolio. The P/E ratio is a good indicator of market expectations about a company's prospects; the higher the P/E ratio, the greater the expectations for a company's future growth in earnings.

prospectus A legal document that gives prospective investors information about a mutual fund, including discussions of its investment objectives and policies, risks, costs, and past performance. A prospectus must be provided to a potential investor before he or she can establish an account and must also be filed with the Securities and Exchange Commission (SEC).

proxy Written authorization by a shareholder giving someone else (such as fund or company management) the authority to vote his or her shares at a shareholders' meeting.

quantitative analysis In securities, an assessment of specific measurable factors, such as cost of capital; value of assets; and projection of sales, costs, earnings, and profits. Combined with more subjective or qualitative considerations (such as management effectiveness), quantitative analysis can enhance investment decisions and portfolios.

real estate investment trust (REIT) A company that manages a group of real estate investments and distributes at least 90 percent of its net earnings annually to its stockholders. REITs often specialize in a particular kind of property, such as office buildings, shopping centers, or hotels. They can invest in real estate, purchase real estate (an equity REIT), or provide loans to building developers (a mortgage REIT).

real return The inflation-adjusted return received on an investment. For example, if the nominal investment return for a particular period was 8 percent and inflation was 3 percent, the real return would be 5 percent (8 percent – 3 percent).

record date The date used to determine who is eligible to receive a company or fund's next distribution of dividends or capital gains.

redemption The return of an investor's principal in a security. Bond redemption can occur at or before maturity; mutual fund shares are redeemed at net asset value when an investor's holdings are liquidated.

redemption fee A fee charged by some mutual funds when an investor sells shares within a short period of time after their purchase.

registered investment advisor (RIA) An investment professional who is registered—but not endorsed—by the Securities and Exchange Commission (SEC) and may recommend certain types of investment products.

reinvestment Use of investment income to buy additional securities. Many mutual fund companies and investment services offer the automatic reinvestment of dividends and capital gains distributions as an option to investors.

return of capital A distribution that is not paid out of earnings and profits. It is a return of the investor's principal.

risk tolerance An investor's ability or willingness to endure declines in the price of investments while waiting for them to increase in value.

R-squared A measure of how much of a portfolio's performance can be explained by the returns on the overall market (or a benchmark index). If a portfolio's total return precisely matched the return on the overall market or benchmark, its R-squared would be 1.00. If a portfolio's total return bore no relationship to the market's returns, its R-squared would be 0.

sector diversification The percentage of a portfolio's stocks that is placed in companies in each of the major industry groups.

sector fund A mutual fund or ETF that concentrates on a relatively narrow market sector. These funds can experience higher share-price volatility than diversified funds because sector funds are subject to issues specific to a given sector.

Securities and Exchange Commission (SEC) The federal government agency that regulates mutual funds, registered investment advisors, the stock and bond markets, and broker-dealers. The SEC was established by the Securities Exchange Act of 1934.

Sharpe ratio A measure of risk-adjusted return. To calculate a Sharpe ratio, an asset's excess return (its return in excess of the return generated by risk-free assets such as Treasury bills) is divided by the asset's standard deviation. It can be calculated compared to a benchmark or an index.

short sale The sale of a security or option contract that is not owned by the seller, usually to take advantage of an expected drop in the price of the security or option. In a typical short sale transaction, a borrowed security or option is sold, and the borrower agrees to purchase a replacement security or option at the market price on or by a specified future date.

short-term capital gain A profit on the sale of a security or mutual fund share that has been held for one year or less. A short-term capital gain is taxed as ordinary income.

size factor The tendency for small cap stocks to outperform large cap stocks by more than can be explained by their higher beta alone.

small cap   A company whose stock market value is less than $2 billion, although the amount varies among index providers.

spread   For stocks and bonds, the difference between the bid price and the ask price.

standard deviation   A measure of the degree to which a fund's return varies from its previous returns or from the average return for all similar funds. The larger the standard deviation, the greater the likelihood (and risk) that a security's performance will fluctuate from the average return.

style drift   When an actively managed fund moves away from its stated investment objective over time.

swap agreement   A derivatives contract between two parties to exchange one security for another, to change the mix of a portfolio or the maturities of the bonds it includes, or to alter another aspect of a portfolio or financial arrangement, such as interest-rate payments or currencies.

tax deferral   Delaying the payment of income taxes on investment income. For example, owners of traditional individual retirement accounts (IRAs) do not pay income taxes on the interest, dividends, or capital gains accumulating in their retirement accounts until they begin making withdrawals.

tax swapping   Creating a tax loss by the simultaneous sale of one investment or fund and purchase of a similar investment or fund that is not substantially identical to it.

taxable equivalent yield   The return on a higher-paying but taxable investment that would equal the return on a tax-free investment. The equivalent yield depends on the investor's tax bracket.

tax-exempt bond   A bond, usually issued by a municipal, county, or state government, whose interest payments are not subject to federal, and in some cases state and local, income tax. See municipal bonds.

total return   A percentage change, over a specified period, in a mutual fund's net asset value, with the ending net asset value adjusted to account for the reinvestment of all distributions of dividends and capital gains.

transaction fee/commission   A charge assessed by an intermediary, such as a broker-dealer or a bank, for assisting in the sale or purchase of a security.

Treasury Inflation-Protected Security (TIPS)   A Treasury security that adjusts its interest and par value with the rate of inflation.

Treasury security A negotiable debt obligation issued by the U.S. government for a specific amount and maturity. Income from Treasury securities is exempt from state and local taxes but not from federal income tax.

Treynor ratio The Treynor ratio, named after Jack L. Treynor, is a measurement of the returns earned in excess of that which could have been earned on an investment that has no diversifiable risk per each unit of market risk assumed.

turnover rate An indication of trading activity during the past year. Portfolios with high turnover rates incur higher transaction costs and are more likely to distribute capital gains (which are taxable to nonretirement accounts).

12b-1 fee An annual fee charged by some mutual funds to pay for marketing and distribution activities. The fee is taken directly from fund assets, which reduces a shareholder's total return.

unit investment trust (UIT) An SEC-registered investment that is an unmanaged portfolio of securities trading as a basket. UITs have a maturity date.

unrealized capital gain/loss An increase (or decrease) in the value of a security that is not yet realized because the security has not been sold.

volatility The degree of fluctuation in the value of a security, mutual fund, or index. Volatility is often expressed as a mathematical measure, such as a standard deviation or beta. The greater a fund's volatility, the wider the fluctuations between highs and lows.

yield curve A line plotted on a graph that depicts the yields of bonds of varying maturities, from short-term to long-term. The line, or curve, shows the relationship between short- and long-term interest rates.

yield-to-maturity The rate of return an investor would receive if the securities held in his or her portfolio were held until their maturity dates.

Notes

Preface

1. John C. Bogle, "The Chief Cornerstone," (speech, Superbowl of Indexing conference, Phoenix, Arizona, December 7, 2005).
2. Charles Ellis, "The Loser's Game," *Financial Analysts Journal* 31, no. 4 (1975): 19–26.
3. Burton Malkiel, interview by Geoff Colvin, *Wall Street Week with Fortune*, PBS, June 20, 2003, www.pbs.org/wsw/tvprogram/20030620.html.

Chapter 1: Framing the Debate

1. Wellington Fund, Prospectus, April 14, 1950, 2.
2. John C. Bogle, "The Economic Role of the Investment Company" (undergraduate thesis, Princeton University Department of Economics and Social Institution, April 21, 1951), 27. The paper points to a Wellington Fund sales brochure as the source for information, "Cost vs. Value," p. 3, n.d.
3. Bogle, 1951, 15, with further reference to *Trusts and Estates, LXXXVIII* (August 1949), 495.
4. Burton Malkiel, *A Random Walk Down Wall Street* (New York: W. W. Norton, 1973), 226.
5. John C. Bogle, "The First Index Mutual Fund: A History of Vanguard Index Trust and the Vanguard Index Strategy," John C. Bogle Research Center, 1996, www.vanguard.com/bogle_site/lib/sp19970401.html.
6. William F. Sharpe, "Indexed Investing: A Prosaic Way to Beat the Average Investor" (speech, Spring President's Forum, Monterey Institute of International Studies, May 1, 2002).
7. William F. Sharpe, "Asset Allocation: Management Style and Performance Measurement," *Journal of Portfolio Management* (Winter 1992): 7–19.
8. Laurence B. Siegel, *Benchmarks and Investment Management* (Charlottesville, VA: CFA Institute, 2003).
9. Richard A. Ferri, *The ETF Book: All You Need to Know About Exchange-Traded Funds*, 2nd ed. (Hoboken, NJ: John Wiley & Sons, 2009).

Chapter 2: Early Performance Studies

1. Cowles Foundation for Research in Economics at Yale University, http://cowles.econ.yale.edu/.
2. Alfred Cowles III, "Can Stock Market Forecasters Forecast?" *Econometrica* 1 (July 1933): 309–324.

3. Alfred Cowles III, "Stock Market Forecasting," *Econometrica* 12, no. 3–4 (July–October 1944): 206–214.
4. John C. Bogle, "The Economic Role of the Investment Company" (undergraduate thesis, Princeton University Department of Economics and Social Institution April 21, 1951), 19. Includes further reference to Securities and Exchange Commission, Investment Trusts, and Investment Companies, p. 508.
5. Bogle, "Economic Role," 27.
6. Ibid., 19.
7. Harry Markowitz. "Portfolio Selection," *The Journal of Finance* 7, no. 1 (March 1952): 77–91.
8. Eugene Fama, "The Behavior of Stock Market Prices," *Journal of Business* 38, no. 1 (January 1965): 34–105.
9. Ibid., 92.
10. William F. Sharpe, "Capital Asset Prices: A Theory of Market Equilibrium under Conditions of Risk," *The Journal of Finance* 19, no. 3 (1964): 425–42.
11. Jack L. Treynor, "How to Rate Management of Investment Funds," *Harvard Business Review* 43 (1965): 63–75.
12. William F. Sharpe, "Mutual Fund Performance," *Journal of Business* 39 (1996): 119–138.
13. Michael C. Jensen, "The Performance of Mutual Funds in the Period 1945–1964," *The Journal of Finance* 23, no. 2 (1967): 389–416.

Chapter 3: The Birth of Index Funds

1. Burton Malkiel, *A Random Walk Down Wall Street* (New York: W.W. Norton, 1973).
2. Paul A. Samuelson, "Challenge to Judgment," *Journal of Portfolio Management* 1, no. 1 (1974): 17–19.
3. Charles D. Ellis, "The Loser's Game," *Financial Analysts Journal* 31, no. 4 (1975).
4. John C. Bogle, "The First Index Mutual Fund: A History of Vanguard Index Trust and the Vanguard Index Strategy," Bogle Financial Market Research Center, 1996, www.vanguard.com/bogle_site/bogle_home.html.
5. Ibid.
6. Wharton School of Finance and Commerce, University of Pennsylvania, Study of Mutual Fund, Government Printing Office, Washington D.C., 1962.

Chapter 4: Advances in Fund Analysis

1. William F. Sharpe, "The Sharpe Ratio," *Journal of Portfolio Management* (Fall 1994).
2. Rolf W. Banz, "The Relationship between Return and Market Value of Common Stocks," *Journal of Financial Economics* 9 (1981): 3–18.
3. Marc R. Reinganum, "A Misspecification of Capital Asset Pricing: Empirical Anomalies Based on Earnings Yields and Market Values," *Journal of Financial Economics* 9 (1981): 19–46.
4. John Burr Williams, *The Theory of Investment Value* (1938; repr., Wells, VT: Fraser Publishing Company, 1997).
5. Benjamin Graham and David Dodd, *Security Analysis* (New York: McGraw-Hill, 1934).

6. Sanjoy Basu, "Investment Performance of Common Stocks in Relation to Their Price-Earnings Ratio: A Test of the Efficient Market Hypothesis," *The Journal of Finance* 32 (June 1977): 663–682.
7. Eugene F. Fama and Kenneth R. French, "The Cross Section of Stock Returns," *The Journal of Finance* 47, no. 2 (June 1992): 427–465.
8. Srikant Dash, interview with SPIVA author at the IMN Super Bowl of Indexing, Phoenix, AZ, December 2009. The SPIVA report is available on line at www.standardandpoors.com.
9. William Bernstein's Efficient Frontier newsletter can be read online at www.efficientfrontier.com.
10. William Thatcher, "When Indexing Works and When It Doesn't: The Purity Hypothesis," *Journal of Investing* 18, no. 3 (Fall 2009).
11. William F. Sharpe, "The Arithmetic of Active Management," *Financial Analysts Journal* 47, no. 1 (January/February 1991): 7–9.
12. Travis Pascavis, "The Morningstar Box Score Report" available from http://corporate.morningstar.com/us/asp/area.aspx?xmlfile=6565.xml.
13. Eugene F. Fama and Kenneth R. French, "Luck versus Skill in the Cross Section of Mutual Fund Returns," *The Journal of Finance* 65, no. 5 (October 2010): 1915–1947.
14. Narasimhan Jegadeesh Sheridan Titman, "Returns to Buying Winners and Selling Losers: Implications for Stock Market Efficiency," *The Journal of Finance* 48 (1993): 65–91.
15. Eugene F. Fama and Kenneth. R. French, "Multifactor Explanations of Asset Pricing Anomalies," *The Journal of Finance* 51 (1996).
16. Mark M. Carhart, "On Persistence in Mutual Fund Performance," *The Journal of Finance* 52, no. 1 (March 1997): 80.

Chapter 5: Passive Choices Expand

1. John C. Bogle, "The First Index Mutual Fund: A History of Vanguard Index Trust and the Vanguard Index Strategy," John C. Bogle Research Center, 1996, www.vanguard.com/bogle_site/lib/sp19970401.html.
2. John C. Bogle, 1996.
3. Christopher R. Blake, Edwin J. Elton, and Martin J. Gruber, "The Performance of Bond Mutual Funds" *Journal of Business* 66, no. 3 (July 1993): 371–403.
4. Marlena Lee, "Is There Skill among Bond Managers?" (working paper, Dimensional Fund Advisors, Austin, Texas, 2009).
5. Eugene F. Fama and James MacBeth, "Risk, Return, and Equilibrium: Empirical Tests," *Journal of Political Economy* 81 (1973): 607–636.
6. Robert E. Cumby and Jack D. Glen, "Evaluating the Performance of International Mutual Funds," *The Journal of Finance* 45, no. 2 (June 1990): 497–521.
7. Christopher B. Philips and Sarah Floyd, "The Case for Indexing: European- and Offshore-Domiciled Funds," Vanguard Investment Counseling & Research, 2009, www.vanguard.com.
8. George Athanassakos, Peter Carayannopoulos, and Marie Racine, "How Effective is Aggressive Portfolio Management?" *Canadian Investment Review,* (Fall 2002): 39–49.
9. Eugene F. Fama and Kenneth R. French, "Value Versus Growth: The International Evidence" (working paper, 1997).

10. Elroy Dimson, Paul Marsh, and Mike Staunton, *Triumph of the Optimists: 101 Years of Global Investment Returns* (Princeton, NJ: Princeton University Press, 2002).
11. Mathijs A. van Dijk, "Is Size Dead? A Review of the Size Effect in Equity Returns" (working paper, Erasmus University, Rotterdam School of Management, 2007).
12. Craig L. Israelsen, "Things Are Not Always What They Seem," *Journal of Indexes* 8, no. 2 (2006): 18–24.
13. William J. Bernstein, "The Big Lie," Efficient Frontier, 2002, www.efficientfrontier.com.
14. Diana B. Henriques, "Wall Street; Straining to Match the Russell 2000," *New York Times*, December 15, 1991.
15. Gary L. Gastineau, "The Benchmark Index ETF Performance Problem," *Journal of Portfolio Management* 30, no. 2 (Winter 2004): 96–103.
16. Richard A. Ferri, *The ETF Book: All You Need to Know About Exchange-Traded Funds*, 2nd ed. (Hoboken, NJ: John Wiley & Sons, 2009).

Chapter 6: Portfolios of Mutual Funds

1. Eugene F. Fama, "The Behavior of Stock Market Prices," *Journal of Business* 38, no. 1 (January 1965): 34–105.
2. Larry Martin, "The Evolution of Passive versus Active Equity Management," *The Journal of Investing* (Spring 1993): 17–20.
3. Allan S. Roth, *How a Second Grader Beats Wall Street: Golden Rules Any Investor Can Learn* (Hoboken, NJ: John Wiley & Sons, 2009).
4. Mark M. Carhart, Jennifer N. Carpenter, Anthony W. Lynch, and David K. Musto, "Mutual Fund Survivorship," (working paper, NYU Department of Finance, September 12, 2000), 16.
5. William F. Sharpe, "The Arithmetic of Active Management," *Financial Analysts Journal* 47, no. 1 (January–February 1991): 7–9.

Chapter 7: The Futility of Seeking Alpha

1. Paul A. Samuelson, "The Long-Term Case for Equities," *Journal of Portfolio Management* 21, no. 1 (Fall 1994): 15–24.
2. Darryll Hendricks, Jayendu Patel, and Richard. Zeckhauser, "Hot Hands in Mutual Funds: Short-Run Persistence of Relative Performance, 1974–1988" *The Journal of Finance* 43 (1993): 93–130.
3. Mark Grinblatt and Sheridan Titman, "The Persistence of Mutual Fund Performance," *The Journal of Finance* 47, no. 5 (December 1992): 1977–1984.
4. Stephen J. Brown and William N. Goetzmann, "Performance Persistence," *The Journal of Finance* 50, no. 2 (June 1995): 679–698.
5. Mark M. Carhart, "On Persistence in Mutual Fund Performance," *The Journal of Finance* 52, no. 1 (March 1997): 57–82.
6. Eugene F. Fama and Kenneth R. French, "Luck versus Skill in the Cross Section of Mutual Fund Returns," *The Journal of Finance* 65, no. 5 (October 2010): 1915–1947.

7. Jeroen Derwall and Joop Huij, "'Hot Hands' in Bond Funds," *ERIM Research Paper Series* (April 16, 2007).
8. Marlena Lee, "Is There Skill among Bond Managers?" (working paper, Dimensional Fund Advisors, Austin, Texas, 2009).
9. Alan Greenspan, *Private-Sector Refinancing of the Large Hedge Fund, Long-Term Capital Management, Testimony before the Committee on Banking and Financial Services, U.S. House of Representatives*, October 1, 1998).
10. Mark M. Carhart, "On Persistence in Mutual Fund Performance," *The Journal of Finance* 52, no. 1 (March 1997): 80.
11. Diane Del Guercio and Paula A. Tkac, "The Effect of Morningstar Ratings on Mutual Fund Flows" (working paper, University of Oregon Department of Finance, 2002).
12. Noël Amenc and Véronique Le Sourd, "Rating the Ratings: A Critical Analysis of Fund Rating Systems," *Journal of Performance Measurement* 11, no. 4 (2007): 42–57.
13. J. A. Adkisson and Don R. Fraser, "Is There Still an Age Bias in the Morningstar Ratings?" (working paper, EDHEC Risk and Asset Management Research Centre, January 2004).
14. Matthew R. Morey, "The Kiss Of Death: A 5-Star Morningstar Mutual Fund Rating?" *Journal of Investment Management* 3, no. 2 (Second Quarter 2005).
15. John C. Bogle, "Nothing Fails Like Success" (presentation, The Contrary Opinion Forum, Vergennes, Vermont, October 3, 1997. The full text is available at http://www.johncbogle.com.
16. Russell Kinnel, "How Expense Ratios and Star Ratings Predict Success", 08-09-10, http://news.morningstar.com/articlenet/article.aspx?id=347327&tl=1282151134&page=2.
17. Judith Chevalier and Glenn Ellison, "Are Some Mutual Funds Managers Better Than Others? Cross-Sectional Patterns in Behavior and Performance," *The Journal of Finance* 54, no. 3 (June 1999): 875–899.
18. Christopher, Wright "Clearing the Bar," *CFA Magazine*, January–February 2010.
19. David, Swensen, *Unconventional Success: A Fundamental Approach to Personal Investment* (New York: Simon & Schuster, 2005), 295.
20. Allison L. Evans, "Portfolio Manager Ownership and Mutual Fund Performance," *Financial Management* 37, no. 3 (August 2008): 513–534.

Chapter 8: Active and Passive Asset Allocation

1. Hoffmann, A. O. I., Hersh M. Shefrin, and Joost M. E. Pennings, Behavioral Portfolio Analysis of Individual Investors, Working Paper Series, June 24, 2010.
2. K. Smith, "Is Fund Growth Related to Fund Performance?" *Journal of Portfolio Management* 2 (1978): 307–328.
3. Richard A. Ippolito, "Consumer Reactions to Measures of Poor Quality: Evidence from the Mutual Fund Industry," *Journal of Law and Economics* 35 (1992): 45–70.
4. Diane Del Guercio and Paula Tkac, "Star Power: The Effect of Morningstar Ratings on Mutual Fund Flows," (working paper, Federal Reserve Bank of Atlanta, March 2001).

5. Diane Del Guercio and Paula Tkac, "The Determinants of the Flow of Funds of Managed Portfolios: Mutual Funds versus Pension Funds" (working paper, Federal Reserve Bank of Atlanta, November 2000).

6. TrimTabs Investment Research, 2010, www.trimtabs.com/global/pdfs/ETF_Flows_and_Market_Returns.pdf.

7. Amit Goyal and Sunil Wahal, "The Selection and Termination of Investment Management Firms by Plan Sponsors," *The Journal of Finance* 63, no. 4 (August 2008): 1805–1847.

8. Jeffrey A. Busse, Amit Goyal, and Sunil Wahal, Performance and Persistence in Institutional Investment Management, *The Journal of Finance* 65, no. 2 (April 2010): 765–790.

9. Del Guercio and Tkac, 2000.

10. Edwin Elton, Martin Gruber, and Christopher Blake, "Participant Reaction and the Performance of Funds Offered by 401(k) Plans" (working paper, New York University, 2006).

11. Swensen, David F. Swensen, *Pioneering Portfolio Management*, 2nd ed. (New York: Free Press, 2009), 172.

12. DALBAR, Inc, "QAIB 2010 Quantitative Analysis of Investor Behavior," 2010, www.qaib.com.

13. Russel Kinnel, "Bad Times Eats Away at Investor Returns," February 22, 2010 www.advisor.morningstar.com.

14. Andrea Frazzini and Owen A. Lamont, "Dumb Money: Mutual Fund Flows and the Cross-Section of Stock Returns" (working paper, NBER, August 2005).

15. Richard A. Ferri, *All About Asset Allocation*, 2nd ed. (New York: McGraw-Hill, 2010).

Chapter 9: Changing Investor Behavior

1. LeRoy Gross, *The Art Selling Intangibles: How to Make Your Millions Investing Other People's Money* (New York: Simon & Schuster, 1988). The firm I worked for was Kidder, Peabody, Inc. The firm was wholly acquired by General Electric in the late 1989 and sold in part to UBS in 1994.

2. John R. Nofsinger, *The Psychology of Investing*, 3rd ed. (New Jersey: Pearson, 2008), 11.

3. Daniel Kahneman and Amos Tversky, "Prospect Theory: An Analysis of Decision under Risk," *Econometrica* 47 (1979): 263–291.

4. Jason Zweig, *Your Money & Your Brain* (New York: Simon & Schuster, 2007), 1.

5. Anonymous, "Confessions of a Former Mutual Funds Reporter," *Fortune*, April 26, 1999.

6. James J. Cramer, "Cramer: Mutual Fund Advertising" April 2, 2008, www.abcnews.go.com.

7. Thierry Post, Martijn J. Van den Assem, Guido Baltussen, and Richard H. Thaler, "Deal or No Deal? Decision Making under Risk in a Large-Payoff Game Show," *American Economic Review* 98, no. 1 (March 2008): 38–71.

8. Calmetta Coleman, "Beardstown Ladies Fess Up to Big Goof," *Wall Street Journal*, Mar. 18, 1998, cl.

9. William N. Goetzmann and Nadav Peles, "Cognitive Dissonance and Mutual Fund Investors," *Journal of Financial Research* 20, no. 2 (1997): 145–58.

10. John Maynard Keynes. *The General Theory of Employment, Interest and Money* (1936; repr., Boston: Houghton Mifflin Harcourt, 1964), 148.
11. Richard H. Thaler, "Toward a Positive Theory of Consumer Choice," *Journal of Economic Behavior and Organization* 1, no. 1 (1980): 39–60.
12. Goetzmann and Peles, 1997.
13. Terrance Odean "Are Investors Reluctant to Realize Their Losses?" *The Journal of Finance* 53, no. 5 (October 1998): 1775–1798.
14. David F. Swensen, *Pioneering Portfolio Management*, 2nd ed. (New York, Free Press, 2009) 3.
15. Richard A. Ferri, "A Steady Hand Pays Off in Unsteady Markets," *Forbes.com*, March 8, 2010.

Chapter 10: The Passive Management Process

1. James Tobin, "Liquidity Preference as Behavior Towards Risk," *Review of Economic Studies* 67 (1958): 65–68.
2. Philip Lawton and Todd Jankowski, *Investment Performance Measurement: Evaluating and Presenting Results* (Hoboken, NJ: John Wiley & Sons, 2009).
3. Charles Ellis, *Winning the Loser's Game*, 5th ed. (New York: McGraw-Hill, 2010), 91.

Chapter 11: The Passive Case for Individual Investors

1. IRS Publication 950, "Individual Retirement Arrangements," Appendix C, Table 1, 2009.
2. David F. Swensen, *Unconventional Success: A Fundamental Approach to Personal Investment* (New York: Simon & Schuster, 2005), 46–147.

Chapter 12: The Passive Case for Charities and Personal Trusts

1. James G. Busse, Blue Line America; and Bennett F. Aikin, *Prudent Practices for Investment Stewards*, Fiduciary360, 2006.
2. Restatement of Trusts 3d, §77, cmt. b. (2007).
3. Massachusetts Court decision, Harvard College v. Amory, 9 Pick. (26 Mass.) 461 (1830).
4. Uniform Prudent Investor Act, Objectives of the Act, page 1, The original act may be found at http://www.law.upenn.edu/bll/ulc/fnact99/1990s/upia94.htm.
5. W. Scott Simon, "Fiduciary Focus: Active vs. Passive Investing (Part 3)," MorningstarAdvisor, www.morningstaradvisor.com, April 7, 2005.
6. Edward C. Halbach, Jr., "Trust Investment Law in the Third Restatement," 77 Iowa L. Rev. 1151 (1992), at 7.
7. Halbach, 10.
8. Edward C. Halbach, Jr., "Trust Investment Law in the Third Restatement," 77 Iowa L. Rev. 1151.
9. Halbach, 10.

10. The Uniform Prudent Management of Institutional Funds Act, 2006, with prefatory note and commentary may be viewed at www.law.upenn.edu/bll/archives/ulc/umoifa/2006final_act.pdf.

11. UPMIFA enactment status is tracked at www.upmifa.org.

12. Uniform Prudent Management of Institutional Funds Act, July 2006, Subsection (d), Rebuttable Presumption of Imprudence, pg. 27, http://www.law.upenn.edu/bll/archives/ulc/umoifa/2006final_act.pdf.

13. Uniform Prudent Investment Act, February 1995, Comment on Section 7, pg.14.

14. Halbach, 11.

15. Charles E. Rounds Jr., Charles E. Rounds, and Charles E. Rounds III, *Loring: A Trustee's Handbook 2009* (New York: Aspen Publishers, 2008), 490.

16. Rounds Jr., Rounds, and Rounds III, 491–492.

Chapter 13: The Passive Case for Pension Funds

1. U.S. Department of Labor, www.dol.gov/dol/topic/health-plans/erisa.htm.

2. Pension Governance Inc. and the Michael-Shake Group, ERISA Litigation Study (company report, April 15, 2009).

3. Investment Company Institute, "Frequently Asked Questions About 401(k) Plans," www.ici.org/faqs/faqs_401k.

4. *Braden vs. Wal-Mart Stores, Inc.* 2009, 588 F.3d 585 (8th Cir. 2009).

5. Edwin Elton, Martin Gruber, and Christopher Blake, "Participant Reaction and the Performance of Funds Offered by 401(k) Plans" (working paper, New York University, 2006).

6. https://www.tsp.gov/investmentfunds/lfundsheet/fundPerformance_L2010.shtml.

Chapter 14: The Passive Case for Advisors

1. Restatement of Trusts 3d: Prudent Investor Rule, § 3, comment.

2. Restatement of Trusts 3d: Prudent Investor Rule § 227, comment m, at 58 (1992).

3. Restatement of Trusts 3d: Prudent Investor Rule § 170 (1992).

About the Author

Richard A. Ferri is the founder of Portfolio Solutions, LLC, a low-fee investment advisor firm located in Troy, Michigan. He is a financial analyst, portfolio manager, financial columnist, and a nationally recognized speaker. He is also a retired Marine Corps officer.

Ferri earned a Bachelor of Science in Business Administration from the University of Rhode Island (URI) and a Master of Science in Finance from Walsh College of Accountancy and Business. He also earned the designation of Chartered Financial Analyst (CFA) offered through the CFA Institute.

Ferri has authored and co-authored seven books on index funds, exchange-traded funds, and asset allocation. He also writes for *Forbes* magazine as "The Indexer" and contributes to other publications. He is a frequent guest speaker at investment conferences around the country. Ferri is often interviewed and quoted in leading financial publications including the *Wall Street Journal, Money, SmartMoney, Barron's, Fortune, Forbes, Kiplinger's Personal Finace*, the *New York Times, Financial Times*, and *USA Today*.

After graduating from URI, Ferri served as an officer and fighter pilot in the U.S. Marine Corps. He has since retired from the Marine Corp Reserve. Ferri started his financial career in 1988 by working at a large Wall Street firm where he managed investment portfolios, analyzed asset management strategies, and created asset allocation models for clients.

In 1999, Ferri founded Portfolio Solutions, LLC, one of the nation's first low-cost advisory firms. The company employs the same efficient investment strategies discussed in this book. Clients include individuals, families, charities, and small pension plans.

Visit Richard Ferri's web site at www.RickFerri.com and the Portfolio Solutions web site at www.PortfolioSolutions.com.

Index